PENGUIN

MOZART AN...

'Anyone wanting to understand how Mozart's operas work need read nothing else' Edward Pearce, *Daily Telegraph*

'Cairns is consistently judicious, giving a detailed account of the commission, the composition and the production of each opera: the chapter on *Idomeneo*, above all, is brilliant and satisfying' Charles Rosen, *New York Review of Books*

'We finish the book realizing that Mozart touches upon all that made us civilized, and that he reminds us both of what we are and of what we might be' Sir Colin Davis

'If you want a book that illuminates the workings of the seven operatic masterpieces within the context of Mozart's life, Cairns's style, wisdom and – crucially – profound love of his subject are unrivalled . . . like all the best writing on music, the chapter [on *Idomeneo*] makes you want to hear the opera again as a matter of urgency' Richard Wigmore, *BBC Music Magazine*

'In the 250th anniversary of Mozart's birth there will be no shortage of idolatrous coverage of [the operas] but there will be no more stimulating or personal a response than David Cairns's' Robert Thicknesse, *The Tablet*

'Over many years Cairns has through his writings contributed greatly to the musical life of this country; his volumes on Hector Berlioz have already achieved classic status . . . He knows well that there is really only one way to write about music and that is *con amore*, as he does about Mozart . . . The presence of Mozart's other music throughout the book is a continual joy and strength' Hugh Wood, *The Times Higher Education Supplement*

'Cairns writes with such beauty and vividness ... he possesses powers of description, a way of employing musical terminology in a succinct, natural and undaunting manner, and a constant flair for finding the right illuminating word or phrase, which make his book a constantly absorbing experience ... a sharp-edged picture emerges of genius at work' Conrad Wilson, *Herald*

ABOUT THE AUTHOR

David Cairns was chief music critic of the *Sunday Times* and the *Spectator*. He has been Distinguished Visiting Professor at the University of California, a visiting scholar at the Getty Center in Santa Monica and a visiting fellow of Merton College, Oxford. His two-volume biography of Berlioz has established itself as the definitive work on the subject and won the Whitbread Biography Award, the Samuel Johnson Prize for Non-Fiction and the Royal Philharmonic Society Prize. He was co-founder of the Chelsea Opera Group and is founder-conductor of the Thorington Players.

DAVID CAIRNS

Mozart and His Operas

PENGUIN BOOKS

PENGUIN BOOKS

Published by the Penguin Group
Penguin Books Ltd, 80 Strand, London WC2R ORL, England
Penguin Group (USA) Inc., 375 Hudson Street, New York, New York 10014, USA
Penguin Group (Canada), 90 Eglinton Avenue East, Suite 700, Toronto, Ontario, Canada M4P 2Y3
(a division of Pearson Penguin Canada Inc.)
Penguin Ireland, 25 St Stephen's Green, Dublin 2, Ireland
(a division of Penguin Books Ltd)
Penguin Group (Australia), 250 Camberwell Road, Camberwell, Victoria 3124, Australia
(a division of Pearson Australia Group Pty Ltd)
Penguin Books India Pvt Ltd, 11 Community Centre, Panchsheel Park, New Delhi – 110 017, India
Penguin Group (NZ), 67 Apollo Drive, Mairangi Bay, Auckland 1310, New Zealand
(a division of Pearson New Zealand Ltd)
Penguin Books (South Africa) (Pty) Ltd, 24 Sturdee Avenue, Rosebank, Johannesburg 2196, South Africa

Penguin Books Ltd, Registered Offices: 80 Strand, London WC2R ORL, England

www.penguin.com

First published by Allen Lane 2006 *2006*
Published in Penguin Books 2007
1

Copyright © David Cairns, 2006
All rights reserved

The moral right of the author has been asserted

Typeset by Rowland Phototypesetting Ltd, Bury St Edmunds, Suffolk
Printed in England by Clays Ltd, St Ives plc

ISBN 978-0-140-29674-7

in memory of my father, Hugh Cairns (1896–1952)

Contents

List of Illustrations

* The illustration shows the double-bass, cello and viola notes prolonged beyond the rest of the orchestra's chords in the second and fourth bars. Modern orthodoxy holds that both here and at the beginning of the overture (where Mozart has again written minims/half-notes in the bass) they should be cut short with the other insruments – partly on the dubious grounds that they are not found in Mozart's catalogue (where the incipit of the overture is notated *in short score*) but only (*sic*) in the autograph, but chiefly because it is claimed that on the instruments and shorter, differently weighted bows of the period the notes couldn't be sustained for the length indicated, and therefore Mozart did not mean what, to the ignorant eye, he appears to mean. Quite apart from the question, why in that case did he write them, it is far from certain that the players of 1787 were unable to sustain them (with the menacing effect that sustaining them creates). To quote an experienced and highly regarded period-instrument player, the instrumentalists of that day "were skilful in bow-control", in contrast to the much more left-hand-oriented players of the twentieth century (when "the use of vibrato had almost taken over all the expression from the right hand"), and "would have had no trouble sustaining those Mozartian minims". Mozart, a string player, wrote "with full understanding of what his players could do", which was why he wrote the passage like that instead of "just writing a crotchet followed by a crotchet rest", as he does for the rest of the orchestra.

Every effort has been made to contact copyright holders. The author and publisher will be glad to make good in future printings any errors or omissions brought to their attention.

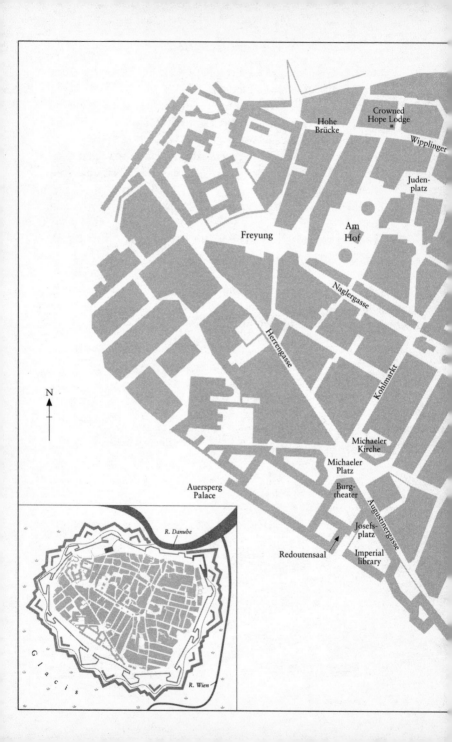

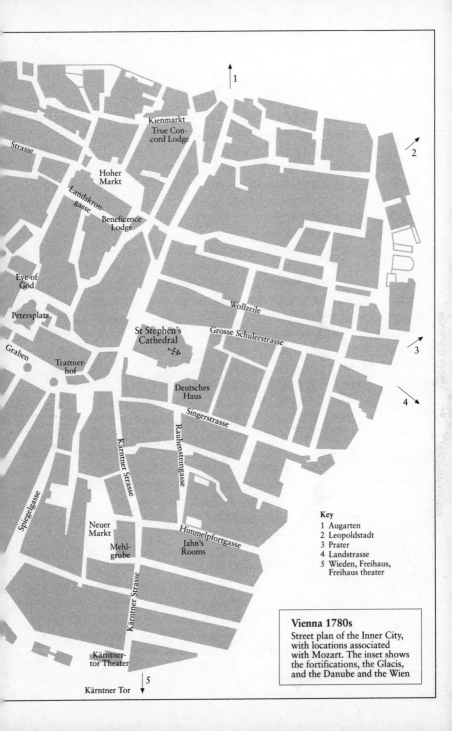

Strasse

Kienmarkt
True Con-
cord Lodge

Hoher
Markt

Landskron-
gasse

Beneficence
Lodge

Eye of
God

Petersplatz

Wollzeile

Graben

St Stephen's
Cathedral

Grosse Schulerstrasse

Trattner-
hof

Deutsches
Haus

Singerstrasse

Kärntner Strasse

Rauhensteingasse

Spiegelgasse

Neuer
Markt

Himmelpfortgasse

Mehl-
grube

Jahn's
Rooms

Kärntner Strasse

Key

1 Augarten
2 Leopoldstadt
3 Prater
4 Landstrasse
5 Wieden, Freihaus,
   Freihaus theater

Kärntner-
tor Theater

Kärntner Tor

Vienna 1780s

Street plan of the Inner City,
with locations associated
with Mozart. The inset shows
the fortifications, the Glacis,
and the Danube and the Wien

Preface

Another book on Mozart and his operas may not be needed. I can only say that I needed to write it – to attempt to put into words what I feel about them, the operas and the man, and what they have meant to me during the sixty years in which they have been at the centre of my life.

Though I have tried to keep track of the latest ideas and discoveries in the extremely active field of Mozart scholarship, the book is addressed not to scholars but to musicians and amateurs – those who know the operas and are happy to go on reading about them or who are interested in the composer enough to wish to hear more.

I am far from alone in my sense of having a personal relationship with the composer of *Figaro* and *Don Giovanni* and *The Magic Flute*. That is the effect Mozart commonly has on his admirers: he is felt as a companion, almost as a friend. And I am certainly not claiming that it gives me special insight into his music – only that that is the spirit in which I have approached the writing of this book.

A good deal of recent research has been devoted to demonstrating the many stylistic links between Mozart's music and that of his contemporaries. This is undeniable, and indeed I refer frequently to his debt to and close study of their works. That was what he did. But it does not make him any less remarkable – if anything more so. Historical context is one thing, quality is another. Appreciation of Paisiello or Cimarosa or Sarti need not inhibit one from acknowledging that Mozart's music left theirs almost immeasurably far behind.

The assumption of the inherently dramatic nature of Mozart's music is also a motif that runs through the book. It reflects my conviction that, whatever (for example) Handel's powers as a dramatist, it was

Mozart who defined and established what we mean by drama in music and who, in *Figaro*, first created complete, living operatic characters.

I have structured the book as a narrative which places the operas in the context of Mozart's life and times, and which, broadly speaking, follows him chronologically through the thirty-five years of his existence. But the conceptual starting-point is *Idomeneo*. The operas up to and including *Zaide* are treated only briefly, as preparations for that great awakening. This is not to say that they do not contain fine, and not merely prophetic, things; but, rather than study each at the length it may be thought to deserve, I have regarded them as stages in Mozart's apprenticeship as a dramatist.

In considering the mature operas, both as a whole and in detail, I have been encouraged by the example of the great Shakespearean scholar Harold Jenkins, editor of the Arden *Hamlet*, who worked on the principle – which he proceeded to justify in practice – that Shakespeare usually understands better than his critics what he is doing and why. Mozart is the dramatic musician nearest to Shakespeare, in achievement, in the accident of living at the ideal historical moment, and in the nature of his art: his capacity to absorb the styles and techniques of fellow-composers and make them his own, his Protean variety of language and form, his masterful mixing of genres, his range, dramatic pacing, unimaginable swiftness of thought, controlled complexity, richness of ambiguity, playfulness and madcap humour, and identification with each and every character – even if he did, Polonius-like, find the Ghost's speech too long. Perhaps it was dully delivered in the performances that he saw. Even the mighty confrontation between Don Giovanni and the Stone Guest can be made to seem too long by an over-deliberate tempo.

Reading James Shapiro's *1599* and Stephen Greenblatt's *Will in the World* with Mozart in mind, one cannot, I think, help being struck by the parallels between the two dramatists. Shakespeare's "curiosity" and "insatiable appetite for books", the way he would "ransack others' styles", his "unequalled capacity to absorb the styles and techniques of his fellow writers", his "gift for reading or hearing something and unspringing its unrealized potential" (Shapiro) are also Mozart's (if for books we substitute scores). What he too achieved "was a product of labour as much as talent". When Greenblatt writes of the transfiguring work of Shakespeare's imagination on the books he read and on the stock figures of popular theatre that he grew up with, one is reminded of Mozart transfiguring and breathing life into his operatic models. When he singles out "one of the prime characteristics of Shakespeare's art" as "the touch of the real", that is Mozart too, to the life. And when he remarks that "the work is so astonishing, so luminous, that it seems to have come from a god and not a mortal", that sense of wonder, of amazement applies no less to the composer – and has provided hardly less fertile ground for fantastic theorizing and the perverse misuse of intelligence. Even in the fortunate chance of their not dying in childhood they are akin: the infant Shakespeare surviving an epidemic of plague that killed two-thirds of the babies born in Stratford that year, the nine-year-old Mozart recovering from typhoid fever after being reduced to pitiful skin and bone.

Behind this book lie many hours not only of performing and listening to Mozart, and reading about him, but of talking, arguing and corresponding with friends – too numerous to name, but all of whom have played a part in it.

Over and above what I owe to the many Mozart specialists I learned from and whose work I have cited in the Bibliography and the Notes, my special debt to Otto Erich Deutsch, Alan Tyson, H. C. Robbins Landon and Daniel Heartz will be apparent in the pages that follow.

For vital help with the illustrations, warmest thanks to Elisabeth Agate, and also to Richard Macnutt and Jo Townsend; for useful information and/or suggestions for further reading, to Gunther Braam, David Charlton, Oliver Davies, Colin Davis, Angela Escott, John Eliot Gardiner, Anthony Holden, Annette Isserlis, Charles Mackerras, John Mathews, Roger Norrington, Chi-chi Nwanoku, Julian Rushton, Michael Steinberg, Edith Stokes, Rémy Stricker and Nicholas Summers. Thanks are also due to Palgrave Macmillan and to A. & C. Black for permission to quote, respectively, from the revised Emily Anderson edition (1988) of Mozart's *Letters* and from Deutsch's *Documentary Biography* (in both of whose translations I have occasionally made changes). The plan of Vienna on pp. xii–xiii is based on material kindly supplied by the Map Room, British Library.

The manuscript was read by Peter Branscombe, Colin Davis, Ian Kemp, Annie Lee, Stuart Proffitt, and my wife Rosemary, and benefited greatly from their comments and criticisms. To all of them gratitude, above all to Peter, without whose wisdom and knowledge of Mozart, ungrudgingly shared, this book would be the poorer.

I have made use, in revised form, of a few of the many Mozart articles that I wrote over the years, in particular the essay on *Idomeneo* in *Responses* and the analysis of *The Magic Flute* in the 1980 English National Opera guide to the work.

The rendering of the titles of the operas follows normal English usage and is therefore not consistent: *La clemenza di Tito, Così fan tutte* and *La finta giardiniera* but *The Magic Flute* and, generally, *The Abduction from the Seraglio* rather than *Die Entführung aus dem Serail*.

References may be found at the end, under Notes, along with further discussion of matters treated in the main text. Each reference is identified by page number and short quotation.

The book is inscribed to my father. In addition I dedicate it to the memory of three exceptional Mozartians, Erik Smith, Alan Tyson and Stanley Sadie.

Prologue

Mozart, like Shakespeare, continues to grow. His music is an ever-expanding universe. The better we know it – the more we explore its heights and depths – the more marvellous it becomes. Yet its exalted status, the central position it occupies today, 250 years after the composer's birth, is of surprisingly recent date. What Misha Donat has called "the recognition of the depth of Mozart's emotional world" was a late-twentieth-century achievement. Until then he was, of course, loved – even deified – but in a particular, limiting way.

Ironically, the composer whose music sounded to nineteenth-century ears too simple, too easy, was regarded by contemporaries as over-complicated and difficult. Few of his fellow-musicians would have exclaimed, with Haydn, "If I could only impress on the soul of every music-lover, and particularly on those of high rank, how inimitable are Mozart's works, how profound, how musically intelligent, how extraordinarily sensitive (for that is how I understand them, how I feel them), the nations would compete to possess such a jewel within their borders." What to us has the stamp of inevitability and – with all its freshly discovered richness of ambiguity – of balance and perfect fitness, to them was disturbingly restless.

With an effort of imagination one can sympathize with them. What doubts must have gone through the startled minds of Anton and Bartholomäus Tinti as they played the twisted, groping introduction of the "Dissonance" quartet, on that famous February evening in Vienna in 1785 when Haydn told Leopold Mozart that his son was the greatest living composer. A few years later, the composer Dittersdorf, who had taken part in quartet parties with Mozart, speaks of the quartets' "extreme, unrelenting cleverness". A genius, no question of that; but a little less frantic profusion of ideas, a little more simplicity, would not come amiss.

Or, what must the second movement of the G major quartet, K387 – the earliest of the six dedicated to Haydn – have sounded like when it was new, with its strange ascending chromatic lines, combined with an alternation of loud and soft every beat, imposing an awkward duple metre on the proper triple time of the dance? What kind of tune was that? What kind of minuet? Even his public works, the piano concertos and the operas, showed a regrettable tendency to excessive abundance. For us, it is precisely this abundance, the richness of texture and harmony, the heart-stopping modulations, that we respond to in Mozart and that in comparison makes the music of most of the other composers of his time apart from Haydn thin and uneventful. But to contemporaries that was precisely the trouble; as one of them remarked, his music was "too highly seasoned" for normal tastes, the writing for wind instruments in particular so "loquacious" that it overloaded the texture and obscured the musical discourse.

As for the G minor string quintet, who had encountered anything remotely like it before: the tormented first movement, with its almost unrelieved darkness of mood, its compulsive chromaticism, the constantly falling melodic lines, the dissonant harmonies, the persistent feverish throb of the accompaniment, which, near the end, stops abruptly, as though exhausted by suffering (to us a wonderful effect)? Or the angular, pathetic minuet, its melodic lines, descending as before, interrupted by sudden brusque offbeat chords and wisps of phrase that aspire weakly upwards only to fall back, disconsolate? And then, after yet more morbid introspection and falling melodies, the manic gaiety of the major-key finale!

That finale, subsequently, raised many eyebrows. How, following the tensions and poignant ironies of the slow movement, could the darkness of the even more sombre fourth-movement adagio suddenly give way, after more than thirty uncompromisingly tragic bars, to light and to a bounding rondo in 6/8 time and in an almost unclouded G major (whose chromaticisms, one might add, are now an expression of vitality, of endless possibility)? The answer, to us, is obvious: because Mozart was not a Victorian moralist; because, in music, above all in music as ambiguous as his, animal spirits do not have to be justified; because his instinct, as a human being and as a dramatist, is for reconciliation and renewal. The finale does not negate the sufferings of the previous movements: they become a springboard to fresh life, like the psalmist's "Who, going through the vale of misery, use it for a well."

To nineteenth-century ears, however, such cheerfulness was a betrayal of the heartache that preceded it; it was not justified, not "earned". Under the impact of Beethoven, and then of Wagner and Brahms, they no longer heard what was in Mozart. As Charles Rosen says, "the sheer physical beauty" of so much of his music masked "the uncompromising character of his art", its subversiveness. His surface perfection was too alien to the values and practices of Romanticism; it was scarcely human. Particular works may have been revered, notably the "daemonic" *Don Giovanni*; such works had an honoured place in the evolution of music from its primitive beginnings to its late-nineteenth-century consummation (for that was how music history tended to be seen, in the age of Progress). Mozart was put on a pedestal – but as an instinctive genius, the unconscious childlike creator of music whose very flawlessness spoke of superficiality, in a period when struggle was the true mark of the artist. He hadn't had to struggle; it came too easily to him, cost him too little. This Mozart could not have echoed Goethe's celebrated phrase, that watchword of the Romantics: "They who never ate their bread with tears, never lay weeping through the night's long agony – they know ye not, ye Heavenly Powers." What he did was exquisite; but in the last resort it failed to rise to the test. It was not deep.

Even admirers were apt to discuss it in terms that limited it, as when Schumann characterized the turbulent G minor symphony (No. 40) as music of "Grecian lightness and grace", or when Anton Rubinstein cried out delightedly that Mozart was "eternal sunshine in music". The oft-repeated description of the E flat symphony (No. 39) pigeonholed it as "the locus classicus of euphony", totally overlooking both the intense rhythmic energy of the music and the shadows that threaten it. As late as 1913 (in Arthur Schurig's biography) the words "blissful peace of mind" could be applied in all seriousness to the deeply troubled second movement of the Jupiter symphony.

At best he was, as Gounod called him, "le divin Mozart", at worst, in the indignant phrase of Bernard Shaw (still unusual, in 1893, for his perceptive admiration of Mozart), "a vapidly tuneful infant phenomenon". Mozart was not allowed to have grown up; he was trapped in the image of "the marvellous boy". The feats of cleverness he achieved when hardly out of his swaddling clouts became a lasting reproach. His miraculous precocity blinded people to the even greater miracle: that the infant phenomenon survived his unnatural early years and, so far from burning himself out, continued to develop, and that to have done so was proof of exceptional strength of character.

To see beneath the beautiful patterns, to realize all that the music's impeccable control concealed – the intensities, the layers of irony, the longing, the undercurrents of sadness, the coexistence of the celestial and the earthy, the sheer intelligence – required not so much a repudiation of Romanticism as a recognition that such convenient but constricting classifications break down before music as transcendent as his. Above all, it required familiarity with the operas. It is they that have transformed our perception of Mozart's art.

That was very much my experience. Perhaps it is a natural and not uncommon experience: to find Mozart superficial until one has lived enough to be able to perceive the truth of him. Until then he can seem trivial, as he did to me. Committed body and soul, from the age of eleven, to Beethoven, and then to Brahms, I couldn't be doing with him. They were the truth and the way; he was an elegant irrelevance. It was not until I was eighteen that light broke and my life changed. A musical mentor since forgotten, or perhaps a guardian angel, prompted me to borrow the Beecham recording of *The Magic Flute* from the local gramophone library. Conversion was instantaneous. From now on I heard Mozart differently – heard him, in fact. And each hearing of *The Magic Flute* revealed emotions yet more intense. I understood dimly that part of Mozart's appeal lay in his music's embodying at one and the same time the perfection our souls long for and the sensation of our longing.

Figaro followed, at the first Edinburgh Festival, in 1947: a moment of instant recognition, of pure delight such as comes rarely, when you sense, from the first note, that this is for you and will be a treasured possession the rest of your life. Then *Idomeneo* (staged by the university opera club in Oxford Town Hall), and *Don Giovanni* and *Così fan tutte*, both at Edinburgh. I became obsessed with *Don Giovanni*, I listened repeatedly to the pre-war Glyndebourne recording, I could not hear it often enough. As Leporello I sang the work with friends round the piano and then in public in Holywell Music Room; I practised speaking his "Mille torbidi pensieri/mi s'agiran per la testa,/ se mi salvo in tal tempesta/è un prodigio in verità" until I had the words securely in my mouth and on my lips and could rattle them off at Mozart's molto allegro. In 1950 came the inaugural concert performance (*Don Giovanni*) of the Chelsea Opera Group, the ensemble founded by Stephen Gray and myself and conducted by the twenty-two-year-old Colin Davis, and, five decades later, this book.

Whether or not my experience is at all typical, there is no doubt that it was the operas, more than anything, that brought about the change in the conventional attitude to Mozart, fostering the gradual growth of understanding. Of course, they had never ceased to be performed in the years following Mozart's death. *Figaro* and *Don Giovanni*, as has been said, were the first operas never to need reviving. But in the age of Wagner and Verdi they did not cut deep. And at least two of them were found fatally wanting: *Idomeneo*, imprisoned in the trappings of an obsolete form; and *Così fan tutte*, tragic case of a divinely gifted musician squandering his talents on a libretto of scandalous frivolity. Wagner actually declared it to be proof of Mozart's genius that the music he wrote for it was – could only be – of poor quality. The more common view was that the score was fine enough to be worth rescuing by marrying it to a more wholesome text (several were manufactured for it), but that it hardly spoke well for Mozart's seriousness that he had been prepared to compose such an opera in the first place. As for *The Magic Flute*, it could only have been the dire need of money – consequence of a feckless style of living? – that induced him to throw in his lot with a suburban pantomime troupe and debase his genius to the lowest common denominator. Where was the artistic judgement, the integrity, in that?

The process whereby the operas came to be accepted on their own terms was long drawn out. As always, conductors were crucial – conductors whose championing of Wagner's vastly more opulent and emotionally explicit music-dramas never blunted their appreciation of the greatness of Mozart's: Hermann Levi, Mahler (who, however, himself put on a doctored version of *Così fan tutte* at the Vienna Opera), Richard Strauss, Beecham, Bruno Walter, Fritz Busch, to name only the most obvious. Thanks to them, to directors of the calibre of Ebert, Klemperer, Strehler, to writers like Abert, Alfred Einstein, E. J. Dent, and to a succession of inspired female singers – Frida Leider, Elisabeth Schumann, Ina Souez, Elisabeth Grümmer, Sena Jurinac, Irmgard Seefried, who in the middle years of the twentieth century helped us to understand the operas' profound empathy with women – Mozart was revealed as the psychologist that we now recognize him to be. Nothing illustrates the transformation more strikingly than the high regard in which *Così fan tutte* is now held. From being the most reviled it has become in some ways the most admired, the modern Mozart opera par excellence, whose ambiguities and exposure of human frailty and heartbreak fascinate audiences, and the most performed – and this not merely because its small cast, minimal chorus role, and undemanding scenic requirements make it the easiest to put on. As for *Idomeneo*, for long relegated to the margins of operatic history, patronized, fair game for arrangers and know-all commentators, it has escaped the museum and become a repertory piece, widely recognized as one of Mozart's greatest works.

Knowledge of the operas has illuminated our whole view of his art. We see that his approach to composition was that of a dramatist through and through. The piano concerto, in his hands, becomes a form of theatre; the great string quartets and quintets are human documents, not mere patterns of perfection, however much their utter rightness of form, within which infinite worlds of expression are bounded, is part of their enchantment.

In the light of Mozart's achievement and its Protean variety, ancient preconceptions and received ideas fall away. How, one wonders, could he have been thought of as pre-eminently a synthesizer, a culmination of other people's work, and not as an innovator? What does the Prague symphony have in common with the symphonies of Carl or Joseph Stamitz or J. C. Bach, of Holzbauer or Cannabich, or even of Haydn at that stage of his career? It and the Jupiter symphony and the Jupiter's companions composed in those brief weeks in the summer

of 1788, the E flat and the G minor, are something new, unprecedented. Certainly, by taking him all over Europe, so that he had the
whole of contemporary music to draw on, his father gave him a
unique advantage and fostered his hyper-acute ear for the novel and
interesting, the extraordinary capacity of his "quicksilver personality"
(in H. C. Robbins Landon's phrase) for seizing on and assimilating
whatever in a newly encountered style will be useful to him. But, with
Mozart, it is what he makes of an adopted form or gesture that is
important, not where it comes from. And though the sense of effortless
inevitability his music conveys might seem to preclude any notion of
breaking new ground, that is what he did. He is simultaneously both
kinds of artist, the assimilator and perfecter and the innovator. It is
Mozart who created the piano concerto as we know it, and the piano
quartet. His writing for wind instruments, especially from 1781 onwards, is highly innovative. Under the influence of the players encountered in Mannheim and then in Vienna, their orchestral role becomes
incomparably richer (so that an astonished observer can declare that
the big E flat and C minor piano concertos are like concertos for wind
with piano obbligato). At the same time the traditional wind band is
metamorphosed from a purveyor of lively noise to a medium of
intensely personal expression, including the expression of a personality with an exceptionally keen sense of the comic: in the finales of
Mozart's E flat and B flat serenades, K375 and 361, sublimity goes
hand in hand with pure clowning – a portent for the later operas.

Parallel with the dawning recognition of all that Mozart's music
contains has come – as both effect and cause – a radically different
idea of his nature and personality. Little by little, strand by strand,
the tangled web of myth woven almost before he was laid in his
unmarked grave is being unravelled. A spirit of healthy scepticism
now examines the legends and the fanciful, credulous theories that
sprang up in the wake of his life and early death, based on stories,
often dubious in the first place, selectively emphasized and embellished
over the years by generations of romantic biographers who could not
accept that the composer of such angelic strains was an unprepossess-
ing, pale little man with popping eyes and a taste for scatological
jokes, and who were driven to invent a mythical two-headed monster,

half god, half beast. A new Mozart has emerged, whom a modern scholar can convincingly describe as "one of the most penetrating intellects of his age".

This Mozart was in all probability not a manic depressive suffering from cyclothymic disorder; was not a drunkard or a compulsive gambler and/or womanizer; was not the mere vessel for inspired music and in all other respects an impractical, incompetent child, "an immortal genius inside a buffoon's, an idle hooligan's, skull" (Pushkin); was as remarkable for his craftsmanship, acquired by long and painstaking hard work, as for his god-given talent; did not indulge in lavatory humour as a consequence of arrested development, still less of acute personality disorder, but from a habit common among natives of Salzburg (even Mozart's mother ends a letter to her husband: "Addio, ben mio, keep well, my love, into your mouth your arse you'll shove, I wish you good night, my dear, but first shit in your bed and make it burst", and Mozart, with the pleasure in wordplay that *is* characteristic of him, simply does it more amusingly); was capable of normal human relationships; did not end by losing his will to live and half-consciously destroying himself through a mixture of dissipation and feverish overwork, but died of diseases that might easily have killed him much earlier, though – fortunately for us – they didn't.

Without doubt, writing music was what he did best and loved best. "I am happier when I have something to compose" (1777); 'I love to plan works" (1778); "my beloved task, composition" (1784); "I like hard work" (1791). We hardly need to be told. Perhaps more than those of any other composer, the works of his maturity, especially, breathe an unmistakable air of enjoyment, of deep pleasure in the act of creation, even when – as with the quartets dedicated to Haydn – there are serious difficulties to be grappled with and overcome. Again and again one senses a delight that is palpable: in – to choose at random – the finale of the quintet for piano and wind instruments, K452, particularly the glorious final pages; in the diabolical humour of the aria "Metà di voi quà vadano", where Don Giovanni disguised as Leporello takes charge of the peasants who are out to kill him – listening to which I feel the presence of Mozart so vividly that I am almost surprised not to see him there, in the theatre or the room; in the quintet with the padlocked Papageno in *The Magic Flute*; in the

chorus in G major for women's voices in *Figaro* Act 3, with its little
chirrups for flute and oboe and bassoon, so innocently sexy; in the
farewell quintet, "Di scrivermi ogni giorno", of *Così fan tutte*, balanced between laughter and sadness; in the gleeful high spirits and
headlong pace, exquisitely poised, of the finale of the G major string
quartet, K387; in the passionate emotions, perfect proportions and
heartbreaking beauty of the *Idomeneo* quartet, of which Mozart said
(in response to the complaint by the tenor, Raaff, that it gave him
"no scope"): "If I knew of a single note that should be altered,
I would alter it at once."

Sometimes, you feel, the delight in composition becomes an ecstasy,
and the composer's mind works at a speed of thought and a pitch of
intensity that even his powers are only just able to control. When the
finale of the Jupiter is played con fuoco, with total commitment, the
creative fury the music gives off is frightening. Is it any wonder that
such a mind needed to let off steam from time to time and play the
fool? The picture of Mozart, in Karoline Pichler's account, suddenly
breaking off an inspired improvisation at the piano and "jumping up
and, in the mad mood which so often came over him, leaping over
tables and chairs, miaowing like a cat, and turning somersaults like
an unruly boy" seems to me evidence of mental health, not the reverse.

The better we come to know *Figaro*, *Don Giovanni*, *Così fan tutte*,
The Magic Flute, the more unlikely, the more grotesquely implausible
that the composer could have been the footling figure of the myths.
Their Shakespearean complexity and depth are only too clearly not
the product of a personality unable to relate to his fellow-men and
women and alienated from society. We do not have to agree with
W. J. Turner that Mozart was that "rarest of all human beings, a saint
who is not a bore" or that "among all the great artists of history
Mozart and Shakespeare were the only ones whose moral superiority
strikes to the core of one's being". His letters show that he could on
occasion be tactless, uncharitable, deceitful, arrogant. But which of
us is never like that? Was Mozart the first or the last son to be evasive
and economical with the truth when dealing with an accusing father?

Leopold Mozart and his anxious, disapproving letters still to some
extent set the agenda, though it is plainly the disapproval and anxiety
of a parent who, having grown accustomed to controlling his son's

life, cannot reconcile himself to his independence: a father, too, who is haunted by the fear that his son will be prevented by lack of good sense and intemperate habits from realizing his promise and will die (as his father warns him in 1778) "an ordinary musician, forgotten by the world". No doubt Leopold Mozart was somewhat reassured when, seven years later, he visited Vienna and heard the D minor piano concerto and the quartets dedicated to Haydn, not to mention Haydn's resounding declaration; yet he continued to fret – and we, even now, to look at Mozart through his eyes.

Gradually, however, despite strenuous discouragement from Peter Shaffer's myth-mongering *Amadeus*, we are learning to see a different picture: not of two contradictory beings, sublime artist and fool, but of one, whom the life as well as the works reveal as fundamentally well integrated – a creature no less miraculous than before, but more human.

In particular, study of Mozart's manuscripts and sketches has made clear the craftsmanship that, so to speak, earthed the genius, the sheer industry which Romantic legends of the preternaturally facile composer, doing it all in his head before writing a note, had no room for. Researches into paper-types and watermarks have given us a Mozart who hesitated, who put works aside and, if he came back to them later, sometimes changed his mind.

The autographs of the six "Haydn" quartets – works more intricate than anything Mozart had yet written – bear out his statement (which posterity usually chose to ignore) that the quartets were "the fruit of long and laborious toil". Their composition covered a period of over two years, and, in Alan Tyson's words, was "not only slow but uncertain"; the manuscripts contain many crossings-out, false starts, afterthoughts, revisions, sketches. We catch him in the act of composing – for example, altering the order of the variations in the andante of the A major quartet, K464, and adding the minor-key variation later, or, in the opening movement of K387, apparently thinking of the clinching dotted-phrase-plus-trill at the end of the exposition only after he has drawn the double bar that concluded it. The rising chromatic passage halfway through the finale of K387 – echoing the similar figure in the minuet (referred to above) – required a lot of tinkering before it reached its definitive form.

Yet, listening to this finale, we have the impression that the whole movement has been shaped in a single decisive stroke. Somehow its disparate elements – strenuously "learned" counterpoint and artless tune plus chugging accompaniment – are fused into one unified discourse of irresistible vitality, ending in the utterly disarming gesture of those last throwaway bars, where the four-note tag with which the movement began is repeated once more, piano, but now harmonized and capped at last by the cadence that – we realize – has been standing patiently in the wings all the time. Mozart has few if any equals for this knack of rounding off a movement with a phrase which is exactly the fulfilment his theme has been waiting for.

Evidence of working-out on paper does not make the resulting work less wonderful – why should it? – any more than, in the C minor piano concerto's opening movement, the seeming inevitability of the orchestral introduction's driving intensity is negated by the sight of the drastic change visible in the autograph manuscript, where a twenty-eight-bar section has been lifted from its original position and placed at a different point in the sequence of events: a startling second thought but one that, knowing the final version as we do, we can only think of as inspired, and inevitable. Such investigations, while they serve to demythologize him, only deepen our sense of love and of awe at the magnitude of what he achieved.

In *The Impossible Adventure* the French explorer Alain Gheerbrant describes the impact of Mozart's music on the Maquiritare Indians of the Amazon forests of northern Brazil. At first, when Gheerbrant and his companions arrive in the village clearing, the inhabitants stay shyly inside and resist all attempts to lure them out. The Frenchmen play various records on their portable gramophone, but there is no response. Finally, they put on their "beloved Mozart". Immediately the villagers, losing all fear, emerge from their huts and sit peacefully round the gramophone, compelled – like man and beast in *The Magic Flute* – by the Orphic power of the sounds.

We too are under the spell. A contemporary of Mozart said that his music would "speak to unborn generations when the bones of kings have long since crumbled to dust". More than two centuries after his death, it speaks as never before. Precisely how it does so we cannot, finally, say. But it speaks, surely, not so much through the charm of its perfect patterns as through its comprehension of life, its penetrating knowledge of women and men, its profound humanity.

I

Imitation, assimilation
The early operas

*I have an inexpressible longing to write another opera. [. . .]
I have only to hear an opera discussed, I have only to sit in a
theatre and hear the orchestra tuning their instruments – oh, I
am immediately beside myself!*
Mozart to his father, 11 October 1777

*As you know, I can more or less adopt or imitate any kind
and style of composition.*
Mozart to his father, 7 February 1778

In June 1765 the Hon. Daines Barrington, barrister, antiquarian,
musical amateur and member of the Royal Society, visited the Mozart
family in their lodgings at 15 Thrift (Frith) Street, Soho, and subjected
the nine-year-old Wolfgang to a systematic examination of "his most
extraordinary abilities as a musician". Barrington had heard him play
and, like many, suspected that he was quite a bit older than his father
claimed. However, in submitting his report to the society a few years
later, he was able to append documentary proof of his age, obtained
from the Salzburg register of births.

The boy had been observed by Charles Burney in April the previous
year, at the house in Cecil Court where they lodged on arriving
in London. Burney jotted his impressions in his musical notebook:
"Extemporary and sight playing, composing a treble to a given base
and a base to a treble, as well as both on a given subject, and finishing
a composition begun by another, his fondness for Manzoli [the Floren-
tine castrato Giovanni Manzuoli], his imitation of the several styles

of singing of each of the then opera singers, as well as of their songs in an extemporary opera to nonsense words, to which were [added] an overture of 3 movements, recitative, graziosa, bravura and pathetic airs together with several accompanied recitatives, all full of taste, imagination, with good harmony, melody and modulation, after which he played at marbles in the true childish way of one who knows nothing."

Barrington's much more detailed report tells a similar story:

[. . .] As during this time I was witness of his most extraordinary abilities as a musician, both at some public concerts and likewise by having been alone with him for a considerable time at his father's house, I send you the following account, amazing and incredible almost as it may appear.

I carried to him a manuscript duet, which was composed by an English gentleman to some favourite words in Metastasio's opera of Demofoonte. The whole score was in five parts, viz. accompaniments for a first and second violin, the two vocal parts, and a base. [. . .] My intention in carrying with me this manuscript composition was to have an irrefragable proof of his abilities as a player at sight, it being absolutely impossible that he could have ever seen the music before. The score was no sooner put upon his desk than he began to play the symphony in a most masterly manner, as well as in the time and style which corresponded with the intention of the composer. I mention this circumstance because the greatest masters often fail in these particulars on the first trial. The symphony ended, he took the upper part, leaving the under one to his father. His voice in the tone of it was thin and infantine, but nothing could exceed the masterly manner in which he sung. His father, who took the under part in this duet, was once or twice out, though the passages were not more difficult than those in the upper one; on which occasions the son looked back with some anger pointing out to him his mistakes and setting him right. He not only however did complete justice to the duet by singing his own part in the truest taste and with the greatest precision: he also threw in the accompaniments of the two violins, wherever they were most necessary and produced the best effects. It is well known that none but the most capital musicians are capable of accompanying in this superior style. [. . .]

When he had finished the duet, he expressed himself highly in its appro-bation, asking with some eagerness whether I had brought any more such music. Having been informed, however, that he was often visited with musical ideas to which, even in the midst of the night, he would give utterance on his harpsichord, I told his father that I should be glad to hear some of his extemporary compositions. The father shook his head at this, saying that it depended entirely on his being as it were musically inspired, but that I might ask him whether he was in humour for such a composition. Happening to know that little Mozart was much taken notice of by Manzoli, the famous singer, who came over to England in 1764, I said to the boy that I should be glad to hear an extemporary Love Song such as his friend Manzoli might choose in an opera. The boy on this (who continued to sit at his harpsichord) looked back with much archness and immediately began five or six lines of a jargon recitative proper to introduce a love song. He then played a symphony which might correspond with an air composed to the single word *Affetto*. It had a first and second part, which, together with the symphonies, was of the length that opera songs generally last. If this extemporary song was not amazingly capital, yet it was really above mediocrity and showed most extraordinary readiness of invention.

Finding that he was in humour and as it were inspired, I then desired him to con ose a Song of Rage, such as might be proper for the opera stage. The boy again looked back with much archness and began five or six lines of a jargon recitative proper to precede a song of anger. This lasted also about the same time with the Song of Love; and in the middle of it he had worked himself up to such a pitch that he beat his harpsichord like a person possessed, rising sometimes in his chair. The word he pitched on for this second extemporary composition was *Perfido*. After this he played a difficult lesson, which he had finished a day or two before; his execution was amazing, considering that his little fingers could scarcely reach a fifth on the harpsichord.

His astonishing readiness, however, did not arise merely from great practice; he had a thorough knowledge of the fundamental principles of composition, as, upon producing a treble, he immediately wrote a base under it, which, when tried, had a very good effect. He was also a great master of modulation, and his transitions from one key to another were excessively natural and judicious; he practised in this manner for a considerable time with an handkerchief over the keys of the harpsichord.

The facts which I have been mentioning I was myself an eye witness of; to which I must add that I have been informed by two or three able musicians, when Bach the celebrated composer had begun a fugue and left off abruptly, that little Mozart hath immediately taken it up and worked it after a most masterly manner.

Witness as I was myself of most of these extraordinary facts, I must own that I could not help suspecting his father imposed with regard to the real age of the boy, though he had not only a most childish appearance but likewise had all the actions of that stage of life. For example, whilst he was playing to me a favourite cat came in, upon which he immediately left his harpsichord, nor could we bring him back for a considerable time. He would also sometimes run about the room with a stick between his legs by way of a horse. I found likewise that most of the London musicians were of the same opinion with regard to his age, not believing it possible that a child of so tender years could surpass most of the masters in that science. [Barrington then reports that he procured the birth certificate.]

All over Europe this was the child that monarchs, musicians and the gaping public became familar with. Leopold Mozart has been severely rebuked by biographers for exploiting the boy's miraculous gifts to his own glory and gain: a man of energy, intelligence, wide reading and independent ideas, the admired author of the leading violin treatise of the age, but in his own eyes scandalously under-valued, a mere vice-kapellmeister in a provincial German town, rest-less, resentful, he fulfilled his unsatisfied ambitions vicariously by controlling and directing his son's career and dragging the frail, undersized little fellow from court to court on journey after exhaust-ing, unhealthy journey – a costly sop for injured self-esteem! In The Hague, a few months after they left England, Wolfgang almost died of typhoid fever. The British Minister, Joseph Yorke, reported at the beginning of October that "we have got the little German boy here who plays upon the harpsichord like Handel and composes with the same facility, he is really a most extraordinary effort of nature, but our professors in physick don't think he will be long lived". Six weeks later they were nearly proved right. For eight days he lay in a virtual coma, unable to speak; his lips turned black; he was, in Leopold's words, "completely unrecognizable". When, after three weeks, his father first ventured to lift him from the bed and carry him to a chair, the body he held in his arms was nothing but "tender skin and tiny bones". One's blood turns cold at the thought. What if he had died then, and not twenty-six years and an Aladdin's cave of compositions later?

But perhaps we should look at it differently and, instead of scolding, be grateful to Leopold Mozart for teaching his son so well, and also try to imagine what he must have felt when he realized what he and his wife Anna Maria had brought into the world. Five of their first six children had died in infancy. Nannerl, the fourth, born in 1751, had survived (and by the age of eight was showing distinct signs of musical talent) – and then came the birth of the seventh child and the revelation of undreamed-of gifts.

Their friend the Salzburg court trumpeter and violinist Johann Andreas Schachtner remembered coming back from church one day, with Leopold Mozart, and finding the four-year-old busily at work:

PAPA: What are you writing?
WOLFGANG: A clavier concerto, the first part is nearly finished.
PAPA: Show me.
WOLFG.: It's not ready yet.
PAPA: Show me, it's sure to be interesting.

His father took it from him and showed me a smudge of notes, most of which were written over ink-blots which he had rubbed out. (NB. Little Wolfgangerl, knowing no better, plunged the pen to the bottom of the inkwell each time, so that when he put it on the paper a drop of ink was bound to fall off, but he was not bothered and, drawing the palm of his hand across it, wiped it off and wrote on.) At first we laughed at what seemed such a galimatias, but his father then began to observe what mattered most, the notes and the music. He stared long at the sheet, then tears, tears of joy and wonder, fell from his eyes. Look, Herr Schachtner, he said, see how correctly and properly it's all written, only it can't be used, it's so difficult that no one could play it. Wolfgangerl said, It's a concerto, that's why, you must practise it till you get it right. Look, that's how it goes. He played, and managed to get just enough out of it for us to see what he intended.

Schachtner also tells a similar story of Mozart, now aged six, wanting to play second violin in some string trios that a friend has brought for Leopold to look at, and being told to go away and stop being a nuisance, at which he "weeps bitterly and stamps off with his little violin". In the end he is allowed to play with Schachtner but "so softly that we can't hear you or you will have to go". Gradually Schachtner realizes that he is "superfluous. I quietly put my violin down and looked at [his] Papa: tears of wonder and relief were running down his cheeks."

Even if Schachtner's memory, recalled more than twenty years later, exaggerated somewhat (his chronology is not always correct), the substance of these and other eyewitness accounts is not in dispute. That is how it was. Before long the child was "soaked in music" (as he described himself many years later). Schachtner said that even "games had to be accompanied by music if they were to interest him. When we – he and I – carried his toys from one room to another, one of us had to take them all so that the other could sing and fiddle a march."

How could Leopold not react as he did? The advent of this being – like a visitant from another world – inevitably changed his life. He could not but dedicate himself body and soul to nurturing and fostering "the miracle which God caused to be born in Salzburg". It was his responsibility; ambitions for his own career must take second place.

The boy was a wonderfully receptive pupil; and Leopold, a born teacher, must have loved instructing him. The troubles which would disturb and undermine their relationship lay far off in the future. Schachtner's testimony that the child Mozart, as well as being tender-hearted, was "susceptible to every attraction" – confirmed by his mother's observation that "when Wolfgang [by then a young man of twenty-two] makes new acquaintances he immediately wants to cede his life and property to them" – was as true of new subjects as it was of people. "Whatever he was given to learn", recalled Schachtner, "occupied him so completely that he put all else, even music, on one side: e.g., when he was doing his sums, the table, chairs, walls, even the floor were covered with chalk figures." Nannerl said the same: "Even as a child he was desirous of learning everything he set eyes on," such as drawing and adding, in which "he showed much skill".

It is not difficult to see how, once Leopold had begun to devote his energies to his son's education and had conceived the idea of showing him to the known world, with all the complex organizing and financing such an operation involved, the role would have grown on him until it consumed him and came to seem ordained. Watching over Wolfgang's first steps in composition, he got used to thinking of himself as his amanuensis, even as his collaborator. Leopold's hand has been traced in many of the youthful Mozart's autograph scores. Erik Smith has argued that the "Chelsea Notebook" of 1765 – a collection of short pieces which Mozart sketched on his own while his father was out of action, ill in bed in the next room – shows greater freshness and invention than the music of the same period that was written under supervision. Yet Leopold's tutelage was not oppressive. Nannerl was emphatic that her brother "was never forced to compose nor to play, on the contrary he always needed to be restrained, otherwise he would have stayed sitting over his clavier or his compositions all day and night". Father and son were of one mind. It was a shared passion. What Cliff Eisen has called their "apparently insatiable curiosity about new music" was mutual.

There is something to be said for the view that the education Mozart received was exactly the one his temperament and particular genius demanded. Undeniably, it had serious disadvantages which would appear later, when he found that doors would no longer open magically as they had once done and that the image of the prodigy, the freak of nature – still fixed in people's minds – was an obstacle to the progress of the adult composer ("they treat me like a beginner," he complained of the Parisians in 1778; "they seem to think I am still seven years old because that was my age when they first saw me.") Leopold did his son no service by passing on to him his lack of social tact, his ill-concealed aversion to authority, his keen sense of injustice, his assumption of superiority. The Berlin *Musikalisches Wochenblatt*, writing about Mozart shortly after his death, said that throughout his career he was a victim of cabals, "which he at times may well have provoked by his *sans souci* manner". The observation of the Irish tenor Michael Kelly, that Mozart had "a thorough contempt for insolent mediocrity", suggests that he didn't attempt to hide it.

But the advantages were priceless; in that regard he could not have had a better upbringing. Leopold's breadth of interests and the lively personality revealed in his letters – "curious, attentive, always ready to give an opinion", as Braunbehrens puts it – ensured that Wolfgang's native intelligence was constantly stimulated and encouraged to expand beyond music. Within music, the preparation was ideal. Mozart was brought into live contact with everything that was going on. Like no other composer, he was given the opportunity to hear and study and absorb virtually every style and trend and to adopt whatever appealed to him – adopt and make it his own.

Superficially considered, you might say that almost everything in Mozart comes from somewhere, someone, else; that is a motif of his whole career. The more you get to know the music of his contemporaries the more you become aware of what he took from them. At the same time he is, paradoxically, in a deeper sense one of the least derivative of composers. The texture of divided violas found again and again in his scores from the time of *Apollo et Hyacinthus* (1767), if not before, was copied from the Salzburg composer Johann Ernst Eberlin; the spine-tingling crescendo near the end of the orchestral introduction of the first movement of the Sinfonia Concertante K364 was his direct response to the recent encounter with the Mannheim style; the haunting opening of the Requiem, his last composition, recalled the Requiem that Michael Haydn wrote for the funeral of Archbishop Schrattenbach of Salzburg in 1771 (and in which Mozart played violin). But these are annexations, not imitations – or rather it is like a natural process. It is not simply that we generally know his music before we hear theirs. The power of his assimilative genius was such that the influences were sucked out of their original context and drawn into his personal style; imperceptibly, they became his. What he did with them is, as always, what matters.

Apollo et Hyacinthus, a Latin play with musical intermezzos performed by the pupils of the Benedictine school and staged in the great hall of Salzburg University in May 1767, is Mozart's earliest theatre music (if we except the slightly earlier *Die Schuldigkeit des ersten Gebots*, a dramatic oratorio to which he contributed an act). By then, barely eleven years old but a veteran traveller, on the road every year since 1762 – eight months in Munich, three in Vienna, seven in Paris, fifteen in London – he had acquired a fascination with opera and the human voice and under Leopold's tuition had begun to cut his dramatic teeth on what would be a long and brilliant series of concert arias. Opera, Mozart's destined goal, was or could be, as Leopold well knew, a composer's richest source of wealth and a possible means to a court appointment.

Apollo has tended to be summarily disposed of by commentators. Dent says it "may be dismissed at once", and even Einstein waves it aside with "we need not occupy ourselves with an analysis". Yet, as Holmes would say, it presents points of unusual interest. The future dramatist peeps out from behind the formalities of the pastoral plot, and for one riveting instant we see him face to face. True, the first few numbers – there are ten altogether, in a score lasting about ninety minutes – are innocent of any special qualities, though we may wonder at their assurance (even if father was looking over his shoulder to correct any mistakes) and note that here and there a twist of harmony or an irregular phrase-length shows the embryonic Mozartian instinct stirring to life. But as the slender action develops and the characters' emotions begin to be opposed in a potentially fruitful tension – Apollo, betrothed to King Oebalus' daughter Melia, is wrongly believed to have killed the king's son Hyacinthus – things start to happen. At the hint of a dramatic situation Mozart's interest quickens. There is a fine thrusting aria for Oebalus, music of whirling energy and vivid imagery, which points distantly to the vengeance arias in *Zaide* and *Idomeneo*. The duet for the angry, bewildered Melia and the pleading Apollo already has, to an unexpected degree, the freedom and direct-ness of musical language characteristic of the mature Mozart. In the following scene the encounter between Oebalus and his dying son prompts the infant dramatist to an accompanied recitative made up of short panting phrases broken by silence and strange chord progressions.

If the tragic sublimity of *Idomeneo* is nevertheless still far off, what are we to say of the andante in which Oebalus and Melia mourn their double loss (Hyacinthus dead, Apollo apparently gone)? A long-breathed melodic line, floating out on muted first violins, then taken up by the voices, slowly unfolds above a pizzicato bass, while plucked chords on the second violins gently mark the intervening beats, and violas in two parts keep up a constant murmur of sixteenth notes. The consoling warmth that the sound of two horns spreads over the musical texture is partly contradicted by the anxious movement of the harmony, circling in and out of C major. The whole piece, in its brief, endless span, seems above and beyond time. There is in it a sense of ritual grieving and of suffering transcended that not only points forward to the sacrifice scene in *Idomeneo* but anticipates it, in style and mood.

During the next eight years Mozart composed eight operas: *La finta semplice* and *Bastien und Bastienne* for Vienna, *Mitridate*, *Ascanio in Alba* and *Lucio Silla* for Milan, *La finta giardiniera* for Munich, and the one-act *Il sogno di Scipione* and the serenata *Il rè pastore* for Salzburg. In them we see the gradual growth of his dramatic talents towards mastery – a mastery which, however, remained incomplete because of factors connected with his youth and with his relative inexperience both of the opera house and of the world. A boy of twelve was, not surprisingly, helpless against the intrigues which kept *La finta semplice* from the stage despite the Emperor's having ordered it. It was only too easy for gossip to hint that the score was actually the work of his father; if anything, Leopold's bitter complaints only made matters worse. Even at eighteen, the age at which Mozart composed *La finta giardiniera*, he was still too young to recognize when a libretto was weak. Einstein remarks that the difference between Mozart and "a hundred Italian contemporaries, not excluding the most famous ones" like Paisiello, Sarti, Piccinni or Cimarosa, was that once he reached maturity "he was no longer satisfied with dramatic nonsense". Meanwhile, though, it was a stage he had to go through.

He had also to learn to curb his natural creative exuberance. From quite early on, Mozart's music stood out from the others'. It was marked by a richness of harmony, texture and orchestral colour, a penchant for modulation (as noted in the earliest accounts), and a hint of the mature works' mercurial variability of mood ("the music changes all the time" in Bruno Walter's phrase): characteristics that were due partly to his being an instrumental composer, not just a composer of operas, but also to his nature. This abundance, which contemporary opinion was forever reproaching him for (and whose complexity, as Leopold Mozart warned, made the music particularly vulnerable to poor performance), is one of the things we relish in him. But in his teenage operas he had yet to control it and to know when not to spread himself. They contain – alongside the formal and conventional – beautiful inventions, arias that are finely shaped musical utterances and dramatically to the point, finales of an eventfulness that no Italian would have been capable of or would have thought proper. By the time of the latest opera seria, *Lucio Silla*, and still more the latest opera buffa, *La finta giardiniera*, the elements of Mozart's dramatic supremacy are in place, waiting. What these works lack is not ability but discrimination, and also luck: he has not met a good librettist, nor has he acquired the authority to bend a mediocre one to his wishes. He does not yet know what he wants. He has not lived enough. With all their beauties, they have a touch of the child who, in Barrington's words, when improvising a recitative and aria on the word *perfido* "worked himself up" to a pitch of mock fury. Sometimes he does seem emotionally engaged with his characters' feelings. At other times it is as if he were playing at it, consummately but not wholeheartedly, perhaps because his own heart has not yet been touched to the quick.

If Mozart had never written another opera – unthinkable thought! – we would surely pay greater attention to these prentice works and perform them more often: the opera serias, in which amid much that is over-elaborate or routine there are passages of striking power, in *Lucio Silla* especially, but still more the comic pieces. *La finta semplice* dutifully conforms to type, setting the commedia-dell'arte-derived characters of the foolish plot to appropriate music. But it is Mozart's music: charming, freshly scored, humorous when it has a chance to be, and from time to time hinting, to our surprise, at the later Viennese operas (whose performance his opponents were unable to prevent, however much they may have tried to). Ninetta, the archetypal saucy servant, is an unmistakable ancestor of Blonde in one of her two arias, and of Despina in the other. There is even a rather touching G major plea for forgiveness, in the Act 3 finale, which makes us think momentarily of the last scene of *Figaro*, and, just before it, an accompanied recitative that shows Mozart already realizing the dramatic possibilities of the form. The composer has learnt his craft and put his models to good use. Perhaps his enemies genuinely believed that the opera could not have been composed by a twelve-year-old.

La finta giardiniera of six years later is on the verge of greatness, held back largely by the inadequacy of its libretto, which is yet another (tepid) *réchauffage* of the war of the sexes, with madness thrown in, and which cannot make up its mind what kind of opera, how comic or how serious, it is supposed to be. Of course, as Einstein sternly declares, a "dramatic musician shows himself not only in how he composes an opera but also in what he deems worthy of composition"; but, as though relenting, Einstein adds that "when one has stated the basic error of this opera, which is that Mozart composed it at all, one must express delight at how he composed it". The characters may, again, be more types than individuals; the five arias of Sandrina, the "pretend gardener" of the title, who is the Marchesa Violante in disguise, in flight from the lover who tried to kill her, vary wildly in style according to which one she is being at the moment. In contrast to the composer of the Viennese comedies, this Mozart still tends to think in stereotypes and categories, in terms of voices more than of actual people. But within these limits and despite the distractions of a muddled, inconsequential plot, what riches he lavishes on their unsuspecting heads. The sharp-tongued servant Serpetta, another proto-Blonde, even has a phrase that is note for note Susanna's "il brando prendete, il paggio uccidete" in the scene where Susanna confronts the Count in the Act 2 finale of *Figaro*.

The aria in which Count Belfiore (another clumsily conceived character, part-serious, part-buffo) boasts of his famous ancestry stretching back to Marcus Aurelius and Cato is in Mozart's true comic vein. At the other extreme are two of Sandrina/Violante's arias, the first a tender cavatina in G major with a flavour of Ilia's "Zeffiretti" in *Idomeneo*, the second – when she has been abandoned in a dark forest – a vivid C minor allegro agitato that is Elettra-like in its bright, baleful orchestration and stabbing offbeat accents, itself followed by an accompanied recitative of exceptional force. The finales of Act 1 and Act 2 have a variety and inventiveness of rhythm, harmony and scoring far beyond anything achieved or attempted by Piccinni or J. C. Bach or by Anfossi, who composed a *Finta giardiniera* a year before Mozart. They are not true finales in the sense of those of *Figaro*, *Don Giovanni* and *Così*; there is little if any counterpoint of voices; the characters do not interact so much as have their say in turn. And, for most of the opera, the aria rules, not the ensemble. But Mozart is ready for the next big step.

*

In the event it will be six years before he has a chance to take it. In that time his mastery grows and, in the family home, the Tanzmeister-haus on Hannibalplatz, he writes works that we recognize as quint-essentially Mozartian in their grace and magical felicity. These are the years of the A major symphony (No. 29), the violin concertos, the Serenata Notturna, the Haffner Serenade, the E flat piano concerto K271, the divertimento in B flat K287, and a host of other instru-mental pieces, church music too, poured out for the delectation of the court and citizenry of Salzburg (who by and large fail to appreciate their immense good fortune), but scarcely at all of music for the theatre. His sole opportunities are the two-act pastoral *Il rè pastore*, composed for the visit of Archduke Maximilian Franz in 1775 and given "semi-staged" in the archbishop's palace – melodious music of great assurance and fluency, elegantly scored, but not what he would have regarded as real opera – and the fiery incidental music to Gebler's play *Thamos, King of Egypt*, performed the following year.

Mozart had seen what the great musical centres had to offer and, though no permanent appointment or further commissions had come, had achieved sufficient success, especially in Milan and Munich, to be hungry for more. No wonder he felt a prisoner in Salzburg. In Salzburg there was "no theatre, no opera". The increasingly fraught relations with his employer, Archbishop Colloredo, only exacerbated a situ-ation which had become deeply frustrating. Colloredo, an authori-tarian but a music-lover, a musician, and a man of culture, imbued with some of the ideas of the Enlightenment, can hardly be blamed for not seeing the case as we do. He was not to know that he would go down in history as the ruler who treated one of the world's supreme treasures like dirt. That he regarded Mozart as a musician of talent and a useful member of his entourage is clear from the fact that he was prepared to have him back as konzertmeister after his sixteen-month absence in Mannheim and Paris and also appoint him court organist, at a good salary. But the insubordination and impertinence of both father and son, in the summer of 1777, were simply not to be tolerated.

The journey on which Mozart and his mother set out in September 1777, in quest of fame and fortune, would prove a catalyst in his life. For the first time he was free of his father (if not of his anxious, admonishing letters); in Mannheim he met the Webers – Fridolin, violinist and singer, his wife Maria Cäcilie, and their daughters – and found in them a surrogate family; he fell passionately in love with the seventeen-year-old Aloisia Weber and with her voice and, to Leopold's alarm, made up his mind that he would marry her and launch her as a famous singer (which she duly became); he heard the Mannheim orchestra and was thrilled by it: "Oh, if only we had clarinets too! You can't imagine the glorious effect of a symphony with flutes, oboes and clarinets"; in Paris he came into contact with the French tradition of choral opera which would be an important influence; in Paris he watched his mother die; in Mannheim, on his slow way home, he was rejected by Aloisia. He came back in January 1779, to Salzburg, a different person. But he came back to the same operatic desert. The town had meanwhile acquired a theatre, but no resident company to go with it. Mozart's career was going nowhere.

He reacted by seemingly doing what he almost never did: composing a work without immediate prospect of a performance. *Zaide* (as it is known, after the name of its heroine) is a singspiel written to a text by his friend Schachtner, based on a contemporary singspiel *Das Serail* (*The Harem*), which was itself derived from Voltaire's *Zaïre*. Mozart probably intended it for Johannes Böhm's travelling company, which was in Salzburg in the winter of 1779–80, when it performed *Thamos* and a German version of *La finta giardiniera*; but he seems also to have had his eye on Vienna, where the Emperor, Joseph II, had created a singspiel company as the musical wing of the German-language National-Theater.

Zaide remained incomplete. Since no libretto and therefore no spoken dialogue has survived and the denouement is missing, presumed not composed, the work is understandably a little difficult to stage, though valiant attempts have been made. Would the angry sultan have ended by pardoning his two escaping slaves and his renegade overseer? Would the hero and heroine, who have fallen in love, have been revealed – just in time – to be brother and sister, as in *Das Serail* and *Zaïre*? Probably not; but who can tell? For that matter, why did Mozart, having completed fifteen numbers, drop it when there was apparently only the overture and the final scene to write? From the fact that he took the score with him when he moved to Vienna a year later, it is clear that he considered it a viable proposition.

Though the putative plot is not impressive, the high quality of the best numbers – the exquisite E major trio, Zaide's lullaby over the sleeping Gomatz, her furiously defiant outburst against the sultan's cruelty, "Tiger, wetze nur die Klauen", and the quartet – is enough to explain Mozart's continuing interest in the work and the regard it is held in today. It also offers the curiosity of two numbers in melodrama form – speech alternating with and heightened by orchestral music – which Mozart was briefly attracted to after he heard Georg Benda's *Medea* in Mannheim in 1778 and studied his *Ariadne auf Naxos*.

Maybe Mozart did after all write *Zaide* for performance, by Böhm's troupe, and there is a simple practical explanation for his abandoning it: he had nearly completed the score when the event occurred which put everything else, *Zaide* included, out of mind – the commission to compose the main opera for the Munich Carnival. He had got his chance at last.

2

"Such great things in so small a head"

Idomeneo

In *Idomeneo* Mozart, abruptly, comes of age. True, there had been a steady deepening of his musical style in the years leading up to it, and one or two individual works in which the artist of the Vienna period stands fully armed before us: the Sinfonia Concertante for violin and viola K364, composed in 1779, and even more startlingly the E flat piano concerto K271 of more than two years earlier, by tradition associated with a visiting French pianist, Mme Jenamy or Jenomé, round whom legend has tried to weave a love affair to account for the brilliance, pathos and liberating boldness of the work. Yet nothing prepares for the explosion of *Idomeneo*. No other opera of Mozart's except *Don Giovanni*, perhaps none by anybody else, starts at such a pitch of emotional intensity, which it then sustains for most of its three-hour duration.

Quite apart from the formal freedom it displays right from the beginning, the richness, force and flexibility of the musical language take the breath away. This is something new, unheard till then. How explain it? What was it that moved the twenty-four-year-old Mozart, when the commission reached him in the summer of 1780 – what moved him so deeply that it released a flood of passion not found in his music before, raised his art to a new level, and transformed serious Italian music-drama out of recognition, creating a work unique in eighteenth-century opera?

Plenty of external factors can be adduced; but they provide a context, not a cause. Certainly, the liberties *Idomeneo* takes with the genre and the expressive demands it makes on singers and instrumentalists would have been unthinkable without the high ideals and lavish conditions which made the electoral court of Mannheim a centre of enlightenment rivalling if not surpassing Frederick the Great's Berlin, and which survived largely intact when the court moved to Munich. The Elector Carl Theodor was a ruler steeped in Enlightenment culture, deeply interested and actively involved in the study of science, philosophy, language and the arts, and he had gathered round him a group of like-minded people who helped generate the serious atmosphere which captivated Mozart when he arrived in Mannheim in 1777. His library, presided over by a statue of Voltaire (whom he received as an honoured guest), had no equal. Carl Theodor maintained a French theatrical troupe, dedicated to performing the great classical dramas. But of all the arts it was music that excited and absorbed him most. Music – in Charles Burney's words, "the chief and most constant of his electoral highness's amusements" – pervaded every activity of court life, its ceremonies, processions, pageants, hunts, banquets, and was at the centre of its entertainments. The Elector, who himself played flute and cello, was a devoted patron of composers and performers, employing some of the leading figures of the day, commissioning important operatic premieres, watching over the development of his younger musicians and sending the most gifted to Italy to refine their education (Christian Cannabich, the violinist and, later, concertmaster who befriended Mozart, was one of them). His orchestra set new standards of virtuosity and expressiveness – Leopold Mozart said it was the finest he had ever heard. Equally exceptional were the opera company's theatrical skills and achievements. The choreographer and stage director Pierre Le Grand and the designer Lorenzo Quaglio were artists of European renown, masters of scenic effect and what the French called "le merveilleux". Their talents were lavished on a succession of grand tragic operas that Carl Theodor and his entourage brought into being, first in Mannheim and then in Munich. *Idomeneo* was far from exceptional in infusing into Italian opera seria values and techniques from the very different tradition of French tragédie-lyrique, above all from Gluck's Paris operas, in particular the two *Iphigénies* and the second version of *Alceste*. That was the pattern of Mannheim–Munich: a loftiness of vision inspired by Racine and the Greek Revival, a large role for the chorus, strong emphasis on stage spectacle, and a predilection for subjects like the Iphigenia myth which showed an all-powerful ruler trapped in an extreme moral dilemma.

In the matter of compositional detail, *Idomeneo*'s overture was by no means the first to be conceived as an integral part of the drama, prefiguring its content. Nor was Mozart the first composer to be concerned to achieve dramatic continuity, to reduce the number of da capo arias, to fill his score with expressive accompanied recitative, and to assign a major role to the orchestra. Such innovations are found in operas by composers active in Mannheim in the 1760s and 1770s like Jommelli, Traetta and J. C. Bach, or like Holzbauer, whose *Günther von Schwarzburg* impressed Mozart when he heard it in 1777 – for serious opera in German was another initiative of Carl Theodor's.

In short, Mozart was writing for an operatic culture whose ideas chimed with those he had himself been developing under the combined influence of French drama, Gluck's operas and his own deepest instincts. His letters from Paris, two years earlier, show him searching through French librettos, old and recent, for possible subjects, and generally preferring the old; and it was a French text of 1712, by Antoine Danchet, that Munich commissioned him to adapt as an Italian opera (a practice common at the time). It was only to be expected that he would jump at the chance offered by orchestral playing and staging of such high quality and that composing for them would have a powerful impact on the way he wrote – composing too for Mannheim musicians who had become his friends and whose abilities he knew and appreciated: the tenor Anton Raaff (Idomeneo), the sopranos Dorothea and Lisel Wendling (Ilia and Elettra respectively), Lisel's husband the violinist Franz Anton Wendling, Dorothea's the flautist Johann Baptist Wendling, the oboist Friedrich Ramm (for whom he would compose the oboe quartet, his first fully characteristic chamber work), Punto the first horn, and the Munich first flute Johann Baptist Becke.

Yet, even given the coincidence of a perfect and longed-for challenge and a Mozart ready to rise to it, the result is astonishing. No one had used the orchestra like that, no one had remoulded the forms of Italian opera to achieve that degree of dramatic continuity, no one, remotely, had created characters as palpably alive and deeply felt as Ilia and Elettra and Idomeneo himself, no one had written such impassioned music before. How did it come about?

*

When, many years later, Constanze told Mary Novello that the happiest time of Mozart's life was when he was in Munich working on *Idomeneo*, she was surely neither inventing nor exaggerating; that was before she married him, when her sister Aloisia, not she, was the one he was in love with. His words must have left a decisive impression on her memory. Constanze also recalled the occasion, two years after *Idomeneo*, when she and Mozart visited Salzburg and the two of them, with Leopold and Nannerl, sang the quartet from Act 3. At the end, "he was so overcome that he burst into tears and quit the chamber, and it was some time before I could console him".

Mozart is far from being the only person to have been moved to tears by the quartet, in which the emotional intensity characteristic of the score reaches its highest point. He, though, had special cause. *Idomeneo* was the fulfilment of a yearning that had been growing for the past five years, and of which he had written to his father from Mannheim in the winter of 1777–8, when he hoped to receive a commission from the court: "Remember how much I long to write operas. I envy anyone who is composing one. I could really weep for vexation when I hear or see an aria." He told the Elector to his face that his "dearest wish" was "to write an opera here".

Perhaps that would have happened but for the dynastic and political upheavals which led to the removal of Carl Theodor and his court nearly two hundred miles south-east, to Munich. If so, the delay was providential. By the time the commission arrived, two and a half years later, the experiences Mozart had lived through had changed him. His compositional powers were at full readiness, waiting; the chosen subject answered his psychological and emotional needs as few others could have done.

Was it Mozart who chose it? However unlikely, it is not impossible. The leading authority on *Idomeneo*, Daniel Heartz, has argued that though the standard procedure was for the ruler and his advisers to select the subject as well as the composer, in this case the suggestion may conceivably have come from Mozart himself. As we have seen, he had made a point, while in Paris, of exploring French dramatic literature in search of potential texts, and had thought "the old ones" the best, though they would have to be "adapted to the modern style". He would certainly have discussed such matters with Friedrich

Melchior Grimm during the weeks when he lodged with him in the rue de la Chaussée d'Antin – Grimm who had stated, in writing, that Idomenée was an excellent subject for tragic opera. Without doubt there would have been a copy of Danchet's *Idomenée* in the well-stocked electoral library, given Carl Theodor's special interest in French drama; but Mozart shared the same interest – a complete edition of Racine was listed among his possessions at his death – and could well have brought with him from Paris a volume containing Danchet's libretto. As Heartz points out, the Jephtha-like situation offered great possibilities:

Its theme of human sacrifice gave him an opportunity to rival Gluck on his own terrain; and to make the libretto all the more Gluckian, Mozart added the final redemption through love (not in Danchet). Moreover, the Idomeneus myth had not seen much operatic use, unlike the parallel story of Agamemnon sacrificing his daughter Iphigenia. Father–son conflicts were rather rare in opera at the time. This kernel of the story, I suggest, was what first attracted Mozart's attention. So much at least is certain: once he became involved in recounting the drama through his art, it called forth some of the most passionate and personal music he ever wrote.

Reading the letters Mozart wrote from Mannheim in 1777–8 and the later ones from Munich, one has the impression that, though the Elector never appointed him to a position at either of his courts, he was intrigued by Mozart and aware that in him there was a talent quite out of the ordinary (as he said after hearing a rehearsal of Ilia's Act 2 aria and the thunderstorm, "who would believe that such great things could be hidden in so small a head?"). May Mozart, on his way through Munich in December 1778 and January 1779, have spoken to someone at court about an opera on Idomeneo, or alternatively have mentioned the idea to Raaff and Cannabich – both of whom, he said, had been "working for me tirelessly" – and they, as important court employees, passed it on? It may be significant that the poet chosen to adapt Danchet's libretto – the Abbé Giambattista Varesco – lived in Salzburg and was a fellow-employee of Mozart's at the archiepiscopal court: in other words, the initiative, the choice of librettist, might have been Mozart's, and the Munich officials merely agreed to it. Both scenarios are, of course, possible: the court commissioned an opera from Mozart on a subject his soul had already "sealed for itself".

In a sense the issue is irrelevant. Even if the choice was the Elector's, it was heaven-sent. To quote Max Loppert, it offered, within a grand "seriosa" frame, "every dramatic situation to which Mozart might be expected to respond most keenly at the time". He had fallen in love, only for that love to be rejected. The death of his mother in Paris had left him bereft and, for the first time in his life, completely alone – the effect of which, in Heartz's phrase, had been to send him "into a kind of creative shock". The whole expensive expedition, lasting sixteen months, from September 1777 to January 1779, had been on the face of it a disaster: no situation secured in Mannheim or in Paris, no opera commission, a meagre harvest of music composed, and relations with his beloved father strained almost to breaking – Leopold angry, hurt, scornful, bitterly reproachful, Wolfgang guiltily evasive, ordered peremptorily home to hated Salzburg but, to his father's exasperation, dragging out the return journey on one dubious pretext after another.

In fact, both Mannheim and Paris were to prove of inestimable benefit, the one through the revelation of a musical environment of a richness hardly dreamed of in Salzburg and through the friendships made there and the allies gained, the other through contact with an operatic tradition whose grandeur and seriousness made a profound impression on him. But that would be for later. For now, it was back to Salzburg and its limitations and discontents. The next eighteen months were hardly barren of compositions: the exuberant Coronation Mass and the other C major mass, K337, the symphonies No. 33 and No. 34, the Posthorn Serenade, the serenade K334, the concerto for two pianos, the great Sinfonia Concertante, and many lesser works. But the lack of a resident opera company remained a constant and growing frustration.

No letters survive from this period; the two indefatigable correspondents were reunited in the Tanzmeisterhaus and reached some kind of accommodation. It needs no imagination, however, to divine what Mozart felt. Salzburg was a prison. Unlike Hamlet, he could not be bounded in a nutshell and count himself a king of infinite space. Salzburg as desert, because opera-less, had been a recurring theme in the letters written over the past few years. To be himself and realize his dreams, he needed the theatre. And then, at last, about midsummer 1780, the commission, and the chance to give out all that he had learned from life and art, all he had experienced of love and suffering and pity and guilt, his comprehensive understanding of the dramatic, his consciousness of unequalled powers, in an opera that was an answer to prayer.

At the heart of *Idomeneo* is the scene where, in music of profound tenderness, the father is reconciled with the son whose fated death he has fought so stubbornly to avert and whom he must now slaughter with his own hand. A broad string passage in A flat major, with the violas rising through A natural, introduces Idamante, robed for the sacrifice. "Padre, mio caro padre, ah dolce nome . . . Now I understand – your agitation was not anger but paternal love." And Idomeneo, in a variant of the same phrase (the violas, with the cellos, now descending in a long chromatic line): "Oh figlio, o caro figlio, perdona." What must Mozart have thought as he set those words, what echoes they sounded in the depths of his soul! He does not tell us – except through his music. Yet there cannot be any doubt that the transformation of Danchet's brutal denouement was his work. Certainly, the Enlightenment would have insisted on nothing less than the same happy ending as crowns Gluck's operas. But the drastic remodelling of the last act, culminating in Neptune's being moved by Ilia's selfless nobility to revoke the sacrifice, is surely attributable more to Mozart than to Varesco or to Count Joseph Anton von Seeau, the intendant of the theatre. The additions in Act 3 of *Idomeneo*, as Heartz observes – crowd scene in front of the palace, high priest's monologue, chorus of lamentation, march, temple scene with priests' chorus, reconciliation, Ilia's attempt to replace Idamante as sacrificial victim, Oracle – are clearly inspired by Gluck's *Alceste*, which Mozart, if he did not see it while he was in Paris (there is no direct evidence), unquestionably studied and pondered. Gluck's dramas were a natural model. They were admired at the Elector's court, where their lofty treatment of the themes of rulers face to face with terrible decisions and sacrifice for the common weal were much in fashion. More than that, they were an example for Mozart to emulate and if possible surpass. *Idomeneo* shows Mozart taking careful note of two defining features of *Alceste*, the dramatic force of the accompanied recitatives and the continuity between numbers.

The Mozart correspondence speaks of the "plan", apparently a detailed treatment agreed with Count Seeau, and perhaps originally drawn up by him but more likely, I think, by Mozart himself: everything we know about *Idomeneo* and its creation points to his being the controlling mind.

We know more about the genesis of the work than we do about the genesis of any other opera of the period, thanks to the long letters exchanged between father and son after Mozart moved to Munich – letters indicating the many changes that Mozart, using Leopold as go-between, wished Varesco to make in the libretto. For the period between the arrival of the commission sometime that summer and Mozart's departure for Munich early in November there are no direct sources – the correspondence between Mozart and the court has not survived – but it is clear that these two or three months were occupied not only with composition but, before that could happen, with hard, concentrated work on transforming Danchet's tragédie-lyrique into the libretto that Mozart required.

The text had, first of all, to be stripped of its allegorical paraphernalia, the intrusive deities and supernatural influences dear to the Baroque but unacceptable to the Enlightenment (preliminary scenes that lasted a good half hour in *Idomenée* as set by Campra). Only Neptune remained. Thus cleared, the first two acts could follow the original fairly closely, with much of Varesco's text a straightforward translation of the French, and for the new arias a resort to the common stock of images and metaphors established by Metastasio, which Varesco could draw on with reasonably practised skill. Some passages bear the mark of Mozart's acute dramatic sense (the recognition scene between Idomeneo and his son on the seashore, for one). Mozart's was the vision and the driving force behind a libretto that was already transcending conventional patterns. In particular, the remodelling of Act 3, along the lines mentioned above, must have involved long and arduous sessions; apart from the opening scene of the act, for Ilia alone and then for her and Idamante, almost everything was altered.

*

When Mozart left Salzburg he took with him a copy of the completed libretto and parts of the score, including some of the arias. Normally a composer would wait till he met his singers and could assess their voices and their capabilities; but Mozart was already familiar with his Idomeneo, his Ilia and his Elettra, and had heard the first two perform music he had written for them. On 8 November, within a couple of days of his arrival, he told his father that Dorothea Wendling (Ilia) was "*arcicontentissima* with her scene [the opening recitative and first aria] – she insisted on hearing it played three times in succession"; shortly afterwards Lisel Wendling (Elettra) was described as having "sung through her two arias half a dozen times" and as being "delighted with them".

In the letter of 8 November came also a demand for changes in the text:

Some slight alterations will have to be made here and there, and the recitatives will have to be shortened a bit. But *everything will be printed*. I have just one request to make of the Abbate [Varesco]. Ilia's aria in Act 2, scene 2, should be altered slightly to suit what I require. "Se il padre perdei, in te lo ritrovo" – this verse could not be better. But now comes what has always seemed unnatural to me – I mean, in an aria – and that is, *a spoken aside*. In a dialogue all these things are quite natural, for a few words can be spoken aside hurriedly; but in an aria where the words have to be repeated, it has a bad effect, and even if this were not the case I should prefer an uninterrupted aria. The beginning may stand, if it suits him, for the poem is charming, and as it is absolutely natural and flowing and therefore as I have not got to contend with difficulties arising from the words, I can go on composing quite easily; for we have agreed to introduce here an aria andantino with obbligatos for four wind instruments, that is, flute, oboe, horn and bassoon. I beg you therefore to let me have the text as soon as possible.

"Just one request" turned out to be the first of many. Five days later:

The second duet ["Deh soffri in pace", in the sacrifice scene, Act 3] is to be omitted altogether – and indeed with more profit than loss to the opera. For, when you read through the scene, you will see that it obviously becomes limp and cold by the addition of an aria or a duet, and very *gênant* for the other actors who must stand by doing nothing; and, besides, the noble struggle between Ilia and Idamante would be too long and thus lose its whole force.

Now that he was in the thick of it, Mozart became aware of considerations that had not been clear to him when he and Varesco first shaped the libretto.

To Act 1 scene 8 Quaglio has made the same objection that we made originally – I mean, that it is not fitting that the king should be quite alone in the ship. If the Abbé thinks that he can be reasonably represented in the terrible storm forsaken by everyone, without a ship, quite alone and exposed to the greatest peril, then let it stand; but please cut out the ship, for he cannot be alone in one. But if the other situation is adopted, a few generals, who are in his confidence, must land with him. Then he must address a few words to his people and desire them to leave him alone, which in his present melancholy situation is quite natural. A propos, shall I soon have the aria for Madame Wendling?

This prompted a long, detailed reply, full of counter-suggestions, from Leopold Mozart. In the meantime, Mozart had asked for a further radical change:

In the last scene of Act 2 Idomeneo has an aria or rather a cavatina between the choruses. Here it will be *better* to have simply a recitative, well supported by the instruments. For in this scene, which will be the finest in the whole opera (on account of the action and grouping which were settled recently with Le Grand), there will be so much noise and confusion on the stage that an aria at this particular point would cut a poor figure – and, besides, there is the thunderstorm, which is not likely to subside during Herr Raaff's aria, is it? The effect, therefore, of a recitative between the choruses will be infinitely better. (15 November)

Like all eighteenth-century composers he was having to satisfy his singers as well as his own dramatic judgement, for their goodwill was essential to the success of the opera. It was a delicate balancing act.

The aria [for Ilia] is excellent now, but there is still one more alteration, for which Raaff is responsible. He is right, however – and even if he were not, some courtesy ought to be shown to his grey hairs. He was with me yesterday. I ran through his first aria for him and he was well pleased with it. Now, the man is old and can no longer show off in such an aria as the one in Act 2 –

"Fuor del mar ho un mar nel seno". So, as he has no aria in Act 3 and as his aria in Act 1, owing to the expression of the words, cannot be as cantabile as he would like, he wishes to have a pretty one to sing (instead of the quartet) after his last speech, "O Creta fortunata! O me felice!" Thus, as well, a useless piece will be got rid of – and Act 3 will be far more effective.

Yet another request followed on 24 November:

Do ask Abbate Varesco if we may not break off at the chorus in Act 2, "Placido è il mar", after Elettra's first verse when the chorus has been repeated – or, failing that, after the second, as it is really far too long! By the next mail coach I hope to receive the recitative and aria for Herr Raaff.

He received it soon afterwards, but neither he nor Raaff liked it.

The aria is not at all what we wanted it to be. I mean, it ought to express peace and contentment, and this it suggests only in the second part. We have seen, heard and felt sufficiently throughout the opera all the misfortunes Idomeneo has had to endure; now he should talk about his present condition. Nor do we need a second part – all the better. In [Pietro Pompeo Sales's] opera *Achille in Sciro*, of which Metastasio wrote the text, there is an aria of the kind in the style which Raaff would like.

Mozart quotes the text, then continues:

Tell me, don't you think the speech of the subterranean voice is too long? Consider it carefully. Picture to yourself the theatre, and remember that the voice must be awe-inspiring – must penetrate – that the audience must believe it is real. Well, how can that effect be produced if the speech is too long? The listener will become more and more convinced that it isn't real. If the Ghost's speech in *Hamlet* were not so long it would be far more effective. The speech of the subterranean voice can easily be shortened, and it will gain more than it will lose. For the March in Act 2, which is heard in the distance, I need mutes for the trumpets and horns, which are impossible to get here. Will you send me one of each by the next mail coach, so that I can have them copied?

Leopold agreed that the subterranean speech was too long. "I have given Varesco my candid opinion and it will now be made as short as possible." He was becoming more and more caught up in the composition of the opera. It was like the old days.

I assume that you will choose very deep wind instruments to accompany the subterranean voice. How would it be if, after the slight subterranean rumble, the instruments sustained or rather began to sustain their notes piano and then made a crescendo of a sort to inspire terror, and then during the decrescendo the voice would begin to sing? There could be a frightening crescendo at every phrase uttered by the voice. [. . .] Why, I seem to hear it and see it!

In the meantime Mozart had reported that Raaff was

as infatuated with [his Act 2 aria] as a young and ardent lover might be with his fair one, for he sings it at night before going to sleep and in the morning when he awakes. As I heard first from a reliable source and now from his own lips, he said to Herr von Viereck, Chief Equerry, and to Herr von Castel: "Hitherto both in recitatives and in arias I have always been accustomed to alter my parts to suit me, but here everything remains as it was written, for I cannot find a note which doesn't suit me," etc. Enfin, he's as happy as a king.

The text of his Act 3 aria still disappointed him, however ("we both want gentler and more pleasing words"), and negotiations continued. On 5 December – after reminders about the trumpet mute ("of the kind we had made in Vienna"), "and also one for the horn, which you can get from the watchmen" – it was the turn of Panzacchi, who was singing the role of Arbace, the king's counsellor:

We must do what we can to oblige this worthy old fellow. He would like to have his recitative in Act 3 lengthened by a couple of lines, which owing to the *chiaro e oscuro* and his being a good actor will have a capital effect. For example, after the line: "Sei la città del pianto, e questa reggia quella del duol" [you are the city of tears and this palace that of sorrow], there is a faint glimmer of hope, and then – how foolish of me, where does my grief lead me? "Ah Creta tutta io vedo", etc. [I see all Crete, etc.] Abbate Varesco need not write out the act again on account of these points – the alterations can easily be added.

The alterations were duly sent (though Varesco was becoming distinctly irritable). The trumpet mute arrived too, and the "black suit" Mozart had requested, as the Empress Maria Theresa had died (the waistcoat's taffeta lining was so torn that it had had to be repaired);

the horn mutes, however, could not be sent, the nightwatchman's apprentices who owned them were away. Eventually a pair was found.

A fortnight later Mozart was still demanding changes.

The scene between father and son in Act 1 and the first scene in Act 2, between Idomeneo and Arbace, are both too long. They would certainly bore the audience, particularly as in the first scene both the actors are bad and in the second one of them is; besides, they only contain a narrative of what the spectators have already seen with their own eyes. These scenes are being printed as they stand. But I should like the Abbate to indicate how they may be shortened – and as drastically as possible – otherwise I shall have to shorten them myself. These two scenes cannot remain as they are – I mean, when set to music.

This time Varesco cut up rough, and Leopold Mozart sent a long and reasoned reply, going through the two scenes line by line and urging against any cuts in either of them; but Mozart was adamant: practical considerations made it imperative. "Raaff and dal Prato [Idamante] spoil the recitative by singing it without any spirit or fire, and *so* monotonously." Raaff, though "the most honest fellow in the world", was "tied to old-fashioned routine" and "too fond of everything which is cut and dried, and he pays no attention to expression" (27 December).

In the same letter Mozart described the "bad time" he had had with Raaff over the quartet in Act 3:

The more I think of this quartet, as it will be performed on the stage, the more effective I consider it; and it has pleased all those who have heard it played on the clavier. Raaff alone thinks it will produce no effect whatever. He said to me when we were by ourselves: "Non c'è da spianar la voce [you can't let your voice go in it]. It gives me no scope." As if in a quartet the words should not be spoken much more than sung. He doesn't understand that kind of thing at all. All I said was: "My very dear friend, if I knew of one single note which ought to be altered in this quartet, I would alter it at once. But so far there is nothing in my opera that I am so pleased with as this quartet; and when you have once heard it sung as a whole you will talk very differently. I have taken great pains to serve you well in your two arias; I shall do the same with the third, and I hope I shall succeed. But as far as trios

and quartets are concerned, the composer must have a free hand." [. . .] I
have had my black suit turned, for it was really very shabby. Now it looks
quite presentable.

Three days later:

Raaff is delighted that he was mistaken about the quartet and no longer
doubts its effect. I am now in difficulty in regard to his last aria, and you
must help me out of it. He cannot stomach [so many i's in] "rinvigorir" and
"ringiovenir" [words that occurred in Varesco's second attempt at the aria]
– and these two words make the whole aria distasteful to him. "Mostrami"
and "vienmi" are also not good, but the two final words are the worst of all.
To avoid the shake on the i in the first rinvigorir I really should transfer it to
the o. In [Metastasio's] *Natal di Giove*, which is, I admit, very little known,
Raaff has now found an aria which I believe is admirably suited to the
situation. [Mozart quotes the text.] He wants me to set this to music. "No
one knows the words," he says, "and we can keep quiet about it." He realizes
that we cannot expect the Abbate to alter the aria a third time, and he will
not sing it as it stands. I beg you to reply immediately. I hope to hear from
you on Wednesday – I shall then have plenty of time to compose the aria.
(30 December)

Varesco, though protesting, did send a third version of the aria, and
this time it was declared satisfactory. Yet, even now, Mozart had not
done. On 3 January, with the first night less than three weeks ahead,
he told his father that

no doubt we shall have a good many points to raise in Act 3 when it gets on
the stage. For example, in scene 6, after Arbace's aria, I see that Varesco
has "Idomeneo, Arbace" etc. How can the latter reappear immediately?
Fortunately he can stay away altogether. But for safety's sake I have composed
a somewhat longer introduction to the High Priest's recitative. After the
mourning chorus the king and all his people exit. In the following scene the
stage directions say: "Idomeneo in ginocchione nel tempio" [Idomeneo on
his knees in the temple]. That is quite impossible. He must come in with his
whole suite [the final version reads: "Enter Idomeneo accompanied by a large
and splendid retinue"]. A march must be introduced here, so I have composed
a very simple one for two violins, viola, cello and two oboes. While it is going
on the king appears and the priests prepare the offerings for the sacrifice.

Then the king kneels and begins the prayer. In Elettra's recitative, after the subterranean voice has spoken, there should be an indication – "Partono". I forgot to look at the copy which has been made for the printer, to see whether there is one and, if so, where it comes. It seems to me very silly that they should hurry away so quickly, for no better reason than to allow Madame Elettra to be alone.

Raaff, as the letters show, was not the only member of the cast to cause problems. At least, though he had never learned to act (he had remained, all his long career, what Metastasio had called him years before, "a block of ice"), he was still, at sixty-six, a distinguished singer, with good breath control and exemplary diction. The same could not be said for the Idamante, Vincenzo dal Prato. Mozart was wrong when he stated that the young castrato – twenty-four at the time of *Idomeneo* – was making his first appearance on the stage. But he might as well have been. He was a wooden actor and a worse singer. Shortly after arriving in Munich Mozart told his father that he would have to teach the whole opera to his "molto amato castrato dal Prato. He has no notion how to sing a cadenza effectively, and his voice is so uneven!" Shortly after that, dal Prato sang at a concert "disgracefully badly". The "wretch" was "a complete wash-out". "I have to sing with him, for I must teach him his whole part as if he were a child." More than a month later, during a recitative rehearsal at Wendling's,

we went through the quartet together. We repeated it six times and now it goes well. The stumbling-block was dal Prato; the fellow is utterly useless. His voice wouldn't be so bad if he didn't produce it in his throat and larynx. But he has no intonation, no method, no feeling, but sings – like the best of the boys who come to be tested in the hope of getting a place in the chapel choir.

That of course was one of the reasons why a composer was expected to be on the spot several weeks before the premiere of an opera: to make sure his singers knew what they were doing and if necessary to teach them their parts. We hear no more of dal Prato in the three and a half weeks between the letter just quoted and Leopold Mozart's departure for Munich, so maybe Mozart succeeded in knocking a little sense and style into him. It looks as if he improved: he had been engaged only for one season, but in the event he would still be there twenty-five years later.

In any case, nothing could damp Mozart's spirits. He was having the time of his life. It was the fulfilment of everything he had dreamed of, of everything he had learned in the past twenty years. As though sensing this, aware too of the magnitude of the task he had set himself and of how far it was beyond what anyone else had done, he came to Munich much earlier than was normal for a composer with a new opera to supervise, arriving more than ten weeks before the first night (then scheduled for 20 January).

From the first the mood of his letters is buoyant. The music he has brought with him is as good as he was sure it was, and it is catching on. Ilia is *arcicontentissima* with her opening scene. Count Seeau is unrecognizable from the curmudgeon they had known six years before ("the Mannheim people have transformed him"). The leading musicians are "one and all" for him, and Cannabich is proving a really good friend. The Elector greets him with "I am glad to see you here again", claps him on the shoulder, and says, "I have no doubt whatever that all will go well." (Mozart comments: "A piano piano, si va lontano" [slow and sure wins the race].) After an orchestral rehearsal in late November, he "cannot tell" his father "how delighted and surprised they all were". Young Count Sensheim says to him that though he had expected a good deal from him he "really did not expect that", and Ramm the oboist exclaims that "no music has ever made such an impression" on him and that he "thought fifty times of your father and of what his delight will be when he hears this opera". (Leopold Mozart, when he comes, will have to get used to a lot of kissing. "When you call at Dorothea Wendling's, where everything is rather in the French style, you will have to embrace both mother and daughter – but on the chin, of course, so that their rouge doesn't turn blue.") Leopold has heard similar reports:

Fiala has just been to see me and has shown me a letter from Herr Becke [Munich flute-player], full of praises of your music for Act 1. He said that "tears of joy and delight came into his eyes when he heard it, and that all the performers maintained that this was the most beautiful music they had ever heard, that it was all new and strange and so forth, and they were now about to rehearse Act 2."

Four days later, on 19 December, Mozart reports that the second rehearsal (held at Count Seeau's, in Prannerstrasse) has gone off as well as the first, orchestra and audience discovering, to their delight, that Act 2 is even more original and expressive than Act 1.

Next Saturday both acts are to be rehearsed again. But this time the rehearsal is to be held in a large hall at Court, which I have long wished for, as there is not nearly enough room at Count Seeau's. The Elector is to listen incognito in an adjoining room. Well, as Cannabich said to me, "we shall have to rehearse like the deuce". At the last rehearsal he was dripping with sweat.

Afterwards the Elector speaks of it "to everyone with whom he converses": "No music has ever made such an impression on me. It is magnificent." Meanwhile Mozart has written to his father that he should "join me in Munich soon, and hear my opera – and then tell me if I am wrong to feel depressed when I think of Salzburg". Leopold and Nannerl will duly join him shortly before the dress rehearsal and will stay at his lodgings, on the second floor of 6 Burggasse (a few hundred yards from the electoral residence and the theatre); a bed, Leopold had written earlier, could be "placed in the room where you have been composing": they can "put up with a little discomfort" and if necessary "live like gypsies and soldiers – no new experience for us!"

The letters from Munich to Salzburg sound a new note. The balance of the relationship between son and father is shifting. Mozart is much less on the defensive. He answers his father's reproaches gently but firmly. He involves him in the progress of his opera, not only as go-between but for his advice, and to please him, and Leopold, as has been his habit, makes endless comments and suggestions. But Mozart takes the decisions himself; he humours him but goes his own way. "I am delighted whenever you send me long letters [. . .] you must, however, forgive me if I do not send you much in return, for every minute is precious."

At the end of December parts of Act 3 still remained to be written. In addition, "as there is no extra ballet but only an appropriate divertissement, I have the honour of composing the music for that as well; but I am glad of it, for now all the music will be by the same composer." (Once again Mozart was emulating Gluck, who, contrary to common practice, was the sole author of his scores.) Four days later, on 3 January: "My head and my hands are so full of Act 3 that it would be no wonder if I turned into a third act myself. It has cost me more trouble than a whole opera, for there is hardly a scene in it that is not extremely interesting."

It is symptomatic both of Mozart's overriding concern for dramatic integrity and continuity and of the artistic seriousness of the Mannheim–Munich court, perhaps too of a growing recognition that in *Idomeneo* they had something of exceptional grandeur and beauty, that it was agreed to forgo the divertissements normally inserted between the acts and instead to make them part of the action. At the end of Act 1 chorus and dancers united in an elaborately choreographed celebration of the king's miraculous escape from death. Act 2, with tragic irony, ended with another choreographic setpiece, this time the Cretan populace's horror-struck reaction to the revelation of the true reason for Idomeneo's escape and to its catastrophic consequences, as, in the words of the libretto, "the chorus express their terror in singing and mime, the whole forming a parallel action which closes the act as the sole divertissement" – in other words, incorporated in the action, not following it. The ballet which concluded the opera, being of his own composition, became an integral part of the whole fabric.

Not long after arriving in Munich, Mozart attended a lunch at Count Seeau's, where he and Cannabich met Quaglio and Le Grand "to make the necessary arrangements for the opera". The experience of working with two such masters of stage spectacle and movement was surely a factor in the electric energy of the finale of Act 2, where the king's evasion of his sacred vow reaps the whirlwind, and in the grandeur of the monumental crowd scenes and rituals of Act 3; it was a stimulus as great in its way as writing for the incomparable Mannheim orchestra. *Idomeneo*, in Heartz's phrase, "is Mozart's Mannheim opera, beneficiary and culmination of many years of superb productions under Carl Theodor". It was no doubt when he discovered how spectacular the staging would be that he realized the absurdity of Idomeneo's singing a cavatina just at that point and of the tempest's dying down obligingly so that he could do so. Quaglio's designs for *Idomeneo* have not survived – a newspaper report praised "the view of the port" [Act 2] and "of the temple [Act 3]" – but there is no reason to suppose that they were any less striking than others that have. The moment in Act 1 when the storm subsided and the cries of the shipwrecked mariners faded must have been worth seeing if the staging lived up to the libretto's instructions: "Neptune rises up over the sea. He signs to the winds to return to their caves. Gradually the sea grows calm. Idomeneo, perceiving the sea-god, implores his potent aid. Neptune, with a grim and menacing glance, plunges beneath the waves and is gone."

As stage rehearsals proceeded and the first night drew near, what Mozart had always been anxious about became obvious: the opera was too long. The rehearsal of Act 3, in mid-January, was a great success; but when it was over it was agreed that drastic measures must be taken to shorten it. Whatever Mozart may or may not have thought, the concluding ballet, involving Le Grand's famous troupe, could not be omitted. But dal Prato's aria, "No, la morte", could. It had been well liked, but its formal cut and leisurely unfolding (complete with slower middle section) made it, as Mozart observed, "awkwardly placed" amid the dramas of the sacrifice scene. Idomeneo's final aria, the text of which (to Varesco's annoyance) had given so much trouble, also went. Its loss was "much regretted; but we must make a virtue of necessity". The Oracle's speech was shortened ("Varesco need know nothing of this – it will all be printed just as he wrote it"). Shortly before the first night, Idomeneo's "Accogli, o re del mar" was cut and the wonderful C minor chorus of lamentation, "O voto tremendo", reduced to half its length, and – even more grievous to modern admirers – Elettra's "D'Oreste, d'Aiace", one of the greatest explosions of psychotic fury in all music, jettisoned. Mozart had long thought it implausible that the other characters should stand about while she sang her aria, and he wielded the knife (replacing the aria, however, with an extended recitative of ferocious power). Even the finest feats of characterization must yield to dramatic conciseness and plausibility.

What was finally heard at the Cuvilliés-Theater on 29 January 1781 – two days after the composer's twenty-fifth birthday – remains one of the marvels of music-drama. Undoubtedly, with a completely free hand, Mozart would have pruned even further. Eight months later, when he had been hoping *Idomeneo* might be given in Vienna, he told his father that, if a performance had been possible, he "would have arranged [the opera] more in the French style". In 1786, when the work was performed privately in Vienna (with Idamante sung by a tenor), both Arbace's arias were removed; in Munich his Act 2 aria survived the last-minute cutting because Panzacchi was an old favourite of the court and, given his position in the hierarchy, could not be left without one. His conversation with the king which opens Act 2 is largely redundant even in the shorter form that Mozart insisted on (against the wishes of Varesco and Leopold), and the sentiments expressed in the aria which follows are of a combined banality and obscurity that Mozart himself was powerless to transcend. Arbace's Act 3 scena is a real oddity. The recitative is as fine as any in an opera remarkable for the inventiveness, power and copiousness of its accompanied recitatives, as Arbace broods on the horrors laying waste the kingdom – music, beginning with a pre-echo of Idomeneo's "Figlio, o caro figlio" in the sacrifice scene, which carries chromaticism and dissonance to its most extreme point in the score. Then comes an aria so uncharacteristic of Mozart, both in its clumsy style and in the total discrepancy between the solemn words and the simpering music, that you almost wonder if it is not the work of another hand.

These are the sole traces of conventional opera seria left in *Idomeneo*. Not even Mozart could have done more. As it is, what he does is amazing. He takes the convention and (with the few exceptions noted) bends it to his transcendent purposes. *Idomeneo* is a classic example of Mozart's ability to inhabit a form with complete artistic freedom and make it his own. Nothing can have prepared the audience for what it heard. Apart from the wholehearted response of the musicians and the members of the local nobility already quoted, there is no direct evidence how the work was received at its three performances; but Mozart would hardly have remembered it as a time of happiness if it had not been received well.

That nothing resulted from it – no permanent position at court, not even the title of Hofcomponist, a looser attachment which would have brought him periodic commissions – does not mean that Carl

Theodor's enthusiasm had cooled, only that enough influential people could testify to Mozart's lacking the deference due in a court servant: Archbishop Colloredo, for one, and Count Seeau, relations with whom had deteriorated during the preparations for *Idomeneo*. Mozart had been too sanguine in believing Seeau a changed person from the haughty, two-faced official he had had dealings with in 1778. In the heady atmosphere of the final weeks he had several clashes with him, culminating in what he called a "desperate fight" over engaging trombones (not otherwise called for in the score) for the scene of the Oracle – a passage which even in the longest of its four surviving forms lasts no more than a couple of minutes. "I had to be rude to him, or I should never have got my way." If he did get his way – and it is possible that in the end the version performed was the one that replaced trombones with clarinets and bassoons – it was at a price. To us it may seem only right and proper that an ephemeral court official should not be suffered to lord it over the creator of one of the masterpieces of art; but in 1781 a lowly musician was not rude to a count, still less to the intendant, if he wanted to make his way in the world. Beethoven's fierce independence lay in the future. Mozart was twenty years too early for that. In fact, Seeau continued to bear Mozart a grudge. Four years later, when *Die Entführung aus dem Serail* was going the rounds of German opera houses, he blocked a proposed production at Munich and had to be overruled by Carl Theodor.

As for *Idomeneo*, it would have to wait more than a century and a half before it could come into its kingdom. Mozart is said to have loved it above all his other works. As we have seen, one of his first moves after settling in Vienna was to try to get it staged. At least once, excerpts from the opera featured at his public concerts; but that was all. The 1786 performance, for which he revised the score, was given in a private theatre. As Heartz remarks, *Idomeneo* "had already become a work dispossessed". In the nineteenth century it enjoyed only the faintest of after-lives. Being by Mozart, it could not be ignored. Breitkopf and Härtel published the full score in 1868, commentators occasionally spoke well of the work, and "Placido è il mar" was a favourite with Victorian glee-clubs. But the opera was of interest much more as a pointer to the greater things to come than for itself. History was against it. The general consensus held that the music's undoubted beauties were suffocated by the work's outmoded form; the "German" seriousness of the best numbers showed what it might have been if Mozart's essentially Teutonic genius had not been forced to conform to the conventions of opera seria. Productions, when they took place, were of suitably doctored versions.

In the twentieth century it continued to provide easy prey for the German passion for performing editions. It now began to crop up all over Germany, but in arrangements whose declared purpose was to free it of its corrupting Italian associations and reclaim it for the German stage. In 1931 Richard Strauss, who had previously done so much for the cause of Mozart, perpetrated a version which Alfred Einstein described as "a gross act of mutilation". As late as 1956, the bicentenary of the composer's birth, the Salzburg conductor and musicologist Bernhard Paumgartner made an arrangement whose main achievement was to demonstrate how little the place had learned since the day Mozart shook off the dust of its stifling provincialism. Among other things, the edition – which for a number of years was the only vocal score of the work in print – removed Idomeneo's Act 1 aria, allocated Elettra's characteristically large-spanned "Soavi zeffiri" to the "two Cretan maidens" who in the previous act had hailed the reign of perpetual peace in pretty thirds and sixths, and rearranged a large part of Act 3 in such a way that Mozart's sequence of scenes was destroyed and a magical change of mood, the transition from "O voto tremendo" to the march, disappeared without trace. The many suggested cuts included one of nine bars in the quartet, a movement so beautiful, and beautifully proportioned, that you would have thought it would humble the most meddlesome kapellmeister. When Paumgartner's version was broadcast, the critic Desmond Shawe-Taylor began his review in the *New Statesman*: "Mozart always hated Salzburg, and if he has been listening in to the celebrations of his 200th birthday he will have found small cause to change his mind. [...] Thus does Austria honour her famous dead."

The review provoked outrage in Vienna and Salzburg. By then, though, *Idomeneo*'s time had come. Opinion had for some years been changing. Edward Dent, in his *Mozart's Operas*, published in 1913, had spoken up for its "nobility and dignity". His advocacy was to bear fruit in the years that followed. Yet even this fervent admirer, who did so much to raise the status of the work, still thought of it as a museum piece, to be revived only "on some special occasion [. . .] which we shall attend in a spirit of pilgrimage".

Dent did not live to see it taken into the general operatic repertory. The Glyndebourne festival had performed it in 1951; but, in Britain, it was the production at Sadler's Wells, in the early 1960s, that showed it could hold the everyday stage. Charles Rosen's assertion, made in 1971, that if the work could have been saved for the repertory that would already have happened, has been overtaken by events. *Idomeneo* has been performed in major theatres all over the world – performances, at their best, of overwhelming emotional impact. A work once dismissed as too remote from real life to have anything important to say, peopled with antique heroes and heroines to whose stylized predicaments it was impossible to relate, has become urgently alive. The destruction of cities, the enslavement of populations, the dilemmas and evasions of rulers, the tragic consequences of their mistakes, are no longer far-off events with no power to touch us. Thanks to the genre-transcending intensity of Mozart's music, they touch us to the quick. *Idomeneo* only needs listening to with ears and mind freed of preconceptions, received ideas, classifications, categorizations, and comparisons with other Mozart operas. Like them it has its unique, compelling voice.

We hear it from the outset. The overture is the score and the drama in microcosm: grand but ominous, driven forward relentlessly as though by the surge and sweep of the sea felt both as physical presence and as the angry Neptune, symbol of the power of malignant fate over human affairs. The commanding D major unisons of the first six bars are immediately undermined by a menacing chromatic growl in the strings, rising from piano to forte and provoking a wild cry from the woodwind – a falling figure that will be heard in various forms throughout the opera (here quoted at its second occurrence, in the more usual triplet form):

As though disoriented, the music finds itself in G minor, and though the commanding mood reasserts itself it is made more hectic by thrashing syncopations in the violins. This is the pattern of the overture: authority threatened by forces beyond its control. In the reprise, tension is further ratcheted up by the common Mozartian device of making an already insistent tutti passage three times as long and intensifying it with rhythmic trumpet and timpani figures (cf. the first movement of the Prague symphony). At the end the music settles on to long, throbbing pedals, piano but interrupted by scrunchingly dissonant chords and with the woodwind cry sounding again and again on flute and oboe, each one a tone or semitone lower than the one before. The tonality is a chromatically inflected D minor; the grand D major of the opening seems far away. At last, via an angular, sighing chromatic phrase reminiscent of Gluck's overture to *Iphigénie en Aulide*, the movement reaches a close in a momentous quietness that prepares us for the drama to come.

The long monologue for the captive Trojan princess Ilia which follows – into which the strings' final piano chords of D major lead without a break – provides even surer proof that Mozart has become a great dramatic composer: he has mastered the art of accompanied recitative. In its flexibility, formal coherence, richness and psychological penetration, the accompanied recitative in *Idomeneo* marks an advance on anything he had written before (remarkable though that often was) or had heard in contemporary opera seria or tragédie lyrique. This is already the familiar expressive idiom of Donna Anna's "Don Ottavio, son morta", "Welch' ein Geschick" in *Entführung*, or Tamino's scene with the Priest. The music Mozart writes while acquainting us with the situation at the rise of the curtain – music now vengeful and resolute, now hesitant, indignation melting into love – charts the ambiguities and cross-currents of feeling in Ilia's heart with moving sympathy, establishes the nobility, purity and passion of her character, and leads by a subtle natural progression into the aria. Its wide expressive range is prophetic of the work as a whole; but note especially the moment when her strenuous "I owe vengeance to him who gave me life [Priam]" yields, at "[I owe] gratitude to him who restored it [Idamante]", to a phrase of exquisite beauty that rises to a soft, full A flat, then descends slowly and caressingly as Ilia luxuriates for an instant in her love for the Cretan prince.

The aria, in turn, introduces us to another quality not encountered before in Mozartian serious opera: a combined terseness and subtlety of expression. The dovetailing of recitative and aria by a simple adaptation of the chords which conventionally close a recitative, the economy with which a heart overflowing with contradictory and half-acknowledged feelings is conveyed, the harmonic freedom, the music's sinuous, seamless flow, the variations in the reprise and in particular the amplification and intensification of emotion at the key words "E un Greco adorerò?" ("Am I then to love a Greek?"), the perfect shape of the whole (which however did not prevent Paumgartner from indicating an optional cut of eleven bars) – these things again announce a new Mozart. We shall find examples of the exuberance of the adolescent, Salzburg Mozart in *Idomeneo* – an exuberance that in his next opera will threaten to overwhelm the drama – but it is rarely if ever that it does not perform a dramatic function, whether directly as psychological expression or indirectly as ironic contrast, or both together. Ilia's Act 2 aria, "Se il padre perdei", is decorated with florid concertante parts written to please the Mannheim principal flute, oboe, horn and bassoon; but in exploiting their exceptional talents Mozart makes them serve the purposes of the drama, in a way that is typical of his whole approach to the composition of the opera; he creates the freedom to indulge his gift for evoking a dreamlike contentment in such a way as not only not to damage realism but to enhance it. The aria marks a crucial point: Ilia no longer hates her Greek captors, and in her new mood of happiness she is ready to acknowledge the reason that has brought about this change of heart – the love she feels for Idamante. At the same time the effect of the music's serene and lavish beauty, in the context of Idomeneo's guilty angst, is one of deep irony, while, dramatically, the king's realization that Ilia is in love with his son gives the tragedy a further twist. Mozart conveys this latter idea in the space of half a bar. Ilia leaves the stage; Idomeneo is alone with his thoughts. The orchestra, without a pause and in the same tempo, softly repeats the aria's second theme, but in a changed colouring which by the simplest shift of harmony turns an image of felicity into an expression of foreboding. The passage, brief as it is, can stand for what is different about the work: its intense self-consciousness (in the good sense), its resourcefulness, its compassionate understanding of the interaction and interdependence of human lives, its sense of the tragic.

The phrase in question is related to the rhythmic figure first heard as a cry from the woodwind in the overture and subsequently in many different incarnations. In Ilia's first aria, transferred to cellos and basses, it takes on a more subdued quality, of inner agitation (the two final beats now subdivided).

Soon afterwards, in the orchestral passage which links Elettra's aria to the shipwreck scene, it is again wild and hectic:

In Act 1, when Idomeneo has saved himself from the god's immediate wrath, it finds a temporary repose,

only to become restless once more as the conscience of the king begins to gnaw.

In Idomeneo's great aria in Act 2, "Fuor del mar", the notes are lengthened and evened out in suitably regal fashion:

At the opposite pole, in the context of Ilia's and Idamante's mutual declaration of love, the motif can lend itself to a sense of bliss blossoming irresistibly

or to a pathetic hesitancy in the scene where Idomeneo, under extreme pressure, haltingly reveals that the victim of his vow is Idamante. Here it is developed, briefly but with great suggestiveness, so as to compress into a few bars the sense of an agonizing decision being taken – the stricken king's acknowledgement of defeat and the submission of his heroic will to harsh necessity:

The motif's appearance in the same form, shortly afterwards, underlines the pathos of Idamante's calm surrender. But its final flowering is reserved for the last scene of all, when the king in the presence of his people hands over authority to his son. Purged at last of all anxiety, the springing phrases add grace to this noblest of recitatives – though the associations the motif has acquired in the course of the opera give an extra poignancy to the drama of Idomeneo's renunciation.

Idomeneo is the first Mozart opera in which thematic and harmonic reminiscences play a vital role. In itself their presence does not make it a great work, though it is one of the reasons – the pictorial use of orchestral colour is another – for calling it a paradoxically forward-looking work. What it does show is the intense seriousness with which Mozart set about his task; it is part of the whole *Idomeneo* spirit. That spirit may be summed up in two words: dramatic truth. Two or three routine arias in an opera lasting three hours represent the sum of his obeisance to convention. For the rest, he has as though at a stroke created a fresh conception of drama through music. It is a matter both of detail and of structure. The smallest touches as well as the largest effects bear witness to the overriding ascendancy of dramatic values. When Elettra echoes Idamante's farewell to Idomeneo at the beginning of the Act 2 trio, melodic, harmonic and textural variations colour the phrase in a way that shows us the emotions of the moment through her eyes; the downward sweep of the vocal line, the momentary turn towards a gloomy D minor, the more broken accompaniment, the chromatic twists followed by wide leaps (suggesting that neurotic fears are active even in the hour of her apparent triumph), and the aristocratic hauteur of the whole ten-bar span of melody – here is music as subtly and powerfully characteristic as is Donna Anna's "Lascia alla mia pena" in the sextet in *Don Giovanni*.

That this was a conscious preoccupation on Mozart's part is clear from the correspondence. The instructions sent to Leopold to pass on to Varesco are all aimed at replacing stilted or prolix utterance and implausible situation with dramatic naturalness and individual emotion. In the most celebrated of all the *Idomeneo* letters we saw Mozart insisting that the cavatina intended for the king between the two choruses in the finale of Act 2 must go. It went, and was replaced by the grand but desperate orchestral recitative that we know – a passage which actually succeeds in heightening the tension, till it erupts in the panic-stricken prestissimo of the final chorus.

The pianissimo conclusion of this chorus is dramatic proof of Mozart's confidence in his powers and in the seriousness of his audience. He is so sure of himself that he will satisfy his instinct – which requires that the music dwindle away to nothing – and not bother courting applause at the end of an act whose continuity of design has almost throughout ignored the demands of popular taste. Not that the pursuit of Gluckian ideals involves, for Mozart, a corresponding musical austerity. All the constituents of musical expression, the techniques Mozart has been acquiring since childhood, are pressed into service. *Idomeneo* is an exceptionally abundant score. Mozart's contrapuntal mastery imparts to the harmonic and instrumental texture an unprecedented energy and richness. Symptomatic is the important part played by the violas – always a favoured instrument with Mozart but here elevated almost to the prominence we associate with it in the later operas. To mention two examples, the quiet but rasping chord, in the introduction to Elettra's first aria, which, held across the restless eighth-note movement of the other instruments, adds an extra colour and tension (dominant against tonic harmony); and the scene, diametrically opposite in character, where Ilia finally declares her love to Idamante and the frustrations of two and a half acts resolve: here the violas, sustained across the bar-line against the violins' triplet movement and the regular detached notes of the cellos and basses, are at the heart of one of the most beautiful expressions of emotional release in Mozart.

Variety and vitality of string texture had long been characteristic of Mozart's style, but never before on such a scale and range: at one extreme the delicate enchantment of Elettra's "Idol mio", at the other the wide-spaced, high-lying chords and furious syncopations of the shipwreck scene and, in between, the sweep and authority of the part-writing in "Fuor del mar", evocative both of the force of Idomeneo's personality and of the sea that has him in its power, and intensifying rather than impeding the music's driving momentum. This is typical of *Idomeneo*; textural elaboration rarely lacks a specific musico-dramatic purpose. It is the same with the work's harmonic invention, whether in large-scale or intimate expression: the audacious means used in Act 2 to depict all nature in upheaval, or the tenderness that floods over the music in the first scene of Act 3 at the modulation from A minor to C major (via a feint towards G) when Ilia speaks of sorrow being overcome by the constancy of her love.

No opera of Mozart's is richer in dissonant harmony, or so strewn with diminished sevenths. In the storm scene of Act 2 he stretches his harmonic idiom to its furthest point in response to the dramatic and theatrical situation. The terror of the populace at the storm's increasing violence is rendered by the unexpected wrench of tonality from the dominant of C minor to B flat minor (a use of shock modulation more commonly associated with Haydn or Beethoven). The chorus's frantic reiterated appeal to the guilty man to declare his identity is set in a series of downward steps from B flat minor to F, linked by diminished seventh chords on A sharp (B flat), G sharp and F sharp, each chord repeated and sustained, amid a vibrant silence, by the full woodwind band reinforced by four horns. Before the chord of F, emphasized for three bars, has had time to die away, the guilty man reveals himself, and the harmony, resolving via another seventh chord, takes two more steps down into a blazing D major, with trumpets and drums, held back till now, in full spate.

It is a moment of revelation, in the music as in the drama. One is tempted to call the whole scene a landmark in Romantic opera. The use of orchestral colour for dramatic and psychological effect looks forward to the discoveries and experiments of Romanticism. It involves more than mere pictures of sea and sky, wind and storm, vivid and apt though they are. Articulation of the larger dramatic structure is in part orchestral. We see it most obviously in Act 2, where constantly varying kinds of sound are an integral part of the progress of the action, and the sea, symbol of a power beyond human grasp, is at first sportive and no more than quietly menacing, its strength for the most part latent ("Fuor del mar"), is then stilled to an illusory serenity, and finally roused to a rage all the more terrible for bursting out of the preceding calm. The contrast between the halcyon peace of the central scene, "Placido è il mar" – a beautiful E-major evocation of Mediterranean felicity, all hazy, murmurous strings, caressing flute and gently mooing horns – and the terror of the storm choruses, with horns in four parts, shrieking piccolo and off-beat violin chords that strike like wind-lashed spray, is only the most obvious manifestation of a principle at work throughout the opera.

In almost every scene Mozart invents fresh colours with which to emphasize the argument and at the same time delight our ears: what nineteenth- or twentieth-century opera surpasses the sheer physical pleasure that *Idomeneo* gives us, from the quiet trumpet entry just before the end of the overture, through the marvellously airy sound of flute, oboe and violins in the introduction to "Fuor del mar", to the volcanic crescendos in Elettra's final recitative or the fury of the full orchestra in her aria? In the third act the feeling of numbed horror that grips the people at the discovery that the victim of Idomeneo's vow is his son gives rise to a sonority unheard in music before, cold, granite-like, made up of muted violins and violas and stark unison woodwind pierced by the gleam of muted trumpets and bruised by the dull beat of the drums; yet this quintessence of desolation leads, with the briefest of transitions, to another dimension of sound, even more solemn in its simplicity. Strings, still sotto voce, joined after a few bars by oboes, play a march that is Gluckian in its quiet intensity, Handelian in its fusion of the learned and the gallant, and purely Mozartian in its finality and in the peace that descends like a benediction on the scene. Once again a new element in the drama – Idomeneo's acceptance of tragedy – has inspired a new colour. Personal decision has been subsumed in ceremony; and in the passage that follows, the sense of immemorial rites is intensified by the luminous texture of woodwind and pizzicato strings encircling the long phrases of the vocal line, as first the king, regal even in defeat, invokes the god he sought to flee, and then the priests repeat the prayer in a high-pitched monotone whose accompanying harmony (diminished sevenths in a glowingly diatonic context) and orchestral colour (bassoons in thirds in their upper register, imitated in turn by the other woodwind) evoke with uncanny immediacy the feel of the ancient world, the otherness of a society dominated by ritual. Throughout all the changes of orchestral colour a clear dramatic purpose is at work. The most spectacular pictorialism is but the outward projection of the human and suprahuman struggles which are the heart of the drama.

If Mozart in his eleven remaining years of life never again approached this proto-Romantic exploitation of orchestral colour, it was much longer before serious opera caught up with what is perhaps *Idomeneo*'s most remarkable feat, its continuity of dramatic construction – a continuity achieved partly by motivic repetition, partly by the shaping of the libretto, but chiefly by the boldest and simplest of means, the running of one musical number into the next. As mentioned above, it was an ideal already pursued in Mannheim opera and elsewhere; but

Mozart went further and deeper. We have seen how, after Ilia's exit at the end of her Act 2 aria, the recitative in which Idomeneo broods on the implications of her avowals begins with a reminiscence from the aria and continues with other thematic allusions to it, darkened with doubt as the king feels the net closing round him. At least the aria comes to the full close expected in an age of singers' opera. Many others in the work flow on into modulations or linking phrases which carry the music-drama forward without a break. In Act 1 the music continues uninterruptedly from Elettra's recitative and aria (themselves joined together) to the shipwreck scene and on to the landing of Idomeneo, his aria, his meeting with his son, his rejection of him, and Idamante's ensuing outburst of grief and bewilderment. Act 2 is even more closely knit. Elettra's "Idol mio", the march, the chorus "Placido è il mar" (enclosing the arioso for Elettra), the trio, the storm, Idomeneo's confession of guilt (joined to the preceding section by the continuation of the stepwise downward movement), the "monster" chorus – the music proceeds in an almost unbroken chain and in masterly progression, through systematic contrast of colour, texture, key, rhythm and tempo, to its astonishing climax.

Act 3, though less consistently well wrought, takes the same principle even further. The first part of the act, concerned with the love of Ilia and Idamante and suffused in the soft radiance associated in Mozart's music with the keys of A and E, performs a function of large-scale contrast similar to that of the central part of Act 2, only deeper. As before, by an exception that has become almost the norm, Ilia's aria "Zeffiretti lusinghieri" does not come to a full close but leads directly into the next scene, in which simple recitative, accompagnato and arioso move in and out of each other in a continuous flow; and as before, the duet is not so much finished as broken into by the arrival of Idomeneo and Elettra. The ensuing quartet is introduced in the same spirit, by a natural progression from recitative to ensemble. Here Mozart uses the momentary suspension of the action, at a point of extreme tension, to develop the different emotions of his characters and at the same time to combine them into a unity-in-suffering above conflict. Note especially how, in the second part of the movement, he characteristically prolongs the reprise of the concerted passage "più fiera sorte, pena maggiore nissun provò" ("no one ever suffered a harsher fate or greater punishment") by two bars whose twisting chromatic lines raise the intensity to an even higher pitch (anticipating similar moments in *Don Giovanni*). Note also the dramatically perfect conclusion: Idamante's final words – "I shall go alone on my wanderings", with which the movement began – trail away to nothing, his next phrase, "seeking death elsewhere, until I find it", unspoken, the vocal line ending on dominant seventh harmony, which the orchestra quietly resolves after the voice has ceased.

The quartet marks a new tone in the tragedy, of transfigured suffering, and so prepares for the turning-point of the drama: the moment when Idomeneo, in bowing at last to his fate, consents to the ritual slaughter of his son. The contrast between "O voto tremendo" and the march has been singled out as an example of Mozart's mastery of varied colour and texture. As an example of continuity it ranks, again, with the finest in the opera, music and drama combining to create what neither could accomplish separately: the sense of extreme suffering giving way to a mysterious repose. Mozart requires only half a dozen bars. At the grim climax of the chorus the music turns, exhausted, into the major, the voices cease, the texture clears, horns sound soft arpeggios, the relentless triplet rhythm dies down, and a long consolatory melody, released on the violins, rises above the hushed orchestra. It is a transition as inevitable as it is unexpected. Gluck, the presiding influence on this part of the work, never united such extremes. The march that steals in softly on the strings breathes a holy stillness that *The Magic Flute* in its different way equals but does not surpass. This is the high moment of the drama; but the scenes which follow do not betray Mozart's lofty conception. Dramatic truth and development by contrast remain the guiding principles behind the culminating sequence of numbers: the sacrifice scene, cut short by the Oracle, Elettra's demented fury, Idomeneo's last appearance as king (for which the warm colour of clarinets returns for the first time since the priests' unison chant), and the dancing and chorus of jubilation which salute the new age.

This account of Act 3, admittedly, is more what Mozart may be presumed to have desired than what actually occurred – Act 3 as it so nearly was but, realistically considered, could never have been. It seems (from a surviving performing score) that, though Arbace's scene was removed before the first night (along with its magnificent recitative "Sventurata Sidon", harmonically the most daring in the whole opera), Idamante's aria "No, la morte", previously suppressed, was restored at the last minute – in which case the sacrifice scene would have been much less effective. Mozart, finally, was not a totally free agent – how could he be? Had he been, he would, he said, have composed the opera "more in the French style". Yet, in the light of the constraints he worked under, what he achieved is only the more wonderful. Again and again he works miracles.

That is as true of the characterization as it is of the other aspects of the work discussed above. When we know *Idomeneo* well, any previous ideas we may have had about the unreality of the people in it vanish. These are recognizably Mozartian creations, warmed to life by the same penetrating and compassionate understanding that makes the characters in the Viennese operas so real, but here seen in tragic, not comic situations. Only poor Arbace, the faithful counsellor always ready with a platitude, failed to kindle the composer's imagination and remains (except in his Act 3 recitative) imprisoned in the stiffest opera seria mode. Otherwise, the portrayal of character in *Idomeneo* continually rises above generalized emotion and conventional gesture. It is not the sharply observed characterization of *Figaro* and the other Da Ponte operas, but on its own terms it is equally valid; Mozart makes us feel for these people in their griefs and joys. The terms are heroic, not those of everyday life; but we realize that on those terms Ilia and Elettra are as consistently drawn and as tellingly contrasted as Susanna and the Countess or as Donna Anna and Donna Elvira, and that the development of Ilia from the unease and desperation of her opening recitative to her exaltation in the quartet and her sublimity in the sacrifice scene is, in its own way, comparable to Pamina's growth from girlhood to womanhood in *The Magic Flute*.

As for Elettra, when did Mozart use his mastery of music as a dramatic language to more devastating psychological effect than in this picture of the formidable but neurotic daughter of Agamemnon and Clytemnestra? Her great scene in Act 1 shows melody, harmony, rhythm, orchestral colour, vocal virtuosity and musical form systematically deployed to evoke abnormality on a grand scale; the traditional rage aria is transformed into something extraordinary, and unique to her. The voice part, alternating great upward leaps with piteous semitonal fragments; the pounding, obsessive arpeggios of the accompaniment; the frequent superimposition of 3/4 time on 4/4 to produce violent syncopations; the baleful orchestration, strangely hollow despite the presence of four horns; the atmosphere of harmonic instability, prefigured in the recitative, with its writhing chromatics, intensified in the introduction to the aria (where the key into which the recitative resolves, A minor, is not the tonic but serves instead as a long dominant pedal across which dissonance flits like the spasms of a tortured mind), and reaching its climax at the reprise in a sudden descent into C minor, the key of the storm music into which the conclusion of the aria rushes with headlong impetus – these things combine to lay bare Elettra's soul and, at the end, with a stroke worthy of the Romantics, to merge its darkness symbolically and actually with the raging of the elements. Similar means are used for the even more explosive outburst in Act 3, where Elettra, now alone in her own tormented world, deprived even of the illusion of hope, is whipped into despairing fury as though by the serpents which the words conventionally and the music most unconventionally evoke.

Yet the picture would be incomplete without her lyrical major-key scenes in Act 2: the aria "Idol mio" and the arioso "Soavi zeffiri". Mozart is not always given credit for this fresh example of his humanity-cum-psychological realism; but who is to say that these pieces are not in character, that this melting mood is not a true aspect of Elettra's complex, unhappy nature, and that she should not dream her dreams and hug her precious illusions for a brief moment? She will lose them soon enough. The music says as much, not only by the immediate context in which it is placed, but also in itself: beautiful as it is, it is touched with the obsessiveness, the withdrawal from reality, that rages openly in the D minor and C minor arias.

Alongside Ilia's growing maturity and depth of feeling and Elettra's near-madness we may place the characterization of Idomeneo, the ruler trapped in the consequences of his rashness. His music, which is endowed with consistent elevation of tone, suggests unmistakably the combination of grandeur and impulsiveness, regal authority and sympathetic insight into the feelings of others, that has brought about his plight. Here is no routine opera seria monarch paying lip service to conflicts between duty and inclination that are as one-dimensional as he is. Mozart's imagination, roused by what is timeless in the story, has seized on the possibilities offered for living dramatic expression. From the moment of his first appearance – remorse already beginning to poison the relief at still being alive – Idomeneo's predicament is painfully real. And, as with Ilia, the music shows us his feelings changing with the development of the tragic action. The superb "Fuor del mar", with typical Mozartian genius, uses the convention of the obligatory bravura aria for consummately realized dramatic ends: the aria, at once majestic and fevered, becomes a mirror of the king's state of mind at this mid-point of the drama, guilt-ridden but defiantly regal, a classical hero on the run but not yet brought to his knees by resentful destiny. By the end of the second act, like Oedipus he is "dans le piège". And as the noose tightens we feel Mozart's pity for him growing. The intensification of Idomeneo's love – against his will – for the son he has discovered only to lose culminates in the wonderfully tender passage in A flat major in the sacrifice scene (mentioned above). At the same time his final submission to fate is all the more moving for be'ng the act of a man who throughout has been characterized as unyieldingly proud and stubborn to the point of recklessness.

Beside him, and beside Ilia and Elettra, Idamante may at first seem a disappointingly lay figure, and it is undeniable that he expresses himself less personally than the others, and that though his music often rises to a poignant eloquence it does so in a more generalized way. Yet I think it is wrong to conclude that Idamante is a failure on Mozart's part, to add to that of Arbace. Looked at in a different way, may he not be, on the contrary, one more example of Mozart's genius for turning convention (and in this case the vocal limitations of dal Prato) to good account? The very plainness, the almost abstract nobility of Idamante's portrayal has, I believe, a dramatic function. It is not only that, in Dent's words, "the self-control, the childlike simplicity and directness of Idamante [are] to save the tragedy from its dreadful completion". If Idamante is a type – the type of heroic, selfless young idealism – it may be because he is meant to be: he is the representative of the new civilization whose dawn is inaugurated at the end of the opera. In the hands of Mozart and his librettist the story becomes a deliberate and noble expression of the Enlightenment.

Danchet's Idamante died, cut down by his father's sword. In Mozart's opera he lives, marries Ilia, and reigns over a revived and contented Crete. The happy ending is no mere convenient evasion of all that has gone before: it is a declaration, an assertion of the power of tolerance, reason and love. Idomeneo, representative of the old order, victim of the old decrees, yields place to his son, the new man who sets his captives free and conquers superstition.

It is Mozart, of course, who makes this resolution convincing. Without him it could not but seem a betrayal of the tragic vision of the rest of the opera. Music can combine or dissolve categories which in spoken drama are mutually exclusive, just as it can give life and shape to Platonic ideas which otherwise would remain abstractions; and no music more than Mozart's. In this, his first great opera, his imaginative insight encompasses an unprecedented range of human experience: love, joy, physical and spiritual contentment, stoicism, heroic resolution; the ecstasy of self-sacrifice, the horrors of dementia, the agonizing dilemma of a ruler trapped in the consequences of his actions; mass hysteria, panic in the face of an unknown scourge, turning to awe before the yet more terrible fact; the strange peace that can follow intense grief; the infinite tenderness of a father's last farewell to his son. *Idomeneo*, finally, moves us because it holds out the possibility of human nobility in a context of unblinking psychological truth.

Humanity may need, as never before, the sanity, the life-renewing laughter of Mozart's comedies. But it needs too the handful of special masterpieces whose qualities of courage, hope, compassion and honesty of vision make them its natural parables and sacred texts. *Idomeneo* is one of those works. Perhaps Dent was right: it should never be taken for granted but always attended "in a spirit of pilgrimage". It is a secular Passion, with power to chasten and uplift a distracted age.

3

Vienna and a new life
Die Entführung aus dem Serail

After *Idomeneo* Mozart could not have gone back to Salzburg. Already, in the heady days rehearsing his Munich opera, he told his father that if he had only himself to think of he would use his latest contract with the archiepiscopal court to "wipe his arse". In the aftermath of the work's success and the consciousness of creative powers in full flow, the idea was still more abhorrent.

This time events were on his side. The Archbishop's aged father, Prince Colloredo, an imperial vice-chancellor, long in poor health, became seriously ill. To be near him and also perhaps to be near the seat of power following the death of the Empress, the Archbishop travelled to Vienna in late January 1781 with his entourage, but without his court organist and most gifted keyboard player. Mozart, extending his original six weeks' leave to four months, had stayed on in Munich with his father and sister to enjoy the pleasures of the Carnival (enjoy them too much, as he later admitted). They had then gone on to Augsburg for a few days. Not till 12 March did the Mozarts finally receive their marching orders: the father to return to Salzburg, the son to proceed immediately to Vienna and rejoin the court at the Deutsches Haus in Singerstrasse, near the cathedral, headquarters of the Austrian branch of the Teutonic Knights (of which Count Karl Colloredo, the Archbishop's uncle, was commander). Mozart arrived there at nine o'clock on the morning of the 16th, after a night journey. At four the same afternoon he was taking part in one of the Archbishop's regular concerts. For the moment he was a court servant again, seated at lunch above the cooks but below the valets, and expected to hover in the antechamber every morning in case he was sent for. But he was in Vienna, and he had other ideas.

It was like a homecoming. This was his fourth visit, but the first as an adult and the first without his father. On the way there, alone in the post-chaise, he had felt an excitement which he could not account for, until he realized why. Vienna was where he belonged. It seemed as if good fortune were "waiting to welcome" him – it was "as if I *have* to stay". "I like being here." Vienna liberated his spirit and his mind. "This is a splendid place, and for my *métier* the best in the world." It was the ideal terrain for the exploitation of his talents. Vienna, by far the largest city in the Habsburg lands, with a population of 200,000, had a musical life of unparalleled richness, watched over by an emperor with a keen and active interest in the art. There was a large public for music, and private patronage on a scale unmatched elsewhere in the Empire. Here if anywhere a gifted musician might make his way. Above all, Vienna was "the land of the clavier".

It was as a pianist and improviser of exceptional brilliance and expressiveness that Mozart first made his mark there. Though the Archbishop forbade him to perform in public – a prohibition symbolic of his servitude which also cost him financially – he could not stop Mozart cultivating the nobility and gentry. That was the world he had grown accustomed to from his earliest years. He was soon a sought-after performer in the households of Countess Thun, Countess Rumbeke, her cousin the state chancellor Count Cobenzl, Baroness Waldstätten, Archduke Maximilian and Prince Dmitri Alexeivich Galitzin, the Russian ambassador. By the time the Archbishop (his father now recovered) left Vienna in May, with most of his retinue but without his rebellious cembalist, Mozart was well advanced in his campaign to capture Viennese society. He had performed, gratis, at the Kärntnertor Theatre – Colloredo had been prevailed on by his peers to waive the prohibition – on the "beautiful Stein pianoforte" lent him by Countess Thun, to great applause (but "what surprised and delighted me most was the amazing silence") and been heard by the Emperor, was beginning to acquire wealthy pupils who paid well, and had played *Idomeneo* to an influential private gathering which included the director of the court theatres Count Orsini-Rosenberg and the court librarian Baron Gottfried van Swieten. Already there was talk of giving him an opera to compose for the German National Theatre (an idea that will result in *Die Entführung aus dem Serail*).

The Emperor, who remembered him well from earlier visits, had his eye on him.

The breach with Colloredo was painful, morally as well as physically – his final encounters with the Archbishop, who lost his temper, boiled over and shouted "Clear out – scoundrel, cretin!", and still more the famous kick-in-the-pants delivered by Count Arco, Colloredo's chief steward, left Mozart seething with rage ("I hate the Archbishop to madness") and brooding on fantasies of revenge for weeks afterwards – but it left him free, free to make his way in Vienna if he could; it severed all but one of the ties that bound him to Salzburg.

The breach with his father that it precipitated was more protracted, and more painful still. Leopold, not surprisingly, took his defection very ill and fought long and hard to keep control, of Wolfgang if not of himself. He had done so for too long to be prepared to give it up – running his son's life for him, handling his money, supervising his compositions and involved in them, to his intense satisfaction, almost as a kind of equal (had he not, only recently, advised Wolfgang how to treat certain passages in *Idomeneo*?), in a word fulfilling the sacred duty laid on him to nurture "the miracle God caused to be born in Salzburg". The habit had grown on him until it had become part of the natural order.

It was a habit Mozart himself did not immediately shake off: we find him, after six weeks in Vienna, begging Leopold's "permission" to return to Vienna for the Lent season of 1782, should he be in Salzburg at the time. As for Leopold, he could not believe in, let alone accept, Mozart's coming of age. He had confidence in his genius but in nothing much else. Wolfgang in his eyes was still, in everything except music, the impractical child his compulsive parenting had done its best to ensure that he remained – Wolfgang had never learnt to fend for himself in matters of money or household affairs, had no idea how to. (As Mozart himself admitted, using it as an argument for marriage, "from my youth up I have never been used to look after my belongings, linen, clothes and so forth".) How could he conceivably manage, adrift on his own in Vienna? Without his father to protect and guide him he would waste his time, dissipate his talent running after pleasure, and fall hopelessly into debt. In the coming months, unable to imagine he could possibly behave sensibly, Leopold would lend a ready ear to all the malicious tittle-tattle that Vienna was so fertile in spawning and that kind friends did not fail to relay to Salzburg.

It seems clear, from the long, flowery letter that Leopold Mozart sent Baroness Waldstätten shortly after the marriage of Mozart and Constanze Weber, that he regarded his son as personally responsible for his not being appointed the Archbishop's kapellmeister. "Having done my duty as a father, having in countless letters made the clearest and most lucid representations to Wolfgang on every point and being convinced that he knows my trying circumstances, which are extremely grievous to a man of my age, and that he is aware of the degradations I am suffering in Salzburg, since he must realize that both morally and materially I am being punished for his conduct, all that I can now do is to leave him to his own resources (as he evidently wishes) and pray God to bestow on him His paternal blessing and not withdraw from him His divine grace."*

No doubt Leopold justified systematically pocketing his son's earnings – it was no more than a fair return for the money he had lavished on his education, an education such as no musical child had ever been granted before. And was he now to be deprived of Wolfgang's salary, which had helped to keep them all comfortable and happy in the Hannibalplatz? The sense of injustice, of ingratitude, was intolerable. To add to it all, the boy's falling again into the clutches of those dangerous Webers was the last straw – for, ejected from the Deutsches Haus, he had of course betaken himself to their apartment and was lodging with them, on the second floor of the house known as the Eye of God, in Petersplatz.†

None of the letters Leopold bombarded him with during all these months has survived – perhaps Constanze destroyed them, perhaps

---

* Yet an earlier letter of Leopold's, to the Leipzig publisher Breitkopf and Härtel, informing them of some of Mozart's recent compositions, suggests a more ambivalent attitude: "As His Grace the Prince [Colloredo] treated my son extremely badly in Vienna and as, on the other hand, all the great noble families marked him out for their special favour, he was easily persuaded to resign a service to which a miserable salary was attached, and to remain in Vienna."

† The family had followed Aloisia from Mannheim to Vienna when she married the actor Joseph Lange.

they were lost during one of the couple's many changes of address –
but their anger is easily detectable behind Mozart's replies. Those
replies – at first shocked and indignant, at the time of the row with
the Archbishop ("I too do not know how to begin my letter, my
dearest father, for I haven't yet recovered from my astonishment and
shall never be able to if you continue to think and write like that") –
became gradually calmer and firmer in tone. Mozart yielded to his
father's insistence that he leave the Webers', which he did at the end
of July 1781 (though the Graben, to which he moved, was round the
corner from Petersplatz), but a month later, as Leopold continued to
scold and admonish, he had had enough:

It saddens me that, from the way you reacted to my last letter – as if I were a
complete scoundrel or else a fool, or both – you clearly have more faith in
the idle gossip and scribblings of others than you have in me – that in fact
you have no confidence in me at all. But I can assure you that all this doesn't
bother me. People may write what they like till they're blue in the face and
you may believe them as much as you please, it won't change me by a hair's
breadth [. . .] But there's no point going on about it, as the absurd tales God
alone knows who puts into your head will always outweigh any reasoning of
mine. But this I do ask you: when you write to me about something I have
done which you disapprove of or think I might have done better, and I reply
to you with my thoughts on the matter, please treat it as something just
between father and son, I mean as confidential, and not as something that
others need to know – as I myself treat it. I therefore beg you to leave it at
that and not involve others, for by God I am not prepared to give the slightest
account of what I do or don't do to anyone, not even the Emperor himself.
Just trust me – I deserve it. (Mozart to his father, 5 September 1781)

The pain of being addressed so scathingly by a father to whom he
had always been so close must have been intense – even in their
worst times during the trip to Mannheim and Paris in the late 1770s
Leopold's reproaches had not been quite so extreme – but Mozart
weathered it. His chance had come and he knew he must seize it; his
art, his life demanded it. In not much over six months he had become
an established part of the musical world of Vienna. He could speak
of "we Viennese"; it was as if he had never lived anywhere else. The
Emperor himself was heard to say: "C'est un talent décidé," and

arranged a contest between him and the visiting pianist/composer
Muzio Clementi, at which he placed a bet on Mozart and won. For
every enemy his talent made him there were two who were attracted
not only by his skill and brilliance as a performer and the audacity of
his music but also by his quick, mercurial mind and open, playful
personality. He was a welcome and frequent visitor at Countess
Thun's, at Count Cobenzl's (in July he spent several days at the count's
country estate at Reisenberg, to the north of Vienna), at the Trattners',
at Baroness Waldstätten's house in Leopoldstadt. "If you really believe
that I am detested at Court," he told his father in December 1781 (the
jealous slander had been fed to Leopold by the violinist-composer Peter
von Winter), "write to Herr von Strack, Countess Thun, Countess
Rumbecke, Baroness Waldstätten, Herr von Sonnenfels, Frau von
Trattner, *enfin* anyone you care to ask."

In the same letter Mozart gives a glimpse of his daily life: "Every
morning at six o'clock my hairdresser arrives and wakes me. By seven
I have finished dressing.* I compose till ten, then I give a lesson to
Frau von Trattner, and at eleven to Countess Rumbecke, each of
whom pays me six ducats for twelve lessons." He was now determined
to marry – and to marry Constanze Weber (the third of the four Weber
daughters), whatever his father's objections. Leopold could only be
furious at this final proof of Wolfgang's independence, but Mozart
was not to be deflected. Marriage had become a physical as well as
moral necessity. "The voice of nature speaks as loud in me as in other
men, louder perhaps than in many a big strong lout of a fellow." In
the event he would wait till after the premiere of his opera, and
then marry without having received his father's consent. Meanwhile,
disapproval from Salzburg rumbled on.

Despite all the ructions, the relationship continued – Mozart kept
his father au fait with his career, sent him his latest scores, or copies
of them, to store in the archive of his music that Leopold guarded in
the Tanzmeisterhaus, asked him to send this or that work for use at

---

* Mozart took great care of his personal appearance, as indeed he had to, given that
he was constantly being received in aristocratic households. A year later we find him
coveting an expensive red coat and planning to unite it with some gem-encrusted
mother-of-pearl buttons he saw at the button factory in the Kohlmarkt – perhaps the
"crimson pelisse" Michael Kelly describes him wearing at a rehearsal of *Figaro*.

his concerts – and, on the surface at least, it grew less fraught. On his side Mozart still found it difficult not to think of the three of them as a unit: he could, he reasoned, be "more useful to the family in Vienna than ever in Salzburg", and he even suggested that Leopold and Nannerl should join him. But the old friendly intimacy and trust had gone, never to be regained. Mozart's replies grew less frequent. Soon he was writing not twice a week but once, and then less often still. And – which must have been for Leopold the most grievous change of all – the letters broke the habit of years by ceasing to confide in him on the subject that mattered most of all, his music. In September 1781 he had sent his father extracts from Act 1 of *Die Entführung*, and written twice about it, the first time to enlarge on what he had done, the second (in October) in reply to Leopold's comments on the quality of the verse he was setting. And after that, silence. That is why we have precious words about Osmin's aria and Belmonte's – the important but comparatively straightforward additions that were made to the libretto of the first act – but nothing about the much more radical modifications to the second and third, made in late 1781 and the early months of 1782: a reference to the "many necessary alterations to the poetry", but no details. This is surely because Mozart had distanced himself from his father's complaints to the point where he could no longer think of him as his mentor, let alone as his collaborator. That Leopold was aware of this and resented it passionately emerges from the letter Mozart wrote him a fortnight after the triumphant premiere of the opera:

I received today your letter of the 26th [July] – but a cold indifferent letter such as I would never have expected in reply to my news of the good reception of my opera. I thought (judging by my own feelings) that you would hardly be able to open the parcel [containing the score] for excitement and eagerness to see your son's work, which far from merely pleasing is making such a sensation in Vienna that people refuse to hear anything else, so that the theatre is always packed. [. . .] But you have not had time.

Having established himself as the leading pianist in Vienna, Mozart was determined to become no less popular as a composer, above all – given his own predilection and the Viennese passion for the theatre –

as a composer of opera. The situation looked promising. Only a month after his arrival he was in contact with Gottlieb Stephanie – Stephanie the Younger, as he was called, to distinguish him from his half-brother, Gottlob – actor, playwright, and director of the National Singspiel, whom he had got to know during his stay in Vienna in 1773, and had shown him his Salzburg singspiel *Zaïde*. Mozart had to agree that the piece was too serious for Viennese taste; but Stephanie, who was "well in with the Emperor", hinted that he would find him a suitable libretto: " 'We're old friends,' he said, 'and I shall be only too pleased if I can be of service to you.' " The man had a reputation for double-dealing as well as extreme rudeness; but Vienna was the home of such reputations. He seems genuinely to have admired Mozart and to have sensed that he was the one to raise native German opera to a higher level.

Five years before, the Emperor, then co-ruler with his mother Maria Theresa, had ended the court's monopoly of theatre in Vienna, keeping only the Burgtheater (attached to the Hofburg palace) and the Kärntnertortheater under imperial control. The consequence was that suburban theatres were built and new commercial companies and troupes came into being, which in turn made possible the large number of orchestral musicians that became a feature of the Vienna musical scene. At the same time he established the German National Theatre, at the Burgtheater. Two years later, in 1778, its musical wing was officially constituted. Joseph's interest was partly aesthetic (he was in the habit of attending rehearsals as well as performances), but it was also political; he saw German theatre, and the German language, as a means of strengthening unity and a sense of national identity.

Joseph II remains a paradoxical and disputed figure. At once ultra-rationalist and impulsive, in his own eyes a supremely benevolent autocrat and the father of his people, a man of the Enlightenment, a rigorous centralizer, the measures he enacted on becoming emperor were aimed at concentrating power in his hands and at the same time liberalizing his still-feudal domains. He waged war on the rights and revenues of the church and the aristocracy, introducing equality before the law and taxation across the board, closing many monasteries and convents, abolishing serfdom, and issuing an Edict of Toleration which allowed a degree of religious freedom to Protestants, Jews and

Orthodox. He was cordially hated by many of the old nobility and the clergy, and, later, the economic recession which was in part the consequence of the Turkish War would cause deep and widespread unrest and turn his former allies against him; but, in his early years at least, his decrees were popular with large sections of his subjects. Vienna in the early 1780s was alive with new ideas for political freedom and social betterment.

For Mozart, there was much in both the person and the policies of the Emperor calculated to appeal to him – his dislike of ceremony and state, his informality and approachability, his hostility to privilege, his encouragement of theatre, the whole drift of his social reforms – and to confirm his belief that Vienna was the place for an artist who knew his own worth and was not going to kowtow to anyone. "It is the heart that ennobles a man," Mozart wrote to his father in June, shortly after the bruising encounter with Arco, "and though I am no count, yet I have probably more honour in me than many a count."

He was also quick to appreciate the abundance of Vienna's theatrical life. The theatre, he told Nannerl that July, was his chief pleasure. "How I wish you could see a tragedy acted here! I don't know of a theatre anywhere where all kinds of play are *really well* performed – but here, they are. Each role, even the smallest and least important, is well cast, and understudied." He made friends with some of the leading actors: Joseph Lange (Aloisia Weber's husband), who was a noted Hamlet and Prince Hal, J. H. F. Müller, Gottlieb Stephanie, Friedrich Schröder the "German Garrick" and a champion of Shakespeare. When Leopold Mozart visited Vienna in the winter of 1785, dinners with Stephanie, Müller and Lange were among the entertainments his son arranged for him.

But if the spoken theatre was flourishing, singspiel had not responded well to the Emperor's expectations. There was simply a lack of good original pieces. For repertoire the company had had to fall back on French and Italian operas adapted and translated into German. During the season just ended when Mozart arrived in Vienna the three most frequently performed works had all been French in origin: Gluck's *La rencontre imprévue* (Germanized as *Die unvermuthete Zusammenkunft oder Die Pilgrime von Mekka*), Grétry's *Zémir et Azor* and Gossec's *Le tonnelier*; and in the following season the most popular was Italian, Paisiello's *I filosofi immaginari*. Mozart might help to remedy that. Hence, I think, the particular interest in the new arrival from Salzburg. In the event, Stephanie got rather more than he anticipated.

The libretto he gave Mozart at the end of July 1781 was not one of his own making, as Mozart had assumed it would be – he was far too busy for that – but one that had had its premiere in Berlin two months before, *Belmont et Constanze, oder Die Entführung aus dem Serail*, by the Leipzig businessman and librettist Christoph Friedrich Bretzner, which Johann André had set to music. Its plot was for the most part the one we know from Mozart's opera. Bretzner's denouement is different – Belmont is revealed, just in time, to be the son of the Pasha, who understandably thinks better of his decision to have him strangled – and Osmin the truculent overseer of the Pasha's country estate is a minor character, conceived more for an actor than for a singer and with only one solo song to his name; but the main outlines were the same. It offered a compliant composer a decent opportunity to show his paces, while reserving the dramatic action largely to the spoken dialogue. Stephanie evidently thought it would do very well as it stood.

Mozart, however, with the experience and discoveries of *Idomeneo* fresh in his mind, was never going to be content with that. True, within days, perhaps hours of Stephanie's handing him the text he had "rushed to his desk" and composed three numbers in Act 1 as they stood, Belmonte's aria, Constanze's in B flat, and the trio-finale in which Osmin attempts to bar Belmonte and his servant Pedrillo from entering the house. A week later, Osmin's song "Wer ein Liebchen hat gefunden" ("Whoever has found a sweetheart faithful to him") and the Janissaries' chorus were both done. There had been, though, a particular reason for such speed. *Die Entführung aus dem Serail – The Abduction from the Seraglio –* was intended by Stephanie for the September state visit of Grand Duke Paul, Catherine the Great's son, heir to the Russian throne, and his consort Maria Federovna. Stephanie reckoned that a German opera would appeal to the royal guests – the Grand Duke was seven-eighths German and the Duchess wholly so – not to mention their imperial host (whom the opera's picture of enlightened absolutism could also be expected to please);

the Turkish setting, too, would be nicely topical, given Catherine's and Joseph's territorial designs on the Ottoman Empire. Then suddenly everything changed. Late in August it was announced that the Russian visit was postponed till November.

Now that there was no longer any need for haste, Mozart – delighted to be able to compose his opera at greater leisure – at once got Stephanie to agree to the first of what would be numerous changes to the dramaturgy of *The Abduction*, all made with the aim of extending the role of the music. Belmonte's spoken monologue which followed the overture became an arietta, and the argument (also spoken) between Belmonte and Osmin, after Osmin's song, was turned into a duet, so that it was music not speech that launched the action. Furthermore, Stephanie found himself obliged to write an aria for Osmin, to cap the angry spoken exchange with Pedrillo – an addition inspired both by the splendid voice of Fischer, who was to sing the part, and by the obvious occasion for music that, in Mozart's eyes, the dramatic situation presented.

The aria features in a letter that is famous for being Mozart's most detailed and explicit account of his musical attitudes:

As the role of Osmin is intended for Herr Fischer, who has a really excellent bass voice (notwithstanding the Archbishop's comment that he sings too low for a bass – I assured him that he would sing higher next time), we have to make use of such a man, especially as he has the public here completely on his side. [. . .] So he's been given an aria in the first act, and will have one in the second as well. I told Stephanie exactly how the aria should go, in fact the essentials of the music were complete before he knew anything about it. You [Leopold] have just the beginning, and the end – which is bound to be effective. Osmin's rage is made comic, as the Turkish music is brought in at that point. In the development of the aria I've let Fischer's beautiful low notes shine (despite our Salzburg Midas). His "Drum beim Barte des Propheten" ["Thus, by the beard of the Prophet"] is in the same tempo but in quick notes, and as his rage increases, then – just when you think the aria is ending – comes the Allegro assai, in a completely different tempo and in a different key, creating what will surely be a very fine effect. For just as a man in such a towering rage oversteps all order, moderation and restraint and completely forgets himself, so the music must forget itself. But since passions, however towering, should never be expressed in such a way as to excite disgust, and music, even in the most terrible situations, should never offend the ear but on the contrary give pleasure, in other words never cease to be music, I've not chosen a key that's foreign to F (the key of the aria) but one related to it, only not the nearest, D minor, but the more remote A minor.

Now Belmonte's aria in A major, "O wie ängstlich, o wie feurig" ["Oh how fearfully, how eagerly"] – you know how I've set that [Mozart had sent his father the opening bars]. But also, his beating heart, full of love, is depicted by the violins in octaves. This is the favourite aria of everybody who's heard it, and mine too. It's written exactly for Adamberger's voice. One can see the trembling, the faltering, one can see how his throbbing breast swells – depicted by a crescendo – one can hear the whispering and sighing, expressed by the muted first violins and flute in unison. [. . .]

Now for the Trio – that is, the end of Act 1. Pedrillo has passed his master off as an architect, so as to give him the opportunity to meet his Constanze in the garden, and the Pasha has taken him into his service. Osmin, the overseer, knows nothing of this, he's a coarse boor, the arch enemy of all foreigners, insolent, and won't allow them into the garden. The first part is very short, and because the text lends itself to it I've written it quite nicely in three parts. Then comes the section in the major, beginning pianissimo – it must go very fast, the end will make a real din, which is just what the end of an act should do. The more din the better, that way the public's applause won't cool off. [. . .]

The overture [. . .] is quite short, and changes from forte to piano all the time, the Turkish music always coming in at the fortes. It keeps modulating. I doubt if anyone could fall asleep during it, even if they hadn't slept a wink the night before. [. . .] Well, I've certainly been chattering enough about my opera. But I couldn't help it. (26 September 1781)

The letter radiates the overflowing exuberance, the zest with which Mozart was composing his opera. The tensions of the last months fell away. He was in his element. Stephanie (no doubt once he had got over his surprise) was exerting himself on his behalf. "Everyone abuses Stephanie. It may be that in my case as well he is only friendly to my face. But after all he is arranging the libretto for me – and arranging it exactly as I want – and by God I can't ask for more than that!"

A couple of weeks later, in reply to his father (who had criticized the verses in Osmin's added aria), he reiterated his faith in Stephanie's dramatic skills: "The verse, I agree, may not be of the best, but it fitted so well with my musical ideas, which were already active in my head, that it couldn't fail to please me." Strictly speaking Leopold might be correct; but "the poetry is perfectly in character with the stupid, surly, malevolent Osmin; and I'll bet that in performance its deficiencies won't even be noticed. [. . .] Best of all is when a good composer, who understands the theatre and has something of his own to contribute, and an intelligent poet, that true phoenix, come together."

The changes continued. Other musical numbers, not in the Bretzner libretto, were added to Act 2: a comic duet for Osmin and Blonde, Constanze's English maid, a swift, jubilant aria for Blonde, rejoicing at the news she is about to bring Constanze, that Belmonte has arrived, and an aria for Belmonte, its text taken from a dialogue scene that was being omitted.

Exactly when Stephanie provided the texts for these three numbers is not known. On top of his work as director of the National Singspiel he had other composers to satisfy, and there were periods during the autumn of 1781 when he kept Mozart waiting. This stage of the composition of *The Abduction* is obscure. In the letter of 26 September Mozart speaks of "the whole story" being "altered" and of "Bretzner's quintet" being moved from the beginning of Act 3 to the end of Act 2, making it necessary for "a completely new plot to be introduced". The quintet did indeed disappear from Act 3, though some of its components were kept, being broken up into separate numbers (a solo for Belmonte and Pedrillo's Moorish serenade); but the ensemble which concludes Act 2 of *The Abduction*, the quartet, is not the same thing at all. It is concerned entirely with the joy of the lovers at being reunited and with the jealous suspicions of the two men, who can't help wondering whether their fiancées have really been faithful – a passing idea in Bretzner which Stephanie developed from the same piece of omitted dialogue as supplied the text of Belmonte's Act 2 aria, and which culminates in the rapt A major Andante in 6/8, one of the holiest moments in Mozart opera. And though the denouement was modified, there is nothing that can be called "a completely new plot". It looks as if Stephanie, "up to his eyes in work" (as Mozart said), drew the line at so radical a change, or that Mozart himself had second thoughts.

For much of October work on the opera was suspended. Not till 3 November was Stephanie able to send word that he had "something ready". In the meantime Mozart had to make do with other compositions, when his "passion", as he said, was for his opera. Prompted by reports that the Emperor was creating a special wind band (*Harmonie*) to entertain himself at meals, he wrote the E flat Serenade K375 for a sextet of clarinets, horns and bassoons (oboes were hastily added later – the Emperor's band turned out to be an octet – to make the version familiar today). Part at least of the great Serenade K361 for twelve wind instruments and double bass may also have been composed at this time.

K375, though written to catch the ear of Johann Kilian Strack, valet-de-chambre of Joseph II and cellist in the imperial chamber ensemble, seems not to have been chosen for any court function, meal or otherwise – the Emperor preferred to dine to tunes from Italian opera – but it enjoyed an airing in less exalted circles. Mozart had it performed on St Theresa's Day (15 October), in honour of Therese, the sister-in-law of Joseph Hickel the court painter, at whose house it was given. "The six gentlemen who performed it are poor devils but they play quite nicely together, especially the first clarinet and the two horns. The main reason I wrote it was so that Strack, who goes there every day, should hear something of mine, which is why I wrote it rather carefully. It was much applauded on St Theresa's night, in fact was performed three times, in different places [for two other Theresas as well]. As soon as they finished in one, they were taken to another, and paid to play it." A fortnight later the piece cropped up again, on Mozart's name-day (31 October), when the same musicians came to the Graben and played it for the composer. They "asked for the street door to be opened, then, positioning themselves in the courtyard, surprised me in the pleasantest fashion with the opening chord of E flat, just as I was about to undress".

By then there was again no need to hurry to complete the opera: it had been decided to honour the Russian guests with a Gluck festival. The sixty-seven-year-old composer, who had returned to Vienna two years before, had revised his *Iphigénie en Tauride* and had it translated into German; both it and *Alceste* (in Italian) were being prepared. Mozart briefly thought of getting the translator of *Iphigénie*, Johann Baptist von Alxinger, whose work he admired, to make a German version of *Idomeneo* with a view to its being added to the celebrations, then realized that with two demanding operas to rehearse the company's singers would have more than enough to do without having a third to learn. For the next four months *Iphigenie auf Tauris* and *Alceste*, joined later by *Orfeo* and *La rencontre imprévue*, monopolized the repertoire at the Burgtheater. *The Abduction* must wait its turn.

Mozart was at most of the rehearsals of *Iphigenie* (which Gluck supervised himself). It may well have been in reaction to them, and to the preface to *Alceste*, that he made his celebrated declaration, that "in an opera the poetry must be the handmaiden of the music", the restraint of Gluck's music having sharpened his own very different convictions. It would be a mistake, however, to take that as his last word on the subject. The same letter, after all, formulates what he considers the ideal: a good composer, who understands the theatre, *working with* an intelligent poet.

Mozart and Stephanie were certainly working together again that winter. In late January 1782 Mozart was still referring to "many necessary alterations which have to be made to the poetry", and Stephanie, we may assume, was agreeing to them. The further delays had given Mozart fresh time to rethink and reshape the text and add more music, which a premiere in September 1781, as first envisaged, would have made impossible. Changes to Bretzner's scheme continued, more far-reaching even than before. Constanze's G minor aria, "Traurigkeit", was given a preliminary orchestral recitative (a practice imported from opera seria); a new scene was created in Act 2 for Constanze and the Pasha Selim, requiring new dialogue to set the added aria, "Martern aller Arten", in context; Belmonte received a long aria, his fourth solo number, at the beginning of Act 3, and Osmin his third, the great "Ha, wie will ich triumphiren"; the duet for Constanze and Belmonte following their failed escape was given a new text (with the lovers now alone, not in the presence of the Pasha); a recitative was added which became the emotional crux of the opera; and the work was rounded off with a concluding "vaudeville" for the five singers, followed by a second Janissaries' chorus. At the same time the climactic (spoken) confrontation between Belmonte and the Pasha was rewritten so as to make Belmonte not the long-lost son of Selim but the son of the former commandant of Oran, Selim's mortal enemy, whose greed and cruelty had destroyed his happiness many years before – thus paving the way for a true Enlightenment denouement of high-minded forgiveness and reconciliation.

These changes kept Mozart busy in the early months of 1782, with the prospect of the opera's being performed in April, "right after Easter" (as he told his father). He had also to organize his first major concert in Vienna. It was given, successfully, in the Burgtheater on 3 March with a programme which (on the advice of Countess Thun and other friends) contained excerpts from *Idomeneo*, together with an improvisation by Mozart at the keyboard and the piano concerto K175 with its catchy new finale, K382, one of the hits of the season. On 26 May, in the refreshment pavilion of the Augarten, the imperial park in the north of Vienna, he conducted Symphony No. 34 and played the concerto for two pianos, K365, with his pupil Josepha Auernhammer, an event attended by Archduke Maximilian and several members of the nobility.*

The Abduction had been postponed yet again. Whether Mozart took advantage of the delay to make further changes we do not know (it is possible that the recitative which introduces the Constanze/Belmonte duet in Act 3 was not written till May, just at the time when Mozart and Constanze were making it up after their first serious quarrel). On 7 May he played Act 2 to Countess Thun and on the 30th, Act 3. Meanwhile he checked and corrected the orchestral parts. Rehearsals began early in June and continued through the month. At length, on Tuesday 16 July, the opera had its first performance.

It was an instant success. Though the partisans of Italian opera hissed the first act energetically, nothing could stop it. Despite intense summer heat the theatre was packed night after night. Already on the day before the second performance there were no reserved seats to be had. The work was popular with every class of spectator: the aristoc-

---

* It is symptomatic of the easy relations between the cultivated nobility and the upper middle class that when Mozart and Josepha played the concerto and the D major sonata for two pianos at the house of her father, Councillor Johann Auernhammer, the previous November, the audience included Baron van Swieten and Countess Thun.

racy in the boxes, the intellectuals and army officers in the *parterre noble*, the middle classes in the upper circle. The performance on 6 August (the sixth) was given at the request of Gluck, who complimented the composer warmly (but what can he have really thought of it?) and invited him to lunch. When the Russian visitors reappeared in Vienna in October *The Abduction* was performed in their honour. "I thought it advisable to resume my place at the clavier and conduct, partly to wake up the orchestra, which had been a bit sluggish, and partly – since I am here – to show myself to the royal guests as the father of my child."*

That autumn *The Abduction* was staged in Prague, and in the next few years made its way all over Germany and the Empire; by the time of Mozart's death it had been performed in more than thirty cities. Salzburg itself heard it. "The whole town is delighted with it [. . .] praises it and calls it a very fine work," wrote Leopold Mozart in November 1784 to his daughter, who had married and was living at St Gilgen, twenty miles away. "Even the Archbishop had the grace to say, 'Really it wasn't at all bad.'"

Mozart, in those pre-copyright days, may have made nothing from the work except the 100 ducats he was paid for it in Vienna, but more than anything it was the popularity of *Die Entführung* that established his reputation in German-speaking lands during his lifetime. Orchestras, not surprisingly, found it difficult, expressively as well as technically, but it was loved and revered. Mozart's first biographer, Niemetschek, recalled its performance in Prague as a revelation (one that would also have fateful consequences for the future of Mozartian opera). From then on "the Bohemians began to seek out his compositions" and perform his symphonies and keyboard works at their concerts. The impact of the work in Prague was such that "it was as if what had hitherto been taken for music was nothing of the kind. Everyone was enchanted, amazed at the novel harmonies, the new, unprecedented way the wind instruments were treated."

The Abduction's abundant woodwind parts reflect both Mozart's experience of the Mannheim/Munich players and the growing popularity

---

* Mozart, as was customary, would have directed only the first few performances.

of wind music in Vienna, and the high standard of performance he found there too. But, as always with him, he took it further than anyone else had done. The opera's wind parts surpass in richness and variety even those of *Idomeneo*. A chart of the scoring of the two dozen musical numbers in the score shows hardly one that does not have its particular, individual colour.

Did he, in this instance, take it too far – not in the actual variety of scoring, whose cunning diversity, as in all Mozart's Vienna operas, is integral and essential to the dramatic meaning, but in the sense that the sheer profusion of the music overwhelms the drama, overloads its fragile structure?

Whether or not the Emperor ever made the remark famously attributed to him – "Far too beautiful for our ears, my dear Mozart, and a monstrous quantity of notes" – it is possible to feel that the back-handed compliment contains a grain of truth. *The Abduction*, not *Idomeneo*, on this reckoning, should be seen as the pointer to the greater things to come; partly because of the conditions and conventions within which the work came to birth, Mozart was unable to achieve the concision, the ideal balance of music and drama so remarkable in his next opera, *Figaro*.

Nothing, however, is less useful, or more presumptuous, than using one Mozart opera as a stick to beat another. Each one creates a world, unbeholden to the others (despite the cross-references that link them), and resists comparisons. We should, rather, marvel that Mozart was able to achieve as much as he did in the circumstances, and recognize that the dramatic principles which drive the other operas are active here, and that *The Abduction* was in its way as ground-breaking, as revolutionary as its fellows. The question is: was it too revolutionary for its own good?

Every change or addition made to the text was made on Mozart's initiative; his was the decisive voice. That much is clear from the evidence. And those changes and additions had almost without exception a common purpose: dramatic truth; greater depth of characterization; greater emotional intensity; the embodiment of the drama in music – music (as he says in the letter about poetry's subordination) which "reigns supreme".

I said almost without exception. Mozart is sometimes accused of being too ready to compromise in order to accommodate his singers, of tailoring the music he writes for them too complaisantly to their demands and vocal styles. But that was what an eighteenth-century composer was, of necessity, expected to do. What matters is, always, what Mozart makes of the obligation, how he turns it to positive account. There are two numbers out of the twenty-four in *The Abduction* that do not serve the drama, that are concert arias pure and simple, examples of the display genre in which Mozart throughout his career was so prolific. Constanze's "Ach ich liebte . . . Doch wie schnell schwand meine Freude" in Act 1, one of the three pieces written in immediate response to the libretto, was – on Mozart's own admission – "sacrificed to the flexible throat of Mlle Cavalieri", the first singer of the role; it expressed "her feelings so far as an Italian bravura aria allows". He could have said "only so far". You would never guess, from the animation and high spirits of the music, that the character's joy has vanished and her eyes are overflowing with tears. Belmonte's "Ich baue ganz" at the beginning of Act 3 ("I build all my hopes on your power, oh Love") is even more superfluous – "Mozart at his loveliest, but exceedingly florid" (Dent), irrelevant to the drama and placed just at the point where it is least wanted, when the four lovers, and the audience, are on edge, waiting for the abduction to begin.

These, however, are the sole lapses. In composing Belmonte's Act 1 aria, as he said, "expressly to suit Adamberger's voice", Mozart was not merely pleasing the singer but exploiting his style in such a way as to create a complete picture of Belmonte's ardent yet anxious, hesitant personality. As for Constanze, once her first aria is passed, her nature is explored with a depth and subtlety worthy of Mozart's more generally acclaimed portraits of women who grow until they become the catalysts of the drama and the bright agents of reconciliation. The progression from her desolate "Traurigkeit", through the heroism of "Martern aller Arten" (where the "flexible throat" is employed to maximum dramatic effect) and through her joyful expansiveness in the quartet, to her nobility in the final scene, is Mozart at his most assured and penetrating.

He undoubtedly asks a lot of a dramatic soprano by requiring her to sing the huge "Martern aller Arten" ("Tortures of every kind")

immediately after "Traurigkeit", but he does so for compelling dramatic reasons. With its long opening ritornello and elaborate concertante parts for flute, oboe, violin and cello, the aria is often
dismissed as another concert aria, magnificent but alien to the drama;
but it is, most emphatically, not that. For one thing, in a good performance it is irresistible, full of thrilling sounds: the measured descent of
the vocal line at "des Himmels Segen belohne dich" ("May Heaven's
blessing be your reward") against an airy texture of suspensions and
high-lying instruments as Constanze pleads for mercy; the rising scales
for the four concertante players and the voice part (a kind of
speeded-up version of Ilia's "Se il padre perdei" in *Idomeneo*), followed by the singer's sustained high C; the blazing excitement and
physical attack of the full orchestra in the coda, like something in an
early Beethoven symphony. But such effects are much more than that:
they have meaning. Coming immediately after the deep dejection of
the G minor "Traurigkeit" (whose exquisitely beautiful writing for
flutes, oboes, basset-horns and bassoons, far from being merely decor-
ative, is a sympathetic reflection and companion of Constanze's grief),
"Martern aller Arten"'s heroic C major marks a decisive moment in
the evolution of her character. As Thomas Bauman points out, the
unusual form of the aria – two contrasting and alternating tempos,
allegro and allegro assai, with the less quick of the two returning
unexpectedly in the middle of the (slightly shorter) reprise of the
quicker – dramatizes Constanze's struggle for a new spirit of resolve.
That resolve, and the moral force by which she wins through to it,
prepare for the Constanze of the great recitative with Belmonte in
Act 3, where her steadfast tenderness calms his anguish with phrases
of noble serenity. "What is death? a pathway to peace." As she sings,
we remember Mozart's own words in the last surviving letter to his
father: "As death, when we come to consider it closely, is the goal of
our existence, I have during the last few years formed such an intimate
relationship with this best and truest friend of humankind that his
image is not only no longer frightening to me but is calming and
consoling." It was surely Mozart who decided on the alteration to
Bretzner's final scene, adding the all-important recitative and demanding a different text for the duet, in which the bliss of being
reunited in death is not the only sentiment, and they acknowledge

that each has brought the other to this pass. But without "Martern aller Arten" Constanze's courage in the final confrontation with death would carry less conviction.

"Martern aller Arten" is integrated musically as well as dramatically with the work as a whole. The alternation of voice part and powerful sustained chords in the orchestra at "shout, bluster, rage!" is echoed in the repeated "nichts" in the final section (Allegro) of the quartet. That is a detail. More significant is the way the music of the aria reflects the opera's "Turkish" style. Mozart, when first announcing the commission to his father, said that he proposed to "write the overture, the chorus in Act 1 and the final chorus in the style of Turkish music". In fact he gave it a bigger role, incorporating it into the musical language of the work. "Martern aller Arten" is full of "Turkish" elements: to quote Bauman, the main motif "unisono, vigorously triadic, duple with firm downbeats and involving immediately the sharpened fourth degree"

and also the rising triad at the beginning of the Allegro assai (associated with the Turkish overseer Osmin) and the whirling scales which bring the aria to its furious conclusion. These were all elements loosely derived from the music of the Janissary bands that featured in European armies of the period (a Western simplification of the real thing). "Martern aller Arten", which is in C, the opera's "Turkish" key, like the overture, the drinking duet and the two Janissary choruses – the key in which the work begins and ends – is in a sense Selim's aria as well as Constanze's. His last words in the preceding dialogue – "(Not death but) tortures of every kind" – give Constanze her cue. The aria is her riposte to his momentary cruelty and his refusal to be moved by her pleading. Though he remains silent, and has only a speaking role in the opera, his voice is behind hers as the music pursues its grand, impulsive progress.

It is typical of Mozart and of his approach to *The Abduction* that he should make so much of what in the hands of another composer might be no more than a pretext for some crowd-pleasing local colour. "Turkish" music was part of the wide range of open-air performances on offer in the Prater and in the streets, and operas and musical plays on oriental subjects were popular. Although Turkey had ceased to be a direct threat to Vienna, the shock of 1683, when the Turks were at the gates, lingered in the folk memory. Vienna was and is a city where pleasures are enjoyed against a background of danger. The scenario of *The Abduction* may strike a modern audience as strictly exotic: for the public of the day it was not so unreal. (In 1782, the year of *The Abduction*, the entire cast of the Malta Opera was captured by Algerian pirates.)

Mozart, however, was not content with a few conventional touches. He uses "Turkish" instruments – cymbals, triangle, bass drum, squeaky-high piccolo – for the overture, the two choruses, Osmin's outbursts of rage in A minor, and the duet where Pedrillo inveigles him into drinking the drugged wine; but he goes further than that. The rising triad, major or minor, occasionally inverted, becomes a motif, and one that is particularly associated with Osmin. We hear it in the first few bars of the overture, in the presto section of Osmin's duet with Belmonte, in the first Janissary chorus, in the trio which ends Act 1, and in the C minor section of the Osmin–Blonde duet. It would perhaps be stretching the point to claim that its reappearance in the orchestral introduction to Pedrillo's "Frisch zum Kampfe" and, inverted, as the theme of Blonde's G major aria shows the influence of their years in Turkish captivity. But it is no accident that we find it at the beginning of the Allegro assai in "Martern aller Arten" and, inverted again, in Osmin's triumph aria and in the final chorus at the words "Let honour be his [Pasha Selim's] due", where the accompanying violins and piccolo play it at the same time in its normal rising form. "Turkish" music and the Pasha's magnanimity have the last word.

The change to Bretzner's denouement is hardly less important than the parallel change to Danchet's in *Idomeneo*. Selim's beneficence, no longer simply that of a father who lifts the death-sentence from his own offspring, achieves genuine moral stature as he forgives the son of the evildoer who destroyed his happiness. The words of the new ending may be Stephanie's – an ending in tune both with the Enlightenment ideal, dear to his employer Joseph II, of the clemency-loving absolute monarch and with the image of the noble Turk often found in eighteenth-century representations of the Orient – but it is not fanciful to see Mozart's reconciling instinct as the guiding force behind them. Mozart's Selim is the antithesis of his Osmin, rising above his desire for revenge where the ferocious overseer lives only and unchangeably for it.

Osmin is of course a caricature, the West's stereotype of the savage Turk – no more nor less stereotypical than the Christian grotesque, Mother of Calamity, in *The Thousand and One Nights* (which Mozart liked Constanze to read aloud to him as he orchestrated his scores). But the caricature is rounded and vitalized into a living portrait. Mozart, it is clear, relished him and hugely enjoyed composing the music for "that grand old rascal", as Beecham called him. Elevating Bretzner's minor character into a central figure had, in addition, a dramatic purpose. Osmin functions as the dark side of Selim (and perhaps, unconsciously, of Mozart himself, as the projection of the fantasies of revenge on Count Arco and the Archbishop that still obsessed Osmin's creator in the months when *The Abduction* was taking shape). But you have the feeling that Mozart did it also because he couldn't resist; like Osmin, he knew no restraint. Though Osmin's role in the plot is minimal, he towers over it. The others, when they sing with him, are as if hypnotized into adopting his manner and style; or he takes their phrases and holds them up to sarcastic ridicule. No other character has so much extra music lavished on him: two arias and two duets not in the original libretto. Fischer's magnificent bass was the occasion ("we must take advantage of it, especially as he has the whole Viennese public on his side"); but as with Adamberger's voice, Fischer's was the spur to greater invention. Osmin's music is an inventory of Fischer's strengths and skills: the beautiful, precisely focused low notes (which, a contemporary said, he could deliver "with a fullness, agility and grace found otherwise only in good tenors"), the rapid repeated notes filled with tone and always sounding, the powerful rising scales, and the widely spaced long notes heard near the beginning of "Solche hergelauf'ne Laffen" ("These prowling puppies who do nothing but ogle women") and again in the middle section of his Act 3 aria; Mozart composes each of these traits into a single comic portrait of unprecedented richness. You can *see* the gloating strides of the slippered, turbaned monster in the hour of his triumph, as he mimics his captives' furtive escape. The opening of the Act 1 aria is no less vivid; the insistent repeated notes followed by the menacing semitones, with angry accents on the lower, shorter notes, and then the lurching run up the stave, suggest nothing so much as a great bull swaying from side to side as it works itself up for the charge.

The lovingly detailed accompaniment to the song Osmin sings in the opening scene as, standing on a ladder, he gathers figs from a tree in front of the Pasha's summer palace, is symptomatic of the serious-ness and fastidiousness that Mozart brought to the writing of the opera. Music "reigns supreme" – but music dramatically inspired, music and drama as one. The song is strophic – Osmin's rumination on how to keep one's women sweet and protect the gullible darlings from predatory young men who lie in wait to tempt them – but Mozart varies the three verses: each is, in turn, differently, more abundantly scored and harmonized. In the third – by which time Osmin has become aware of Belmonte hovering below him – the Andante tempo breaks into an angry Allegro at "Some young gallant is often lurking, ready to seduce the little fool". The dovetailing of song into duet (with Belmonte exasperatedly repeating Osmin's interminable refrain in a new tempo and metre), the repeated staccato string figures, expect-ant, impatient, accompanied by sustained oboes and horns, as Belmonte asks if this is Pasha Selim's house and Osmin affects not to hear him, the recitative interrupting the duet and Osmin's menacing reaction to the mention of Pedrillo, the wide range of keys, reflecting Osmin's ungovernable character – all this is masterly and brilliantly inventive, Mozart the comic dramatist at full stretch. If it overshadows the plot, who can really object?

The more you study *The Abduction* the more you find in it. Again and again convention, transformed, is harnessed to the dramatic situ-ation. The traditional slow middle section of the tripartite overture becomes a foretaste of the action: surrounded on either side by the fizzing, buzzing "Turkish" presto, the music of Belmonte's C major arietta, here prefigured in a hesitant C minor, suggests the traveller who has reached his goal but finds himself in a strange, perhaps hostile environment.

Similar examples can be cited from all over the opera. Pedrillo's midnight signal to the ladies, with its stealthy pizzicato, its ambiguous tonality drifting between B minor, D major, A major, C major, F sharp, and B minor, its sudden breaking-off in mid-phrase, and its lilting but at the same time nervous siciliano rhythm, makes of the conventional operatic serenade something both magically atmospheric and apt to the situation: the very moment of escape. Another popular form, the vaudeville, becomes in Mozart's hands a subtler, more satisfactory rounding-off, thanks to the variants in each of the verses sung by the two pairs of lovers and by Osmin: Belmonte's with strings only, Constanze's with added bassoon, Pedrillo's with oboe and Blonde's with flute (the two servants' a plainer version of the F major tune announced by Belmonte), and finally Osmin's version, beginning with a brusquer form (to words not of gratitude for the Pasha's benevolence but of rage – "we should burn these dogs"), only for the tune to lose control completely and explode into a repeat of the A minor "Turkish" coda of his F major aria from Act 1, before he storms out. Instead of a simple reprise of the vaudeville, Mozart proceeds to write a beautiful fourteen-bar passage of block harmony, as the four beneficiaries of the Pasha's generosity draw the moral: "Nought is so hateful as revenge; but to be humane and kind and selflessly forgive is the mark only of noble souls." Then the vaudeville resumes, ending in a new, clinching two-bar phrase, before the final Janissaries' chorus restores C major.

Nothing is perfunctory, and almost nothing without a clear dramatic purpose. The music for the two servants is as characteristic in style and colour as the music of Belmonte and Constanze and has no less affection and care lavished on it (though not clarinets, which except in the drinking duet are reserved for the gentry).* Blonde is the equal of her mistress – the first notable member of the long line of spirited soubrettes who have enlivened German opera. Unlike Pedrillo she is not afraid of anyone. She can manipulate Osmin with ease and worst him at his own game of sarcasm: see her reply in the duet, parodying his sepulchral "swear to obey me" with "not if you

---

* The drinking duet uses the bright, forceful C clarinet; the clarinet in Belmonte's music is generally the warmer B flat instrument.

were the great Mogul himself", going down to low A flat. In the quartet, when Pedrillo pleads to be forgiven for his suspicions (to a warm-hearted tune whose second phrase recurs in the piano concerto in the same key of A major, K414, which Mozart composed not long afterwards), her reply – "No, I can't forgive you for thinking me capable of that, with that stupid old fool" – is set in a skittish triple time (12/8) against the common time and legato phrases of the other three, a remarkable piece of writing that is perfectly in character. The orchestral accompaniment to Blonde's two arias is equally character-istic: strings, alternately caressing and perky, for the A major aria in which she coaches Osmin in how and how not to treat a woman, airy flutes, bassoons and horns for the breathless G major aria that she sings after learning that Belmonte has arrived.

But accompaniment is no longer an appropriate word. The orches-tra is a central player in the drama, an active and vital contributor to the richness of the score, interacting with the human voice so that, to quote Bauman, "together [they] create the sense of a living organism".

Is the score too rich? Some critics have thought so. Dent maintained that in *The Abduction*, beginning with Osmin's "Solche hergelauf'ne Laffen", Mozart "yielded to his besetting temptation – the tendency to make all his arias too long", a tendency that "becomes more and more disastrously pronounced as this opera proceeds". That is unquestionably true of Belmonte's fundamentally undramatic "Ich baue ganz" (which in many productions is omitted); but I do not find it so, in performance, of any of the other arias, or of any other movements except the rapturous Constanze–Belmonte duet, which makes the mistake of falling in love with its own rapturousness. The huge dimensions of "Martern aller Arten", as I have tried to argue, are justified dramatically; the difficulty it presents – strictly one of staging: what to do with Constanze during the long ritornello and with the Pasha during the whole aria – is not one that can't be overcome by an imaginat-ive director. Belmonte, in his "O wie ängstlich" in Act 1, may indeed take longer to "get through his devotions" than Tamino in *The Magic Flute* in his aria of a similar "devoted and adoring type" (Dent), but that does not make the aria too long. It needs to be longer than Tamino's: it is a much more detailed piece of characterization, and *The Abduction* is a different work.

Dent also called the Constanze–Belmonte duet "enormously long for the type of opera in which it occurs", and complained that Mozart, in composing the work, provided his virtuoso singers "with songs [far] outside the scale of German *Singspiel*". This judgement has been followed by many commentators. But that implies that there are precise rules governing singspiel, when there are no rules for it or for opera generally, or for that matter for musical composition, but only (as Shaw says) "rules of thumb". The Constanze–Belmonte duet is too long not because it occurs in a singspiel but because it is too long *tout court*. There is nothing fixed and immutable about the singspiel form. No one, at least no one in their senses, would complain that the trio in Act 1 of *Fidelio* or Leonore's "Abscheulicher . . . Komm, Hoffnung" – both of them substantial pieces – are too long because *Fidelio* is a singspiel. The problem of *The Abduction* lies not in the singspiel form itself but in this particular example of it.

In setting the text he was presented with, Mozart did not have complete freedom to "remould it nearer to the heart's desire", as he was able to in his three Italian comedies and in *The Magic Flute*. He showed from the first that he was determined not to be bound by the limitations of the genre, as everyone else had been – insisting on the opening scenes being carried on almost entirely in music and, once he realized he had time to play with, constantly enlarging the role of music in the scheme of the opera – but there was a point beyond which even he could not go. Bretzner's libretto, designed for a genre which had its roots in spoken drama, could be adapted only so far; the great symphonic structures which reflect and forward the dramatic action in *Figaro* and *Don Giovanni* are almost entirely absent. The German tradition of comic opera as a play with musical numbers also left a strong mark on *The Abduction* in the protagonist's being represented by an actor with not a note to sing. Ten years later the wisdom and magnanimity of his equivalent in *The Magic Flute*, Sarastro, will be incarnated in one of the great bass roles in opera. Here, however, music could not "reign supreme", much as Mozart might have wished it.

Indeed, in Stephanie's and Mozart's remodelled Act 3 the main action, the focus of the drama – the elopement and its frustration by Osmin and the guards – takes place largely by means of the spoken word: the play-with-music, the genre from which *The Abduction* sprang, has reasserted its primacy. Mozart's instinct to create a multi-movement ensemble (the quartet) as a finale to Act 2 was a sound one – the shape of the score, you can say, demanded it – but it left the first part of the following act impoverished. To that extent his dramatic touch, so sure by the time he came to write *Figaro*, was not yet faultless. Yet if the climactic confrontation between the Pasha and the lovers could have been embodied in music, that would have mattered much less. The ambiguous nature of the Pasha which we are asked to believe in – essentially noble but with a cruel side which he has to struggle to subdue and transcend – could have been made convincing if expressed in Mozart's music. As it is, we are not convinced of it, and the drama is weakened in consequence, losing vital tension.*

In short, I doubt if we would hear so much about the weaknesses and over-indulgence of *The Abduction* were the plot stronger. Those weaknesses belong not to a score that is too luxuriant, let alone to one that combines too many different styles, but to a libretto which, even when worked over and changed, is not strong enough to support it. The music's stylistic diversity would not have struck contemporary Viennese audiences as anything unusual; the singspiels which preceded *The Abduction* at the Burgtheater typically mixed the serious and the comic, popular German song and no less popular Italian coloratura. Mozart merely took the accepted convention further, as was his wont, and then proceeded to forge the diverse elements into a homogeneous whole.

In any case, how much do those weaknesses, which loom so large in the study, bother us in the theatre? When the opera is sung and played well, and the director refrains from foisting on it alien, heavy-handed conceptions, the combined verve and finesse of the music carries all before it. From the opening of the overture, with its dazzling pace and audacious orchestral activity (epitomized in the whizzing moto perpetuo second violin part), what Weber called "the gaiety and spendthrift youthfulness and warmth of *Entführung*" delight the

---

* Nor do we hear again of the interesting idea mooted in Selim's soliloquy after "Martern aller Arten", that since both threats and kindness have failed he must resort to cunning. It is simply left hanging.

willing listener. (The same qualities overflow into the brilliant Haffner symphony of late July 1782, written to celebrate the ennoblement of Sigmund Haffner, the Salzburg burgomaster's son, a work whose joie de vivre, conscious compositional mastery, and presto finale theme – adapted from Osmin's triumphant Act 3 aria – come exactly and appropriately from the time when the opera was drawing full houses at the Burgtheater.) Mozart will write greater comedies than *The Abduction*; but, while we are experiencing this one, that is for the moment beside the point. The ability to create comedy in its widest and deepest sense, which will be demonstrated in *Figaro*, is already his.

As in *Idomeneo, Die Entführung aus dem Serail* ends on a note of reconciliation which resounds with echoes of the composer's life. Mozart, like Belmonte, was united at last with his Constanze, after months of heartache, tension and misunderstanding and in the face of opposition and meddling from both sides of the family. But that was over now. They married on 4 August, between the fifth and sixth performances of the opera that celebrated her namesake's deliverance, and without his father's blessing; Leopold's grudging consent arrived the day after the wedding. The symbolism is apt. Both of them had slipped the ties binding them to their families; as they began life together they were on their own. Mozart had chosen a wife without parental consent. Constanze was fully as ready to free herself from a parent's interfering grasp. But now, in the apartment in the Hohe Brücke (the same building where the Mozarts had lodged sixteen years before), all that no longer mattered, in the absorption of mutual companionship and sexual discovery. They had each other.

That autumn and early winter *The Abduction* continued to figure on the Burgtheater playbill. Yet despite its success, perhaps partly because of it, the National Singspiel's days were numbered. There were not enough good composers and poets interested in writing for it; the best that Umlauf or Gassmann or Gallus could produce was pallid in comparison. Mozart would have liked nothing better than to compose another German opera – "Every nation has its own opera, so why not Germany? Isn't German as singable a language as French or English?" – but the Emperor had already decided to bring the experiment to an end and install an opera buffa company in its place. His ambassador in Venice was ordered to engage singers for it.

In early 1783 Mozart, his mind still on German opera, had Goldoni's comedy *Il servitore di due padroni* translated for him; but though he seems to have composed two arias the project went no further. Meanwhile, the previous December, at a gathering at Prince Galitzin's, Count Rosenberg had called him over and had a word in his ear: would he write an Italian comic opera? Whatever Mozart's preference for German, this was a chance not to be missed: opera in whatever language was the thing. If that was where his future lay, so be it. Within hours, he was sending to Italy for the latest librettos.

4

Lorenzo Da Ponte and the
perfect marriage
Le nozze di Figaro

On 7 May 1783 Mozart wrote his father a letter that is one of the prime documents in the history of opera. "Another short letter! I intended to put off writing till next Saturday, as I have to go to a concert today; but as I have something to say that is of special importance for me I must snatch the time to write at least a few lines." The new Italian company at the Burgtheater – which he had thought would not last long – is doing excellent business; the buffo bass, Benucci, is particularly good. He cannot wait to get involved. But he has "looked through at least a hundred librettos" and found scarcely one that will do: so many changes would have to be made that it would be easier to write a new text, which would be better anyway. Mozart goes on:

Our poet here is now a certain Abbate da Ponte. He has a huge amount to do, revising pieces for the theatre, and he has to write *per obbligo* an entirely new libretto for Salieri, which will take him two months. He has promised after that to write a new one for me. But who knows whether he will be able to keep his word – or whether he will want to. As you are aware, these Italian gentlemen are very charming to your face . . . Enough, we know them! If he is in league with Salieri I shall never get anything out of him. But I should dearly like to show what I can do in an Italian opera.

The historic meeting between Mozart and the man who was to have a decisive influence on his career and art took place courtesy of the banker Baron Raimund Wetzlar von Plankenstern, a converted and ennobled Jew in whose house in the Hohe Brücke Mozart and Constanze had lodged the previous winter, and who was godfather to their first child. Lorenzo Da Ponte, born Emmanuel Conegliano in 1749, the son of a Jewish tanner and shoemaker from the Veneto, took the name of the officiating bishop when his father and he and his two brothers were baptized into the Catholic Church. After a chequered career as priest, preceptor, radical thinker, and frequenter of married women, Da Ponte had recently settled in Vienna. The two versions of his memoirs, written many years later in America, are seriously unreliable; but his talent, and his passion for poetry and the theatre, were genuine, and his charm and good manners did the rest. In Dresden he talked his way into working for Caterino Mazzolà, poet to the Italian opera at the Saxon court, who in turn gave him a letter of recommendation to Salieri. Da Ponte arrived in Vienna in the winter of 1780–81, where he courted the aged Metastasio, renewed acquaintance with Mozart's admirer and patron Count Cobenzl (who had helped him earlier), and endeared himself to Count Rosenberg. When the Italian company was set up at the Burgtheater he was appointed resident librettist.

Mozart's letters are tantalizingly silent about him – the letter just quoted is the only one to mention him by name – and there are none addressed to him. We know nothing about a partnership that must have been close, except what its fruits tell us. This is, first, because almost no letters from Mozart to his father – the chief source of information about his doings – survive from later than mid-1784, well before he began working with Da Ponte, and, second, because he had no need to write to a collaborator who lived in the same city. In the months when *Figaro* was taking shape, Mozart's lodgings were in Grosse Schulerstrasse (the modern Domgasse), a short walk from Da Ponte's office in the Burgtheater.

Why did two artists who in retrospect seem destined for each other take so long to connect? Here, much more than with Stephanie, was Mozart's ideal partnership made flesh: "a composer who understands the theatre and a true poet, that phoenix, working together". Yet Da Ponte had been in Vienna four years before they began collaborating. "I should dearly like to show what I can do in an Italian opera." Precisely. Why did it not happen sooner?

For several different reasons. The first – before there could be any question of a collaboration with Da Ponte – was Mozart's fastidiousness and his increasingly acute dramatic sense which could not be satisfied with the less than first-rate, or at any rate with the mediocre.

It is hard to imagine even the best of his contemporaries looking through 100 librettos without finding one they were prepared to set. Count Rosenberg might well have him in mind for a commission, and Mozart might long to respond. But if no libretto appealed to him, what then?

Another reason was his identity and reputation. The most successful and frequently performed composers at the Burgtheater between 1783 and 1789 were all Italians, or were regarded as one of them, as was the Spaniard Vicente Martín y Soler. Mozart, a German, was not one of them. At the same time his exceptional talents made them, understandably, wary. As his friend Sigmund Barisani wrote in Mozart's album, "Latins envy thy composer's skill." The leading Italian composers of opera buffa were highly skilful, but in a much simpler musical idiom than Mozart, whose operatic style was deeply permeated, and facilitated, by his non-operatic compositions, and for that reason, in their view, over-complicated. He was a composer of instrumental music, which by and large they were not.

It is often said that, influenced by his father's "habitual paranoia", Mozart saw enmities and conspiracies where none existed. But no paranoia was required. They were endemic to the theatre in Vienna. He could not have forgotten that an Italian cabal prevented his opera *La finta semplice* from being put on there in 1768, though the court had commissioned it, or that the Italian faction had tried to hiss *The Abduction* off the stage. It was not only Leopold who spoke of "powerful cabals" intriguing against *Figaro* and of "Salieri and all his supporters" planning to do the opera down: the Mozart family's Bohemian friends the Duscheks testified that people were "plotting against him" because of the reputation which his "outstanding talent and ability" had won. There was nothing unusual in that. It would not have needed a full-scale conspiracy to slow things down nicely.

Mozart, having just met Da Ponte, could not of course know what the future held. He only knew that he wanted to write a comic opera for the Italian company. Da Ponte might or might not produce something for him – for the moment he was not free to, and Mozart did not feel inclined to wait till he was, nor to search for someone else to alter one of the less unsatisfactory librettos he had been studying. As he said, a brand-new text was better.

Hence the strange idea broached (presumably with Count Rosenberg's assent) in the letter of 7 May already quoted: that Leopold Mozart should see if he couldn't persuade Varesco – assuming he wasn't still feeling sore about *Idomeneo* – to collaborate with him again and write him a comic libretto (for which he would receive a decent fee, the takings of the third performance). Varesco could jot down a few ideas – "the essential thing is that the story should be really comic" – and they could work on it together when he and Constanze paid their visit to Salzburg, planned for that summer. A fortnight later he repeated his request: "Please keep on reminding Varesco [. . .] The chief thing is the comic element – I know the taste of the Viennese."

The nookshotten result was *L'oca del Cairo*, *The Goose of Cairo*, an abortive project if ever there was one. It is perhaps a measure of Mozart's desperation that he should not only be prepared to consider collaborating on a comic opera with a man who, as he admitted, had "not the slightest knowledge or experience of the theatre" but should actually work on so barren a tale off and on for six months before finally acknowledging that it was hopeless: the story of an old Marquis who keeps his daughter – betrothed to a man she doesn't like – and her companion shut up in a tower, from which the daughter's true love rescues her by entering it concealed inside a large mechanical goose.

We know from a letter written by Mozart after his return to Vienna that he and Varesco discussed the opera during the Salzburg visit. Varesco set to work at once and provided him with a draft of the libretto of the first act. Some of the eight numbers which survive, mostly in sketch form and all from Act 1, were written in Salzburg, some on the journey back to Vienna, in Steyr, and in Linz where Mozart and Constanze spent three weeks as guests of old Count Thun, father and father-in-law of Mozart's Viennese patrons. The finale was sketched in Vienna in December. By then, not before time, he was having serious doubts about the mechanical goose: "my only reason for not objecting to this whole goose business", he told his father, "was that two people of greater penetration and judgement than I had no objection to it – that is, yourself and Varesco."

This, though surely meant ironically, is a lame excuse. He should have realized much sooner that the Abbate was out of his depth and incapable of creating a comedy with characters and situations he could get his teeth into. You can feel his scorn when, on receiving part of the text of Act 2, he finds that Varesco has written, in the margin of a cavatina, "the music of the preceding cavatina will do for this": "That is out of the question. In Celidora's cavatina the words are disconsolate and depressing, whereas in Lavina's they are comforting and full of hope. Besides, for one singer to echo the song of another is completely out of date. [. . .] Further, the audience would hardly be able to tolerate the *same aria* from the second singer, having already heard it sung by the first." Mozart soldiers on – the letter is full of fresh suggestions for improving the libretto – but the next letter (10 February 1784) reveals that *L'oca di Cairo* has been put on one side: Mozart has other "works to compose which are bringing in money *now*". By this time the *Goose* is well and truly cooked, and nothing further is heard of it.

Another opera which remains a fragment, *Lo sposo deluso* (*The Deluded Bridegroom*, subtitled "Three women's rivalry for one lover", and adapted from the text of Cimarosa's *Le donne rivali* of 1780), probably dates from about the same time, or from 1784, after the *Goose* was abandoned. It may be the libretto which Mozart mentions in a letter of July 1783 as having been brought him by "an Italian poet", which "I shall perhaps adopt if he agrees to adjust and tailor it to my liking". The poet is often assumed to have been Da Ponte, but the very moderate quality of the dramaturgy and verse of the four numbers that Mozart either completed or sketched makes that unlikely.

Though neither of these attempts got anywhere (and any foretaste they give of what was soon to come is surely much fainter than is sometimes claimed), it was not all wasted effort. Writing the ensembles – the *Goose*'s finale especially – provided him with useful experience towards acquiring the mastery of the contemporary style of opera buffa, infused with his own inimitably personal voice, that would burst forth fully armed two years later. That he had to wait so long must have been intensely frustrating for Mozart, watching and hearing what Paisiello and Salieri and Martín and Sarti and Cimarosa could do and knowing he could do better. In fact the delay was as providential as it was with *Idomeneo* and, to a lesser extent, *The Abduction*. Those two intervening years were to prove, paradoxically, an ideal preparation for *Figaro*. While he waited to "show what [he] could do in an Italian opera", he studied the works of his contemporaries that were put on at the Burgtheater and the Kärntnerthor and took note of the changing conventions of opera buffa, the increase in the number of ensembles, the greater flexibility permitted in the forms of arias. Above all, two Paisiello operas premiered in Vienna, *Il barbiere di Siviglia* (1783) and *Il rè Teodoro in Venezia* (1784) – together with Haydn's *La fedeltà premiata* (1784), with its carefully organized multi-movement finales that would inspire the greater finales in *Figaro*, and Bianchi's *La villanella rapita* of 1785, for which Mozart composed two inserted numbers, a trio and a quartet – helped him to understand where his true bent lay: in comic opera that was a drama of real-life characters and a critique of society, not a mere string of farcical situations.* Even if he was not himself composing the opera he longed to write, he was exercising his powers in readiness for it. In addition to the pieces added to Bianchi's opera, the dramatic concert aria "O misero! o sogno!", sung by Adamberger (Belmonte in *The Abduction*) at the Society of Musicians' Burgtheater concert on 22 December 1783, illustrates, in Robbins Landon's words, "the intensity, passion and personal involvement in the text" that he will bring to the writing of *Figaro*.

Mozart's non-vocal compositions exerted an influence that was still more potent. By the mid-1780s he had become a composer who could do exactly what he wanted, find whatever he needed for each new conception, and who was as true to himself in a work like the A major string quartet, where the merest thematic tag could be made to dance for him and yield untold riches, as he was in the bounteousness of the first movement of the piano quartet in E flat, where melodies follow one after the other in reckless profusion. The conversational ease of *Figaro* springs at least partly from the experience gained through the music he put aside *The Goose of Cairo* to write – above all, through the piano concertos. It was as if the pent-up operatic longings, denied

---

* *La villanella rapita* anticipates *Figaro* in its attack on aristocratic abuses.

their desired outlet, were concentrated with redoubled creative force on a medium that became, unprecedentedly, a dramatic form in its own right.

1784 is the year of the piano concerto. In the thirteen months between February 1784 and February 1785 Mozart composed eight (and the first hundred bars of a ninth, the A major K488), works which changed the whole idea of the piano and the concept and status of concerto form out of recognition. Not even the trio of concertos, K413–415, published the previous year, which carry the elegant, limited display-vehicle of J. C. Bach into a new dimension, hint at the magnitude of development found in the great series beginning with K449 in E flat and ending with K467 in C major – a work which, as Charles Rosen says, belongs as much to the history of the symphony and even the opera as of the concerto.

It is hardly accidental that the period of this intense activity, as well as coinciding with the gap in large-scale operatic composition, includes no symphonies – none between the Linz of November 1783 and the Prague of three years later. The piano concerto becomes a symphonic form, with the soloist and the orchestra involved together in a single integrated, highly wrought argument. It also becomes a form of theatre. Each is a separate instrumental drama, with its own colour and its own compositional processes. The diversity of forms as well as of moods is extraordinary – operatic, in fact. Only because there are so many concertos is it possible for a work like the grand D major, K451, and its companion from March 1784, the B flat K450, to be as neglected as they are; it is simply that the next one, composed for Mozart's pupil Babette Ployer, the G major K453 (whose chirpy finale tune Mozart's pet starling could whistle with only one mistake), is even more obviously appealing.

The last two of the series, the D minor K466 and the C major K467, take the symphonic and operatic further still. In K467's richly comic finale, orchestra and piano engage in repartee that is almost speaking: oboe and bassoon, echoing the soloist's four notes (part of the main theme), are as irreverently subversive as Harpo Marx. On the other hand the mysterious F major andante is an opera seria aria without words, or rather goes beyond even the most magically evocative opera: music of intense yet dreamlike emotion as – above the steady tick of the bass and the regular pulse of the accompanying triplets (which cease only once, memorably, for three bars) – the strange gleam of the woodwind textures, the plangent dissonances arising from continuous suspensions, and the soloist's flowing declamation and wide vocal leaps combine to create an unbearable tension, yet experienced as though through a veil. The spacious opening movement, at once grand and relaxed, is one of the longest in Mozart, but surprises us by its quiet ending, with the commanding march theme melting into thin air.

If K467 was unlike any C major trumpet-and-drum symphonic work heard before, what can Mozart's audiences have thought of its companion, the fiery D minor, the most operatic of all his works that are not, ostensibly, operas? Its opening allegro, too, ends in a whisper, a suitably dramatic conclusion to a movement which from the first creates an atmosphere unique in Mozart's instrumental music, eerie, driven, possessed. In shadowy, pulsating syncopations the violins pick out Mozart's favourite D minor motif, D-A-F-E-D,

while beneath them the cellos and basses paw the ground like beasts waiting to spring – the whole gesture and mood and texture a presage of the opera Mozart will write for Prague in two years' time. At intervals horns, trumpets and drums lend a menacing *Don Giovanni*-like colour to the orchestra, and the single flute (as prominent here as in the opera) adds its pale, haunted character. In the finale, begun by the piano with a rocketing arpeggio, the music rises to a wilder desperation, with tuttis of "brilliant violence" (Rosen), brusque modulations, huge leaps by the first violins, and echoes of the sudden pauses which were a feature of the first movement. The mood seems confirmed when the piano's transitional theme appears not, as normally, in the relative major but in F minor. But Mozart has one more dramatic stroke in store. In the reprise, though the unexpectedly cheerful second theme duly reappears in D minor, that is not to be its final goal. The violins' vertiginous leaps are heard once more, ushering in the cadenza. When it is over, the soloist, not the orchestra, takes up the story, beginning as if to restate the rocketing theme in full. But the storm has blown itself out. The music breaks off on a series of powerful diminished seventh chords, whereupon, after a pause, oboe, bassoon and horns give us the cheerful theme in an unambiguous D major. The coda is still grand but now unequivocally high-spirited. Only those who insist on judging music in moral terms can possibly feel offended that a work which began with *Don Giovanni* should end with *Figaro*. In any case, that is one aspect of the concerto that will not have bothered the Viennese audience which heard it for the first time in February 1785.

Leopold Mozart was in the audience, having arrived that morning to stay with his son and daughter-in-law in the Grosse Schulerstrasse apartment. He was plunged straight into a whirlwind of musical activity that must have forced him to reconsider his assumptions about Wolfgang's indolence, if he still harboured them. The pattern had been set the previous year, when in the three months from February to April Mozart composed four piano concertos, the quintet for piano and wind and the violin sonata K454 and, during Lent (when theatre was in abeyance), gave more concerts than we will probably ever know. A letter of 3 March 1784 detailed twenty-two that he was involved in between 26 February and 3 April, a mixture of gatherings at Prince Galitzin's or Count Johann Esterházy's, private events organized by Mozart himself in the big room at the Trattnerhof, where he and Constanze were then living, and public concerts at the Burgtheater. (As he wrote to his father, "Well, I've enough to do, haven't I? This way, I doubt if I'll get out of practice.") Add to that list the concert given on 23 March, also at the Burgtheater, by his friend the clarinettist and basset-horn player Anton Stadler (at which four movements from the serenade for twelve wind instruments and double bass were played), and perhaps others too, for Mozart was as generous in contributing to fellow-artists' programmes as he was in letting them share his own. Another letter in March gave the names – more than 150 – of the subscribers to his private concerts, a list brimming with princes and princesses, barons and counts, which reads, in Landon's words, "like a cross-section of those appearing in the *Almanach de*

Gotha, including the cream of Viennese society". Mozart's concert at the Burgtheater on 1 April 1784 was thus only one of many, though the grandest: a programme which included two symphonies (probably the Linz and the Haffner), a new piano concerto (K450 or K451) and the piano-wind quintet.

It may well have been because of this surge in activity that the Mozarts left their apartment in the Trattnerhof that September and moved, a few hundred yards, to a larger one in Grosse Schulerstrasse. With new works being performed almost as soon as they were composed, and therefore orchestral material having to be prepared in double-quick time, more space was needed for the copyists who laboured under Mozart's and Constanze's eye – not to mention the pupils who came for lessons, the quantity of paperwork required by the organization of so many concerts, the resident billiard table (if Michael Kelly is to be believed), no doubt a dog or two, and the new baby, Carl Thomas, who had arrived just over a week before, on 21 September 1784.*

It was there that Leopold Mozart arrived, in the freezing winter of 1785, to add his substantial presence to the busy household. The letters he wrote to his daughter Nannerl during the ten-week stay give the most detailed picture we have of Mozart's life at the high point of his career. Leopold brought with him a pupil, the thirteen-year-old violinist Heinrich Marchand, son of the Munich theatre manager Theobald Marchand (who provided a coach from Munich and paid the expenses of the journey). They reached Vienna in time to attend the first of six Friday concerts that Mozart was promoting at the Mehlgrube, the casino in Neuer Markt, as Leopold reported:

We arrived at 846 Schulerstrasse, first floor, at 1 o'clock on Friday. That your brother has very fine quarters with all the necessary furniture you may gather from the fact that his rent is 460 gulden. The same evening we drove to his first subscription concert, where a large number of members of the aristocracy were present. Each person pays a souverain d'or or three ducats for these Lenten concerts. Your brother is giving them at the Mehlgrube, he pays only half a souverain d'or each time for the use of the hall. The concert was magnificent and the orchestra played splendidly. In addition to the

* Their first child, Raimund Leopold, born in June 1783, lived only three months.

symphonies there was a female singer from the Italian theatre who sang two arias. Then we had a new and superb concerto by Wolfgang, which the copyist was still writing out when we arrived – your brother had not even had time to play through the rondo, as he had to supervise the copying. [. . .] On Sunday evening the Italian singer Madame Laschi, who is leaving for Italy, gave a concert in the theatre at which she sang two arias. A cello concerto was performed, a tenor and a bass each sang an aria and your brother played the marvellous concerto which he wrote for Mlle Paradis for Paris [K456]. I was sitting only two boxes away from the beautiful Princess of Würtemberg; I had the great pleasure of hearing all the interplay of the instruments so clearly that tears of delight came into my eyes. When your brother left the platform the Emperor waved his hat and called out "Bravo, Mozart!" When he came out to play there was great applause. Yesterday we didn't go to the theatre – there is a concert every day. Just now I began to feel the effects of the cold during the journey. Even on Sunday evening I drank elder-flower tea before the concert and dressed up very warmly. On Monday I had tea again in bed, stayed in bed until 10 o'clock, drank tea again in the afternoon and this morning as well. Then a doctor came to my bedside, secretly arranged by your sister-in-law, took my pulse, said it was good, and proceeded to prescribe what I was taking anyway. This evening there is another concert in the theatre – your brother is again playing a concerto. I am now feeling much better; I shall drink another good portion of elder-flower tea. I shall be bringing back several of his compositions. Little Carl is the picture of him. He seems very healthy [Carl lived into his seventies] but children have teething troubles from time to time, and yesterday he wasn't so well – today he's better again. The rest of the time he is charming, extremely friendly and laughs whenever he's spoken to. I've seen him cry only once, the next moment he started laughing. Now his teeth are hurting him badly again. Yesterday, the 15th, there was another concert in the theatre, for a girl [Elisabeth Distler, of the Italian company], who sang charmingly. Your brother played his grand new concerto in D minor – magnificent. Today we are going to a concert given at the house of the Salzburg agent von Ployer. (16 February 1785)

Vienna, Monday 21 February 1785

You will have received my first letter. I thought I had completely shaken off the cold I caught on the journey; but yesterday evening I had pains in my left thigh and before I went to bed I discovered that I had indeed got rheumatism. So this morning I drank some burr root tea in bed and didn't get up till half past one, just in time for lunch, at which I had the company of your sister-in-law's youngest sister, Sophie. She's still with me now at eight in the evening, because your brother, his wife and Heinrich [Marchand] had lunch today with Herr von Trattner, an invitation I had, sadly, to refuse, and this evening your brother is performing at a grand concert at Count Zichy's, at which Herr le Brun and his wife [members of the Mannheim court orchestra] are appearing for the first time; your sister-in-law and Marchand, however, have gone to the concert given by Herr von Ployer, our agent. As usual it will probably be one o'clock before we get to bed. On Thursday the 17th we lunched with your brother's mother-in-law Frau Weber. There were just the four of us, and Frau Weber and her daughter Sophie – the eldest daughter is in Graz. I must say the meal, which was neither too lavish nor too little, was cooked to perfection. The roast was a fine plump pheasant, everything was excellently prepared. We lunched on Friday the 18th with Stephanie the Younger, the four of us and Herr le Brun, his wife, Carl Cannabich, and a priest. I have to tell you that fast days are not observed here. Only meat dishes were offered. There was a pheasant as an additional dish, with cabbage, the rest was fit for a prince, and at the end oysters were served, then delicious glacé fruits, not to mention several bottles of champagne. I need hardly add that coffee is de rigueur. From Stephanie's we drove to your brother's second concert at the Mehlgrube, at 7; it too was a splendid success. [. . .] Tuesday the 22nd. [. . .] As I write this it is already 5 in the afternoon, it's snowing heavily. I've not yet gone anywhere out of doors on foot except to go to Mass at St Stephen's, which is very near. I'm so worried about the cold wind that I certainly won't travel home till the weather gets milder. I've met various people at the concerts, among them Baron van Swieten, to whose place I've been invited, the sisters Countess Thun and Countess Wallenstein, Baron Freyberg, Baron Nagl [father of Mozart's piano pupil Theresia von Trattner], the Prussian ambassador Herr von Jacobi, Benedict Edelbach, Herr von Sonnenfels and his wife, Herr Starzer and Herr Aspelmayr, Prince Paar, Prince Auersperg, and others whose names I can't remember.

Your brother made 559 gulden at his concert [at which the concerto K467 was played for the first time], which we never expected, as the six subscription concerts at the Mehlgrube have more than 150 subscribers, each of whom pays a souverain d'or for the six [i.e. the 559 gulden were taken at the door]. Also, he has been frequently playing at other concerts in the theatre as a favour. [. . .] We never get to bed before one o'clock and I never get up before 9. We lunch at 2 or 2.30. The weather is horrible. There are concerts every day, and the whole time is given up to teaching, music, copying and so forth. I feel rather out of it. If only the concerts were over! I can't describe the rush and bustle. Since I have been here your brother's fortepiano has been taken to the theatre or some other place at least a dozen times. He has had a large fortepiano pedal made which stands under the instrument and is about two feet longer and extremely heavy. It too is taken to the Mehlgrube every Friday and has also been taken to Count Zichy's and Prince Kaunitz's. (12 March 1785)

If my son *has no debts*, I think he can now deposit 2,000 gulden in the bank: he certainly has the money, and so far as eating and drinking is concerned, the housekeeping is extremely economical. (19 March 1785)

As I write, the weather is changing from sunshine to heavy snow. A few days ago it snowed heavily and the wind whistled, and then it changed to bright sunshine, and the streets were frozen solid just as if it were New Year. I've ordered the copyist to come here and he's at work on three different sets of variations for you, which I shall pay for. Then I shall press to have the cadenzas [for Mozart's concertos] and shall buy whatever is engraved. (25 March 1785)

I must stop now as the sandpaperer or floor-waxer is dancing round the room and I don't know a single warm place in the whole apartment where I can write, and it will soon be six o'clock, when we're going to the banker's [Wetzlar] where we ate on Easter Day, to play the quartets. (2 April 1785)

Leopold, who was sixty-five, was finding the pace too hot. That he stayed on till late in April was no doubt so that he could complete his initiation into the masonic order at the lodge Zur Wohltätigkeit (Beneficence) to which his son had belonged since the previous December. Leopold Mozart was made a master on 22 April; two days later, a few hours before Leopold left Vienna, father and son attended a joint meeting of several lodges held at Zur gekrönten Hoffnung

(Crowned Hope) in honour of Ignaz von Born, the famous mineralogist, Master of the leading Viennese lodge Zur wahren Eintracht (True Concord), who had just been created Knight of the Empire by Joseph II. During the celebrations Mozart conducted *Die Maurerfreude* (*The Mason's Joy*, K471), the cantata for tenor (Adamberger), three-part male chorus and orchestra which he had completed four days before. The attendance record at the previous meeting of True Concord lists "Leopold Mozart and Wolfgang Mozart of the Beneficence" among "visiting brothers" on 16 and 22 April.

One might have expected Mozart to join the order earlier than he did; its ideals of humanity, tolerance, egalitarianism, freedom of expression, good works and social justice were those he believed in, there was nothing in the practices of Zur Wohltätigkeit, the most Catholic of the lodges, to conflict with his religious observances, prominent figures in Viennese society, writers, men of science, and noblemen with whom he was on friendly terms like van Swieten, Gemmingen, Count Thun and Prince Paar, were members, and it gave him a sense of belonging to a community of like-minded idealists. Once he had joined he took an active part in the movement. Perhaps it was what seems to have been a quite serious illness, and the intimations of death it may have prompted, that made him decide to apply. We know of the illness only from a letter of Leopold's, relaying to Nannerl the news that at the first night of Paisiello's *Il rè Teodoro in Venezia* (23 August 1784) her brother was overcome with such violent sweats that all his clothes were soaked, and afterwards while waiting in the cool night air for his servant to fetch his coat he caught a chill. Leopold goes on: "My son writes as follows: 'Four days running, at exactly the same hour, I had a dreadful attack of colic which ended each time in violent vomiting. So I have to be extremely careful. My doctor is Sigmund Barisani, who since he arrived in Vienna [from Salzburg] has been to see me almost every day. People here praise him very highly. He is very clever too and you will find that in a short time he will make his way. When you write to St Gilgen please send millions of kisses to our brother-in-law and to my sister, etc.'"

He was ill for several weeks – dangerously ill if we are to judge by two entries in Mozart's album, one a poem by Barisani which speaks of his pride and happiness at having "saved" him "for the world's delight", the other a note of Mozart's calling Barisani the "preserver of my life". On 21 September Carl Thomas was born, on the 29th they moved to the new apartment, on the 30th Mozart celebrated his recovery by completing the B flat piano concerto K456, a work of outrageous inventiveness and exceptionally rich woodwind writing, which he entered in the catalogue of his works that he had been keeping since February. Two months later "Kapellmeister Mozart"'s name was submitted to the Beneficence lodge; its Grand Master was Baron Otto von Gemmingen, whom Mozart had known since his stay in Mannheim six years before.

It was natural that a man of Leopold Mozart's enquiring mind and wide interests should, like his son, be attracted to Freemasonry. Though it would soon have passed its peak in Vienna and started on a steep decline, it was still a force in the cultural and intellectual life of the city. The list of famous men involved in the movement received fresh lustre when Josef Haydn was initiated, at True Concord, on 11 February, the day of Mozart's opening concert at the Mehlgrube and Leopold's first evening in Vienna.

Haydn was at the Grosse Schulerstrasse apartment the following evening when the string quartets K458, 464 and 465 were played, and told Leopold (as reported to Nannerl) that in his opinion – the opinion of the great Haydn himself – his son was the greatest living composer. (Haydn, who had been in Vienna since December, had heard Mozart and friends play the first three of the set, perhaps all six, a few weeks before.) Copies of the first three, composed in 1782–3, were already in the Salzburg archive – the letter of 16 February refers to "the three which we have". Leopold had thus had ample opportunity to study them and admire the richness and audacity of his son's invention and the quartets' complexity and mastery of workmanship. It may have been his intimate knowledge of these three quartets and constant marvelling at all they contained that prompted what has always struck me as his surprising response on first hearing the other three: that, though "excellent compositions", they were "somewhat easier" than the first three – a judgement which might apply to K458, the Hunt, if one were being pedantic, but hardly to the A major and the Dissonance.

On 25 April Mozart and Constanze accompanied their visitors as far as the village of Purkersdorf, seven miles west of Vienna, where they had lunch. Then they parted, and the Marchand coach continued towards Linz.

What contradictory impressions and feelings Leopold Mozart must have carried away from those tumultuous, intense ten weeks! He had with him glorious evidence of his son's greatness: "I shall bring back several of his new compositions [having had them copied]," he told Nannerl; and "I shall buy everything that has been published." He had, perhaps, seen for himself that Wolfgang had not after all married the wrong wife; he acknowledged that his daughter-in-law ran the household economically (having been highly sceptical whether the couple would be able to manage their affairs); and Constanze had taken it on herself to arrange for her doctor to see him when he was unwell. He had shared his son's public triumphs; his eyes had filled with "tears of delight" as he listened to the interplay of the instruments. But he was no longer part of it. He was not necessary. Freemasonry, for a moment, had brought them closer together; but Wolfgang was leading his own life and didn't need him.

Despite all he had witnessed, Leopold could not quite bring himself to accept that his advice, his guidance were no longer required. His letters to Nannerl continue to veer between admiration and resentful carping; the attitude of mind was too deeply ingrained to be given up.

He is up to his eyes in work on his opera *Le nozze di Figaro*. [. . .] No doubt, as is his usual charming habit, he will have kept putting it off.

The journalist [Lorenz Hübner] met me a few days ago and said: [. . .] "in all the announcements of musical works, I see nothing but Mozart. The Berlin announcements, when quoting the quartets, merely add the following: 'It is quite unnecessary to recommend these quartets to the public. Suffice it to say that they are the work of Herr Mozart.'" I had nothing to say as I know nothing, for it is more than six weeks since I had a letter from your brother.

But he had Haydn's words. Nothing could take that away. It was like a vindication of his whole life.

The immediate stimulus to the composition of Mozart's six "Haydn" quartets, begun in late 1782, was the publication of the older man's set of six, the so-called Russian quartets, Op. 33, issued a few months earlier (and dedicated to the same Grand Duke Paul for whom *The Abduction* was put on later the same year). Just as Haydn's Op. 20 had inspired Mozart's set, K168–173, ten years before, so now, "prick'd on thereto by a most emulous pride", he must strive to equal or surpass the master from whom he had learned to write quartets. But the resulting six are the fruit not only of the "long and laborious toil" cited in the dedication to Haydn printed in the score but also of the study of Bach and Handel and the immersion in counterpoint that had been going on since the spring of 1782 if not earlier. On 10 April of that year Mozart told his father that "every Sunday at noon I go to Baron van Swieten's [his apartments in the Imperial Library on the Josefplatz], where nothing is played but Handel and Bach. I am collecting Bach's fugues – not only Sebastian's but Emmanuel's and Friedmann's as well." When Mozart was younger, "Bach" had meant Johann Christian, the youngest Bach. Now it stood for an earlier art, above all the baroque art of Johann Sebastian.

Van Swieten had acquired a taste for Bach and Handel, and a collection of their works, in the 1770s when he was Viennese ambassador in Berlin. Mozart, having been trained in fugue as a boy by Padre Martini, was no stranger to the form; but the expressive power of Bach's fugues was a revelation. His response to the discovery was shared with Constanze, as he explained to his sister ten days later: "My dear Constanze is really the cause of this fugue's coming into the world [K394]. Baron van Swieten, to whom I go every Sunday, gave me the works of Handel and Bach to take home (after I had played them to him). When Constanze heard the fugues she absolutely fell in love with them. Now she will listen to nothing but fugues and particularly (in this kind of composition) the works of Handel and Bach. Since she had often heard me play fugues out of my head, she asked me if I had ever written any down and when I said no she scolded me thoroughly for not recording some of my compositions in this most artistic and beautiful of all musical forms, and didn't stop begging me to write down a fugue for her. So that is its origin."

The influence of Bach and of Handel can be heard in the C minor Mass, composed, though never completed, in fulfilment of a vow made sometime in the first half of 1782, when Constanze was ill. But the real significance of Mozart's discovery of their works was his applying its lessons to instrumental music: first and foremost to the six string quartets but then subsequently to his output as a whole. The coincidence of the study of fugue and the publication of Haydn's Op. 33 – in which, in Rosemary Hughes's words, "the fugal element is no longer an isolated feature but has passed into the growing fluency and felicity of the part-writing" – was crucial for Mozart. The flexibility and freedom from convention of Haydn's music and his concept of chamber music as (in Rosen's phrase) "dramatic action" could only make the deepest impression on a mind as receptive as Mozart's. At the same time, having fallen in love with "this most artistic and beautiful of musical forms", he had to master the technique and make it an integral part of his personal style. If the effort shows occasionally, in the six "Haydn" quartets, how richly is it rewarded! Mozart, in these mercurial works, is more than ever himself. Independent part-writing had long been an element in the vitality of his musical textures; but from now on their systematic contrapuntal enrichment marked a new stage in his development, demonstrated not only in the private world of chamber music but in his public compositions, in concerto and symphony, and not least in opera: the ensembles that are among the glories of the three Da Ponte works depend on the contrapuntal mastery which allows the characters to express their individual thoughts and feelings within a composite whole.

About the time of the publication of the "Haydn" quartets in the autumn of 1785 Mozart finally got his chance to "show what [he] could do in an Italian opera". The exact process by which Beaumarchais' *La folle journée, ou le mariage de Figaro* came to be accepted as a fit subject for an opera at the imperial court theatre is obscure. Da Ponte's *Memoirs* cast more darkness than light. The cardinal role he gives himself in persuading the Emperor to overcome his objections is contradicted by evidence that Joseph II was already interested in the project. At the end of January 1785 the Emperor sent a note to Count Pergen, president of the government of Lower Austria, notifying him that the performance of Beaumarchais' play shortly to be given, in German, at the Kärntnertortheater should not be allowed to proceed unless the text was purged of the "objectionable" material it contained. A day or two later *Die Hochzeit des Figaro*, which had been announced by the actor-manager Emanuel Schikaneder's company for 3 February, was prohibited and the performance cancelled. But the censor passed it for publication uncut and it appeared the same year, as *Der närrische Tag* (The Crazy Day), with a foreword by the translator Johann Rautenstrauch, who dedicated it to the memory of the 200 ducats he had lost by the play's non-performance. This was in fact one of two German translations printed at about the same time. Beaumarchais' play was the talk of Europe. Its scandalous and prodigiously successful Paris production, the previous spring, had taken place only after several years of argument and prohibition. Louis XVI had at first banned all public performance – though, interestingly, the Queen, Marie Antoinette, Joseph II's sister, thought it should be allowed. That her brother should have approved the opera while prohibiting the play is not really so illogical.* The effect of such a drama, played in the vernacular to a bourgeois audience at the Kärntnertor, could well have been inflammatory. On the other hand an Italian operatic version with a suitably amended text, performed at the Burgtheater, could be just the thing; its home-truths would be far from displeasing to a ruler who had been conducting a campaign against aristocratic privilege and its abuse. Whatever Beaumarchais' influence – if any – on the events that led to the French Revolution, the conflicts in his play are resolved without change to the social order.

If Da Ponte is to be believed, it was more the play's moral than its political content that Joseph II found objectionable. But he was in no need of Da Ponte's eloquence to convince him that an operatic version was worth commissioning. It had been thanks to his insistence that Paisiello's setting of Beaumarchais' *Le barbier de Séville* was given at the Burgtheater soon after its St Petersburg premiere. The work was the perfect vehicle for Francesco Benucci, star of the Italian troupe

---

* Two years later, in Prague, when an application to put on Beaumarchais' play was refused, it was stated that there was no objection to the piece being "performed as an Italian opera".

and darling of the Viennese public. Joseph's correspondence with Count Rosenberg contains glowing references to the bass – who was as excellent an actor as he was a singer – and how imperative it is to keep him in the company: good as the soprano Nancy Storace is, he says, "this man is worth more than two Storaces". Benucci's Barber, as expected, was a huge hit. But the opera itself delighted Joseph, as well as the public (it had seventy performances between 1783 and 1788), and it was natural that he should welcome the idea that his theatre should follow it with the sequel, a second Figaro opera – controversial though the play might be – and with Benucci again in the title role. Even if Count Rosenberg was against it (as Da Ponte claims and as some authorities maintain), the Emperor was in favour, and it happened.

When *Il barbiere* was first performed at the Burgtheater, Mozart, having looked through "more than a hundred librettos", was in the middle of negotiations with Varesco for what became, briefly, *The Goose of Cairo*. Once the *Goose* was dead and buried, he found *The Barber*, and the lessons it taught and the possibilities it suggested, increasingly instructive – not merely Benucci's musical and dramatic powers but still more the example Paisiello and his librettist Petrosellini had given by putting a play more or less directly into music and by structuring it, unusually, so that there were almost as many ensembles as there were solo numbers. Mozart had mixed feelings about Paisiello's music (though their personal relations seem to have been cordial – we hear of him fetching the Italian in his carriage so that he can attend a concert where he and his pupil Babette Ployer, the dedicatee of the concertos K449 and 453, are performing). But his regard for *The Barber* and his close study of it are manifest in the score of *Figaro*. This is more than a matter of diplomatically alluding to an opera which was a favourite of the public's and concerned with the same familiar characters, and with which the new work was in clear competition. At several points in *Figaro* Mozart can be seen using Paisiello as a model. The Countess's aria "Porgi, amor" – not merely written in the same key as her younger self's "Giusto ciel" in *The Barber*, E flat (the conventional key for the so-called *aria d'affetto*) but with the same time signature, 2/4, the same tempo, larghetto, and an orchestration that like Paisiello's has a prominent part for clarinets and bassoons – is not the sole example. There is nothing slavish in this. It is emulation, not imitation. And Mozart knows very well how far he can surpass his model. What he can do in an Italian opera will, necessarily, be different.

Sometime in 1784 or early 1785 the realization of how to do it must have come to him: *Figaro* was the way. The choice was Mozart's – Da Ponte's *Memoirs*, a book otherwise intent on casting glory on its author, makes no bones about it. It was a shrewd choice, given the enormous popularity of Paisiello's setting of the companion work and the huge notoriety of the play. But it may also have appealed to Mozart's deep instinct for reconciliation: *Figaro* is an opera of reconciliations – between Figaro and Marcellina, Figaro and Susanna, the Count and the Countess and, at the end, the whole little community of souls who inhabit the castle. It is the theme of the work.

Exactly when Mozart and Da Ponte began working on it we don't know. It was Da Ponte who supplied the texts of the arias which Mozart added to the Kyrie and Gloria of the C minor Mass to create the cantata *Davidde penitente*, K469, performed at the Society of Musicians' concert in the Burgtheater on 13 March 1785. A date sometime that summer for the inception of the opera is likely. No documentation survives – the two men had no need to correspond. But we can be sure, and in one or two cases can demonstrate, that Mozart was deeply involved in the shaping of the libretto. That had become his practice and he was not going to abandon it, least of all now. As Leopold Mozart observed, "it [*Figaro*] will cost him a lot of running back and forth and arguing before he gets the libretto exactly as he wants it". That Da Ponte was an intelligent man and a clever and elegant poet only made their close interaction the more desirable: there was a chance to create something exceptional.

Mozart had never had such a collaborator. The adaptation is masterly, even in the last act, where some commentators have detected a falling-off. Beaumarchais' five acts became four, the plot was pruned of minor characters and subplots, some incidents were modified, others, in obedience to the demands of music-drama, were moved to a different point; but the essence of the action remained intact. In consultation with the composer Da Ponte chose which scenes to turn into duets and trios, where to place the arias which would articulate emotions only hinted at, if at all, in the play, what should become recitative, and how to fashion the larger ensembles, in particular the complex finales of Act 2 and Act 4, out of equivalent passages in Beaumarchais that lent themselves to extended musical treatment. At the same time they worked out the verse forms and metres for the various musical numbers.

People have never stopped accusing Da Ponte of emasculating the play by drawing its political teeth. But the sole major change in that respect was suppressing Figaro's class tirade in the last act – "Monsieur le Comte, what have you done to earn your exalted position? Put yourself to the trouble of being born, nothing more," etc., a speech that also attacks magistrates and censors – as a result of which, only the outburst against the deceitfulness of women was left. Da Ponte could hardly have done otherwise if the libretto was to pass this particular censor. Even so, class conflict remains at the centre of the work; as Rosen says, "the call for the renunciation of unjust aristocratic privilege is sufficiently underlined as it stands". And, as it happens, the music puts the social criticism back. By giving a valet (and shortly afterwards a chambermaid) an accompanied recitative – the prerogative of high-born characters – and an aria scored for that well-born instrument the B flat clarinet, Mozart was sending a clear political message: the servant is as good as his master. Right at the beginning, in Figaro's "Se vuol ballare" (an aria derived from a single line in a different part of the play – "et puis, dansez, Monseigneur"), the subversive second-beat accents cutting across the rhythm of the minuet – an upper-class dance – are like a kick up the aristocratic backside. As the opera proceeds, the conventional musical distinction between the two is progressively eroded. The Countess, in the Act 3 Letter Duet, adopts her maid's musical idiom.

Other initiatives too are clearly Mozart's. The structure of the opera was necessarily dictated by the composer. If he wanted to end the acts with the full orchestra including trumpets, he was limited to the keys of D, C and E flat (trumpets could also play in B flat but had fewer notes available). Having chosen D as the key of the opera, he could divide the other three finales only between C and E flat. But it was also, surely, Mozart's decision to end Act 1 with a martial air for

Figaro, the C major "Non più andrai" – Beaumarchais' first act ended inconsequentially – as it was his to introduce the Countess for the first time at the beginning of Act 2, with a soliloquy in E flat, balancing the E flat of the act's conclusion; in *La folle journée* the Countess had already made her appearance in Act 1. The evidence of the autograph score suggests that Mozart, again, decided to make a through-composed scene of the wedding festivities in Act 3 – superimposing words originally intended for simple recitative on orchestral music (the march and the fandango) – and also to add the little song for Barbarina about the missing pin at the beginning of Act 4, where only a recitative had been planned.*

It is in the last act that the opera diverges most from the play – not so much in the actual events as in their emphasis, above all the emphasis on the role of the Countess in resolving the conflicts of the crazy day. The deepening of her character is the one major change made by Da Ponte and Mozart. Perhaps it was, in the first place, in deference to the Emperor's moral scruples that they downplayed the dangerous *tendresse* Beaumarchais' Countess feels for Cherubino (and that will lead, in the next play, *La mère coupable*, to her bearing his child). If so, it became part of a greater transformation. Mozart's Countess is a nobler, less light-hearted, less equivocal character. I say Mozart's because the music is what makes this transformation real and because her progression from passive sufferer to active agent of reconciliation aligns her with other Mozart heroines, Constanze, Pamina and Ilia. There is no equivalent in the play to either of the Countess's arias: the first listless, despairing, self-regarding, the second beginning in deep nostalgia, then, after a pause which is the turning-point of the drama, rousing itself to heroic exertion. A moment before, she had been outraged at being forced by her humiliating situation as betrayed wife to intrigue with a servant. Now she is ready for any-thing; she has taken charge of her destiny. The ecstatic reaffirmation with which the second aria ends resolves, musically and dramatically, the questions left hanging in the first. From now on she is the moral focus of the action. A moment later, in the exquisitely playful Letter

---

* In the play the crucial conversation between Barbarina and Figaro comes at the end of the penultimate act.

Duet, in full control of her feelings and even beginning to enjoy herself, she dictates to Susanna the note which will entrap the Count "beneath the pine-trees". And in the following scene her glacial response to the discovery that the Count has been groping the twelve-year-old Barbarina cements her determination. The last act is hers as much as it is Susanna's. The marriage of Figaro, so long in doubt, is now assured. It is her marriage that has to be rescued.

There is other unfinished business, of course. Figaro, who has been so busy lecturing others – the Count in "Se vuol ballare", Cherubino in "Non più andrai", Antonio in the Act 2 finale – has an important lesson of his own to learn. But Act 4, with all its dark cross-currents, its mistaken identities and alarms and excursions, belongs to the Countess and her ally Susanna; it leads inevitably to the transcendent moment of healing – so different from the worldly tone of the play's denouement – when she forgives the kneeling Count.

Commentators who object that the fourth act of *Figaro* fails to sustain the dramatic momentum of the first three, or even that it prolongs a work that is really over by then (like those who argue that Verdi's *Falstaff*, properly considered, comes to an end with the knight's ducking in the Thames, and the rest is mere plot), completely miss the point. The opera absolutely requires that the drama leave the castle and move out of doors, into the night – the final stage of the crazy day – and into a new dimension of poetic enchantment and human awareness, so that reconciliation may be achieved. Mozart prepares for the nocturnal atmosphere of Act 4 by means, first, of the anxious, slightly sinister fandango in Act 3 (its A minor tonality linking it with the beginning of the act) and then of Barbarina's F minor cavatina, a dusky, plaintive sound unheard in the opera till then.*

The reconciliation is the work of the Countess; but in an even deeper sense the protagonist of the drama is Susanna. To quote Nicolas Hytner:

The house, the paradigm for a whole society, needs to dissolve before the conflicts can be resolved. And so *Figaro* ends with its own Forest of Arden,

---

* Schubert used it twenty years later as the starting-point of his four-hand piano Fantasy in the same key.

under the pines in the garden. There at least the tensions of the first three acts can be put aside. There with the help of a liberal dose of disguise people can be themselves, and there Susanna, the one person who never worries about her role, her job, her position, can make time stand still. For everyone but Susanna, the opera is a voyage of self-discovery. Susanna seems to know herself from the first bar of the opera; and at the end of it, joined by Marcellina who has discovered motherhood and the Countess who has rediscovered herself as a wife, she stands as a glorious reproach to the whole world of men.

The women, as so often in Mozart, are so much wiser and shrewder and more civilized than the men, and Susanna, who takes part in every ensemble, is of all of them the pearl. Mozart is at pains to establish her personality – warm-hearted but sharp-eyed, resourceful, alert, a woman of strong feelings but fully in command of them, and cleverer than Figaro, for all his invincible belief in his cleverness – from the beginning of the opera. Susanna was the only principal character not already familiar to the Viennese public from *The Barber*, in which she doesn't appear. She springs immediately and fully to life in scene 1, in the duet where Figaro is absorbed in measuring the room to see if it will accommodate the large bed that is the Count's somewhat equivocal wedding present. She is trying on her hat and wanting him to admire her in it, which he duly does. He has met his match. The Count will dance to Figaro's tune but *he* will sing to hers.

The realistic contemporary subject and closed community of individuals was the perfect focus for Mozart's gifts at this stage of his career. After four years of studying the human comedy in Vienna's teeming, complex society he had exactly the scope his fully matured comic powers demanded. Like the "three or four families in a country village" which for Jane Austen was "the very thing to work on", the libretto of *Figaro* was all he needed. It was heaven-sent. On it he could concentrate his sympathetic but non-illusioned understanding of women and men and their loves, jealousies, ambitions, furies, longings and sexual desires, seen both as representatives of their rank and status and as distinct human beings, but interacting in the intricate dance of existence. (The rhythms of the dance run through the score.) This is the respect in which *Figaro* is a truly revolutionary work, all questions of politics and society aside. For the first time music has found the means of embodying the interplay of living people, the feelings and passions and thoughts of rounded human beings, servants and masters, as they arise in response to life, each speaking in their own characteristic idiom, all inhabiting an actual world, enchanted yet recognizable, companionable but full of danger.

The music is alive with this sense of discovery. Like Jane Austen in *Pride and Prejudice*, Mozart seems consciously to revel in his new mastery of the comic style. Right from the beginning, in the overture, he celebrates it with dazzling vivacity. Unlike the overtures to *Don Giovanni*, *Così fan tutte*, *The Magic Flute*, *The Abduction* or *Idomeneo*, it contains no obvious foreshadowing of the musical material of the opera; but in its mixture of energy, brilliance, mystery, and directness of musical style, it is the ideal introduction to the drama of the *folle journée* in the life of the Castle of Aguas Frescas. It is symbolic of the difference between Mozart and his rivals that the overture should begin with a 7-bar phrase instead of the conventional 4 or 8. Mozart is not like the others. Originally, as the autograph shows, he planned to interrupt the music's swift current with a slower middle section (as in the overture to *The Abduction*), and then resume the Presto. Happily, he thought better of it.

From then on there is no trace of hesitation. The confidence is total; the flexibility and resourcefulness of the musical language are seemingly infinite. The tunes come straight to meet us. At the same time Mozart's inventiveness is such that the most undistinguished material yields treasures. Nothing is too trivial to be put to fruitful use. The way in which seemingly commonplace figures, weaving through a movement, take on ever-changing colours and moods in response to the text (fruit of the mastery of musical language achieved in the concertos and the quartets) is one of the fascinations of the work: to cite only two examples, the nine-note staccato string figure which runs through the scene where the Count challenges Figaro to identify and explain the papers Antonio picked up in the garden, and, a little earlier in the Act 2 finale, the arpeggio phrase which dominates the exchange between the Count, the Countess and Susanna, after the Count, having failed to find Cherubino in the dressing-room, begs Rosina to forgive him.

In the Act 4 finale the climactic scene between Susanna, disguised as the Countess, and Figaro – following the magnificent Larghetto where the jealous valet compares himself to Vulcan about to enmesh Mars and Venus in his net – begins in a way you would think could hardly be less promising; but what a movement this Allegro molto is, what riches flow from its banal downward, dominant-tonic four-note phrases, how naturally it responds, at high speed, to the twists and turns of the action, external and internal, constantly throwing up new ideas, how gloriously it flowers into extravagant melody as Figaro pretends to be wooing the Countess – and then how beautifully its tensions relax into the lilting andante, music whose serenity and sense of complication resolved depict to the life the lovers reunited in new understanding. Yet the same andante, a moment later, can without effort take on a different tone as the Count comes into view, still searching for Susanna. This finale is less often praised than the more celebrated finale of Act 2. But if its eight linked movements do not exhibit the same cumulative growth as the other finale's do (from two voices to seven), it is as finely balanced and as apt to the changing dramatic situation, and its musical invention is if anything even richer.

By the time *Figaro* was written, opera buffa conventions were allowing a far greater variety of formal procedures than before; but Mozart, characteristically, went further. Often, though the harmonic framework of tonic-dominant-tonic is preserved, strict form is replaced by continuous development. When, in the Countess's "Porgi, amor", the music returns to E flat, what happens is not a resumption of the opening melody (though the words are the same) but new music, complete with poignantly dissonant G flat on first bassoon, as the Countess sinks into deeper melancholy. Susanna's F major invocation to love, "Deh vieni, non tardar", passes through the dominant, C major; but, though the return of the tonic key is marked by the first violins changing their plucked notes to caressing bowed phrases – the moment when Susanna "moves from the irony of 'teaching Figaro a lesson' to genuine desire" (Jessie Waldoff and James Webster) – there is no reprise, only a single ecstatic unfolding of melody; all that is repeated are the woodwind's two bars which completed the short introduction to the aria and which return at the end. Similarly, the frantic whispered duet in G major for Susanna and Cherubino, before the page jumps out of the window of the Countess's room, goes from tonic to dominant and back to tonic (after flashing through E minor and C major), but is structured as one continuous, distracted development of the same endlessly repeated four-note motif.

Some numbers are in a miniature sonata form; however, we are never made to feel that the repetitions inherent in the form are a drag, an implausibility. Thanks to the reprise of the Countess's "Dove sono" after the middle section – a return that portrays her as still willingly imprisoned in the past – her sudden resolve to take action, and the consequent breaking off of the music in mid-phrase before the change to a quicker tempo, becomes doubly dramatic.

If the situation is static, as in the C major trio in Act 2, where the Count stands at the locked door of the dressing-room and orders Susanna to come out while, unseen, she comments breathlessly from the doorway to her room, the return of the imperious opening phrases in the tonic key is appropriate. But Mozart varies them in response to the new words. In particular, at the Count's "Consorte mia, giudizio!" ("Be careful, my lady!"), the music moves into a smoothly menacing A flat major with an effect that screws the emotional tension and physical excitement of this vivid, headlong movement still higher. The trio is at once a completely satisfying formal entity and a riveting articulation of the drama, a perfectly shaped movement that makes our pulse beat faster as we listen to it.

Sometimes Mozart composes what Erik Smith calls a "vestigial recapitulation", as in the sextet, the blissful ensemble which follows the revelation that Figaro is the long-lost illegitimate son of Bartolo and Marcellina. The point where the reprise should come is also the point where Marcellina needs a new tune, to explain to the bewildered Susanna that she is Figaro's mother; so she has one, and the opening theme returns only as an accompaniment to it in the woodwind, thus meeting the demands of both drama and formal symmetry at the same time. According to Michael Kelly, who played Basilio and Curzio in the first production, the sextet was Mozart's favourite number (and was loudly bravoed by the Emperor at the premiere). The music, which in a thoroughly Mozartian way contrives to laugh both with and at the dramatic situation, embraces within one hilariously harmonious whole the reactions of the unsuspecting parents (Marcellina's, delight,

Bartolo's, embarrassed, furtive pleasure), the stupefaction and exasperation of the Count and the stuttering Curzio, the relief and high spirits of Figaro, who had come within an ace of being married off to his mother, and the sequence of sharply contrasting emotions in Susanna, from cheeky satisfaction through amazement and outrage to complete contentment.

Structure and musical gesture arise each time as though naturally to fit situation and character. Dr Bartolo's revenge aria, "La vendetta", begins grandiloquently, but the orchestra is soon revealing him as the overblown windbag he is; as his rage masters him the vocal line degenerates into the patter that is conventionally associated with buffo characters, making unintentionally ironic his pompous "All Seville knows Dr Bartolo". For Cherubino's canzonetta "Voi che sapete", his hymn to his amorous feelings, Mozart seems to have taken as model the Count's serenade in the first scene of Paisiello's *Barber* (whose accompaniment, like the canzonetta, includes plucked strings). But the model is left far behind. The musical setting is not strophic – that is, arranged in equal, repeated stanzas, as the form of the verse might suggest it would be – but through-composed; the opening phrases return only at the end. In between, on reaching the dominant (F major), the music flits butterfly-like – the "farfallone amoroso" of Figaro's "Non più andrai" – through C, D minor, A flat, G minor, E flat, and eventually back to B flat. The unprecedented range and rapidity of modulation is an exact musical mirror of the page's confusion, perpetually in love but at a loss where to fix his affections.

When a movement is in clear sonata form, like the Act 1 trio where the Count, having himself previously been hiding behind the armchair, discovers Cherubino hiding in it, the formal disciplines seem only to inspire Mozart to still greater freedom. Here a structure of strict musical logic, moving at speed (allegro assai), articulates a quite complicated series of events while at the same time giving graphic expression to the different feelings of the three participants: the Count, by turns angry, suspicious, commanding, lecherous, Susanna's agitation both feigned and genuine, and the leering Basilio in an ecstasy of malicious delight.

Figaro is a fast-moving score – as it had to be, to cover the complex events of such a long play, even expertly trimmed by Da Ponte. The slow or slowish numbers – "Porgi, amor", "Dove sono" (first part), "Deh vieni", one or two sections in the finales, none of them long – provide just the right amount of stillness or repose in all the bustle. But even in the quickest movements Mozart always seems to have time to do what he wants.

The wealth of dramatic incident and emotion, including humour, is phenomenal. *Figaro* is a wonderfully funny opera, not simply because of the situations themselves but because of the way the music takes possession of them. Think of the passage in the trio just mentioned where the Count, describing how he discovered Cherubino hiding under the tablecloth at Barbarina's, lifts the dress from the armchair and discovers him again. The irony of having the Count use the unctuous descending phrase to which Basilio sang the words "My suspicions about the page were mere speculation" enhances the comedy. At the same time the tension that accumulates in the soft accompaniment, with the violas' E flat sustained over two and a half bars while the other strings continue their pattern of descending phrases, makes the moment of revelation all the more effective. Or think of the sly, butter-wouldn't-melt-in-its-mouth innocence of the music as Susanna appears in the doorway of the dressing-room and asks the astonished Count: "My lord, why so amazed?" – music by which the drama of the coup de théâtre is marvellously enhanced.* Or the comedy of that other encounter between Susanna and the Count at the beginning of Act 3, where she pretends to agree to meet him in the garden and, as the temperature and the pace increase, her answers to his panting questions get mixed up – music that is funny, erotic and fraught with peril at one and the same time. (The repeated "sì" and "no", like Figaro's "sì" in "Se vuol ballare", are Mozart's addition, not provided for in Da Ponte's text.) Finally, and not least, in the sextet, the absurdity of "his mother", "his father", tossed from voice to voice, accompanied by chortling violin trills on the offbeat and then by syncopated woodwind, followed by Figaro's expansive "and this is my mother/father" – once again the composer's development of an idea not explicit in the verse.

---

* The phrase is derived from an opera of Grétry's, *L'amant jaloux*, that was performed in Vienna in the early 1780s.

A single note can transform the atmosphere, like the dissonant D flat and G flat on oboe and bassoons in the opening scene of the opera, when Susanna's warnings about the Count's intentions shake Figaro out of his complacent good humour. The mood can darken in a moment, or deepen, as it does memorably in the scene in the Act 2 finale where the Count confronts Figaro with the anonymous letter, and the disarming phrase to which Figaro denies the charge ("Then my face is lying, not I") becomes, sublimely, an intense sotto voce prayer to forgive and forget, solemnized by a resounding C, like a bell, on horns and double basses.

Instrumental colour in *Figaro* is as varied, and expressive and subtle, as an enlightened music-lover who had heard *Idomeneo* or *The Abduction* would have expected – from Mozart but from no one else. The orchestra is a leading player in the drama. Flutes, oboes, horns, bassoons and strings – the basic group – are used in eleven of the forty-five movements or sections, and the full complement, including clarinets, trumpets and drums, in four. The remaining thirty involve no fewer than fourteen permutations. Among them we may note that the sensuous sound of clarinets, horns and bassoons (without oboes or flutes) is reserved for three numbers: Cherubino's "Non so più", "Porgi, amor", and Figaro's "Aprite un po' quegl' occhi", in all of which the characters express in different ways – puzzled, anguished or bitterly angry – the sense of being deprived of the love for which they long or on which they had counted.

Love is at the centre of the opera, in every imaginable guise and degree: the Count lustful and avid for sexual adventure, Cherubino in love with love, the Countess nostalgically reliving her lost romance, Figaro consumed with jealousy, Susanna rapturously anticipating physical fulfilment. Yet, above and beneath and around and within the passions unleashed in the work, we feel Mozart's unique quality of divine play. With all the reality of the conflicts and tensions absorbing the inhabitants of Count Almaviva's household, and the perils lurking in every corner of the castle, that quality infuses everything in the opera. Perhaps it is this that gives the work its special claim on our affections. *Don Giovanni* may be more haunting, *Così fan tutte* may probe human beings' frailties even more deeply, *The Magic Flute* may be more beautiful: no opera, by Mozart or anyone else, quite equals *Figaro*'s sense of fitness, of being in total harmony with itself, and – with all its detailed, vigilant craftsmanship – of complete naturalness. It is as if these tunes, these motifs and phrases and no others were the only possible ones and they had sprung from the text by spontaneous generation.

Perhaps, too, it is this perfection that makes some people feel, perversely, that they must search out weaknesses in it: it is more than their scholarly reputations are worth to be caught praising unreservedly. Thus, because the second half of the Susanna–Marcellina duet in Act 1 is a more or less exact repeat of the first, the form of the piece has to be compared unfavourably with the freedom shown elsewhere in the opera – when we should be grateful for the opportunity Mozart has given us to enjoy their deliciously bitchy exchange twice over.

Even more strangely, fault has been found with the vivacious aria in G major sung by Susanna as she dresses the kneeling Cherubino in women's clothes and coaches him in his role – an aria in which, we are told, Mozart "relies upon an obviously Italianate musical gesture" because he is "less inspired than usual", and which doesn't "project her emotions, unlike her other music". But it does: the attraction she feels for Cherubino as she touches and clothes him is manifest; she scolds him for fidgeting and staring at the Countess but she is almost ready to fall in love with him. The long, ravishing melody variously played by oboe, bassoon and flute which arches over the busy strings, the skittish first violin part, Susanna's brief, snatched phrases, precisely apt for someone giving hurried instructions while their hands are occupied – all this brings the scene unmistakably before our eyes. No music in *Figaro*, Italianate or not, is more graphic.

As for the arias for Marcellina and Basilio in Act 4, it is commonly objected that we do not need to know more about these two characters so late in the drama – in Julian Rushton's words, "major statements by minor characters are out of place when everything is tending to a conclusion"; the arias are there only because the original singers had to be satisfied, and they hold up the denouement of an opera that is already dangerously long. I suppose it is arguable that Basilio's is one aria too many, with Figaro's and Susanna's great, and absolutely essential, scenes to come; but it could also be argued that Mozart's profoundly non-exclusive humanity demands that Basilio's character too be explored and any redeeming features in it identified. In any case, the question of length has more to do with audience stamina than with the dramaturgical correctness in whose name Act 4 is declared unduly protracted. That some people tire and their concentration flags before the end of *Figaro* is not by definition the fault of the opera. There is no law decreeing that four consecutive arias, or even three, are not permitted in a final act.

If Basilio's aria is expendable, Marcellina's is not. From having been Figaro's and Susanna's sworn adversary she has become their friend and ally – a vital shift of allegiance that needs the emphasis Mozart gives it. The sentiments the aria expresses – women "wrongfully oppressed by men", "even wild beasts treat the female of the species well" – prepare for a finale in which women play the predominant role. That is the whole thrust of the denouement: it is the women who will set things right and restore amends. The end of *Le mariage de Figaro* is worldly-wise, light-hearted, witty, ironic, in keeping with the tone of the play. But such a conclusion was out of the question for Mozart. He had gone too far for that. The final allegro assai may be as fizzing as the overture which inaugurated his *folle journée*, but the true climax is the andante that precedes it, as the Count twice begs forgiveness (the second phrase intensifying the first), the Countess grants it in six bars of noble magnanimity, completing the melody he began, and the whole company takes it up in words that are banal – "Ah tutti contenti saremo così" ("Then let us all be happy") – but in music that is on the heights.

Does this denouement ring true? Some have claimed that it does not. Without Mozart's music no doubt it wouldn't. But Mozart has Shakespeare's balanced, controlled complexity. *Figaro* is both reality and ideal – antitheses too deeply interfused to be separated. True, beneath this most felicitous of scores runs the persistent Mozartian undercurrent of sadness. We sense it at the outset. As the curtain rises and the orchestra evokes with lightest hand the domesticity of the scene and the mutual affection of Figaro and Susanna, something in the sweetness and simplicity of the music takes us unawares and tugs at the heart. Maybe we feel it too at the end of the drama, because of the impermanence of all happy endings, this one not excluded. All the same I do not hear or see the final resolution as hollow. Figaro has his beloved Susanna at last; Bartolo and Marcellina have got each other – the last thing they expected, but discovering their son could conceivably be the making of both their existences; Cherubino's life lies before him, in all its excitements and disillusionments; and the Countess has given an object-lesson in human charity, gentleness and large-heartedness. Only if one insists on being literal is the Count's reformation unlikely to outlast the night by many hours. But he has, publicly, asked his wife's forgiveness, an astonishing concession by so proud and touchy an aristocrat and male chauvinist. Besides, how can we be literal after experiencing this miraculous opera? And, even on the most hard-headed reckoning, the Countess, in recapturing the liveliness of Rosina and playing and beating her husband at his own game, may well have rekindled her attractiveness. As for the Count, he is no longer the man portrayed a few hours before, in the ranting and raving of his superb aria. Taught, like Figaro, by Susanna and the Countess, he has had the limitations of masculine dominance forcibly demonstrated; he has acquired greater self-awareness and, in Tim Carter's words, has learnt "the perils of male power-play, and come to a higher understanding of the strength and value of a woman's love". This is the opera's clear message.

Mozart's reconciliations are real. They invoke the good in human nature. His vision embraces the pain and cruelty as well as the compassion – the darkness and the light; but it is the light that prevails.

The score seems to have been composed mainly in the late summer and autumn of 1785, in the gap recorded in Mozart's thematic catalogue between 27 July (the G minor piano quartet) and 5 November (the quartet written for Bianchi's *La villanella rapita*). Around the end of October Count Rosenberg, as reported by Leopold Mozart, was "prodding him" to complete it, which suggests that the premiere may well have been intended to take place during the 1786 Carnival if not at the beginning of the year. For whatever reason, a new opera by Martín, *Il burbero di buon cuore*, with a libretto by Da Ponte, was put on instead.

The postponement may have been due partly to the absence abroad of Luisa Laschi, who was to play the Countess; but delaying tactics by Mozart's Italian rivals, Salieri included, cannot be ruled out. Salieri's name figures or is implied in several such references. Leopold Mozart and the Duscheks have already been cited. Michael Kelly described him as "a clever, shrewd man, possessed of what Bacon called crooked wisdom". The Salzburg gossip-sheet *Pfeffer und Salz* of 5 April, a few weeks before the premiere, alluded to "plots" by "Ro+g's [i.e. Rosenberg's] favourites" and wondered whether they would affect Mozart's opera, adding ironically, "Long live Salieri and Casti [Salieri's librettist]!" And the *Wiener Realzeitung* of 11 July, in its review of *Figaro*, stigmatizing those journalists who claimed that the opera "had not pleased at all" (a "blatant lie"), stated that "now, after several performances, one would have to *belong to the cabal* [italics added] or be devoid of taste to maintain that Herr Mozart's music is anything but a masterpiece of art".

Whatever the truth, Mozart made good use of the time. He was busy in February and March not only with the completion of two of his greatest concertos, the A major K488 and the C minor K491, and with the private production of the revised *Idomeneo* at the Auersperg Palace, but also with composing and directing *Der Schauspieldirektor*. This one-act comedy with music, written by Stephanie, was part of an entertainment put on by the Emperor at Schönbrunn on the afternoon and evening of 7 February for his sister, Princess Marie-Christiane and her husband Duke Albert of Sachsen-Teschen, governor-general of the Austrian Netherlands, who were in Vienna on a visit. After the eighty-two distinguished guests had banqueted at an enormous table in the long hall of the Orangery (regaled, as they ate, by Joseph's wind band playing music from Salieri's *La grotta di Trofonio*), they watched the singspiel, given on a specially built stage at one end of the hall, then moved to the other end for Salieri's one-act opera buffa *Prima la musica e poi le parole*, which, like *Der Schauspieldirektor*, had been composed for the occasion.

The two new pieces were intended to show off the actors and singers of the court theatre. Mozart was writing for three of the artists he knew best – Adamberger, Cavalieri, and Aloisia Lange. He made the most of his opportunities. The play – about the vanity of singers and an impresario whose attempt to form a touring company is hampered by the rivalry of the two leading ladies, each out to upstage the other and secure the bigger fee – is somewhat crude and pedestrian; but Mozart's five numbers momentarily raise it to a higher plane. They consist of an incisive, powerfully argued overture; an aria each for the battling prima donnas, the one (for Madame Herz) a parody of the pathetic style, the other (for Mademoiselle Silberklang) an exuberant rondo, both exploiting the singers' strong top registers; a brilliantly comic trio in which the ladies trump each other with higher and higher notes while protesting their selfless devotion to art, before the tenor (Herr Vogelsang) imposes a truce; and a cheerful concluding quartet in which the three are joined by Herr Buff, who has absolutely no doubt that he has no rival.

Figaro, directed by Mozart from the fortepiano, eventually opened on the symbolic date of 1 May – the first time the notorious drama had been given in any form in the Habsburg dominions.

It would not be so surprising if the work faced opposition, before and after the premiere, from people who were jealous of the composer and felt threatened by him. But Niemetschek's contention that the cast tried to sabotage the first night is hard to credit, when it included friends such as Nancy Storace (Susanna) and Michael Kelly. It is possible that some of the singers were hostile to begin with. If so, the rehearsal of "Non più andrai" described in Kelly's famous account may have been the moment when they came round to it, which was why he recalled the incident so vividly: it was an instant of shared electricity, when the genius of Mozart's music fully dawned on them for the first time, like the moment in the film *Shakespeare in Love* when the company stand spellbound at the rehearsal of the balcony scene in *Romeo and Juliet*.

Mozart was on stage with his crimson pelisse and gold-laced cocked hat, giving the time of the music to the orchestra. Figaro's song, "Non più andrai, farfallone amoroso" Benucci gave with the greatest animation and power of voice. I was standing close to Mozart, who, *sotto voce*, was repeating "Bravo! Bravo! Benucci"; and when Benucci came to the fine passage "Cherubino, alla vittoria, alla gloria militar", which he gave out with stentorian lungs, the effect was electricity itself; for the whole of the performers on the stage and those in the orchestra, as if actuated by one feeling of delight, vociferated

"Bravo! Bravo! Maestro, Viva, viva, grande Mozart." Those in the orchestra I thought would never have ceased applauding, by beating the bows of their violins against the music desks. The little man acknowledged, by repeated obeisances, the distinguished mark of enthusiastic applause bestowed on him.

Whatever their first response to the music, the singers seem to have tried their best. As for the public, the *Wiener Realzeitung* says that its reaction on the first night was mixed – the performance "was none of the best, owing to the difficulty of the composition" – but that by the third performance (8 May) there was such a demand for encores that next day the Emperor had to order Count Rosenberg to post a notice at the Burgtheater stating that "no piece for more than a single voice will be repeated", in order to "prevent the excessive duration of operas", and this was done. Five numbers had been encored at the second performance and at the third seven: the little duet for Susanna and Cherubino had to be given three times. Joseph II evidently liked *Figaro* enough to order a special performance at the Laxenburg Palace in June. The success of the opera is also attested by the prompt announcement of full scores and piano reductions by two different music-copying firms. There was a further performance (the fourth) on 24 May, followed by five more between July and December. But the one given on 18 December was the last. Whether because Nancy Storace was shortly leaving for England, with a party which included Kelly (Don Basilio and Don Curzio) and Mozart's young English pupil Thomas Attwood, or because of the runaway success of Martín's *Una cosa rara*, which had opened on 17 November, or for both reasons, *Figaro* disappeared, not to be heard in Vienna again till it was revived in 1789.

Mozart would have his revenge on *Una cosa rara* a year later, in the supper scene of *Don Giovanni*, where the stage band plays a tune from it, followed by one from Sarti's *Fra i due litiganti* (another Viennese favourite), and then puts them both in the shade by playing "Non più andrai", which the Praguers loved. Prague's enthusiasm would compensate him for any Viennese inadequacy. *Figaro*, performed at the Estates Theatre in early December, took the city by storm. Soon afterwards the composer was invited to come and hear it, with consequences that were to be momentous for him and for the future of opera.

5

Prague and "the opera of all operas"

Don Giovanni

On the morning of Monday 8 January 1787 Mozart and Constanze set out on the three-day journey to Prague. With them in the coach were Anton Stadler, the violinists Franz Hofer (who a year later would marry Constanze's sister Josepha) and Kaspar Ramlo, the thirteen-year-old prodigy Maria Anna Crux and her aunt Madame Quallenberg, the Mozarts' servant Joseph, and their dog Gauckerl. They made a merry party, playing funny word games and inventing mad names for each other: Constanze Schabla Pumfa, Wolfgang Punkitititi, Stadler Natschibinitschibi, equally fantastic pseudonyms for the others, and the dog Schamanuzsky.

The reception Prague gave Mozart confirmed his high spirits. It was his first visit to the city of which he would later say "my Praguers understand me", but he felt instantly at home. The music at Count Johann Thun's palace in the Mala Strana (to which the Count insisted they move, after a night at the Three Lions) was "real entertainment", he told his friend Gottfried von Jaquin, and when an "excellent pianoforte" was placed in Mozart's room the whole evening was given up to an improvised concert, including one of the piano quartets (probably the E flat K493). The same day the *Prager Oberpostamtszeitung* splashed the news of the composer's advent across its front page:

Last night [sic] our great and beloved composer Herr Mozard arrived here from Vienna. We do not doubt that in honour of this man Herr Bondini will have *The Marriage of Figaro* performed, that well-loved product of his musical powers. Our famous orchestra will then not fail to give new proofs of its art, and the inhabitants of Prague will surely assemble in large numbers, notwithstanding that they have already heard the piece frequently. We would dearly like to be able to admire Herr Mozard's playing for ourselves.

On his first evening in Prague he had proof of the opera's popularity when Count Canal, a fellow-mason and, like Count Thun, a music-loving aristocrat with his own private orchestra, drove him to the Seminary Hall for one of the fashionable balls given by Baron Breitfeld, where (Mozart reported to Jaquin), "the cream of the beauties of Prague is wont to gather".

I neither danced nor flirted with any of them, the former because I was too tired, the latter owing to my natural bashfulness. But I watched with the greatest pleasure while all those people flew about in sheer delight to the music of my *Figaro*, arranged as contredanses and German dances. Here they talk of nothing but *Figaro*. Nothing is played, sung or whistled but *Figaro*. No opera is drawing the crowds like *Figaro*. Nothing, nothing but *Figaro*. Certainly a very great honour for me!

Figaro in fact had been the salvation of Pasquale Bondini and his company, which had been on the point of abandoning Prague when the success of the work restored their fortunes. At a performance on 4 January, given for the benefit of Ponziani (Figaro), the theatre was "so crowded that people could hardly move". Mozart was present when the opera was revived on the 17th. Two days later the general wish to hear him play was granted when he put on a concert at the theatre, conducting the D major symphony, No. 38 (composed in Vienna in December but universally known as the Prague), and giving three piano improvisations, the third on Figaro's "Non più andrai". On the 20th he conducted the opera.

Niemetschek was at the concert. "The theatre" (he recalled some years later) "had never been so full as on this occasion; never had there been such unanimous enthusiasm as that awakened by his heavenly playing. We did not know which to admire most, the extraordinary compositions or his extraordinary playing; together they made such an overwhelming impression on us that we felt we had been bewitched. When Mozart had finished the concert he continued improvising for half an hour." The symphonies he conducted were "masterpieces", particularly the one in D major, "which is still a favourite in Prague, although it must by now have been heard a hundred times". Mozart "likewise counted this day as one of the happiest of his life".

Just before they left, Mozart composed six Teutsche or German dances (K509) for the ball of the Society of Nobles, scored for an orchestra without violas but with an exceptionally large woodwind ensemble including piccolo as well as flutes, and clarinets as well as oboes, plus bassoons, horns, trumpets (and drums) – a wind group bigger even than that of the C minor piano concerto of March 1786, the most richly orchestrated of all Mozart's symphonic scores. That he thought highly of Prague's wind players would be demonstrated in dramatic fashion nine months later.

Mozart left Prague with 1,000 gulden in his pocket (according to Nancy Storace, the Vienna Susanna) and, less ephemerally, with a commission from Bondini and his fellow-director Domenico Guardasoni to compose a new comic opera for the following season.

We shall probably never know for sure how the subject of *Don Giovanni* came to be chosen. Da Ponte's *Memoirs* claim that it was his idea; but in his earlier *Extract* it is Guardasoni who suggests it, offering Mozart the libretto of *Don Giovanni Tenorio* by Giovanni Bertati which had just been premiered in Venice, with music by the Venetian composer Giuseppe Gazzaniga. Librettos travelled fast, as well as being considered fair game for resetting by other composers – Stephanie handed Bretzner's *Belmont und Constanze* to Mozart two months after that opera's premiere. Even so, Guardasoni could hardly have had a copy to give Mozart before he left Prague, only three days after the first performance, 250 miles away.

In the *Memoirs* Da Ponte suppressed all mention of Bertati. But *Don Giovanni*'s debt to Bertati's text is irrefutable. The version in the *Extract* sounds altogether more plausible. The Prague directors were eager for another opera, another *Figaro* from the team that had rescued them. Why not Don Juan, a story traditionally treated as a comedy and, though frowned on by the cognoscenti, of proven popular appeal? Guardasoni no doubt sent Mozart the libretto some weeks later, or brought it to Vienna himself, by which time he had acquired a copy, perhaps from Antonio Baglioni who had sung the title role (a tenor part) in Venice and would soon take the role of Don Ottavio in Mozart's opera.

Being in only one act, Bertati's *Don Giovanni* would obviously need to be enlarged. But Mozart would never have been content with a patched-up version of a libretto so loosely constructed and so relentlessly frivolous in tone; he was always going to want to treat it differently and compose to a text that, even if it took Bertati as its starting point, was reworked from top to bottom. There is no reason to doubt what the *Extract* claimed: that Mozart "insisted on having a book written by Da Ponte on the same subject *and not by any other dramatist*". He too wanted another *Figaro*. It had been a near-ideal partnership. What better than a chance to renew it?

Yet *Don Giovanni*, of all operas, is surely the last one you would want to imagine coming into the world haphazardly, by the mere accident of another composer's having written one a few months before. It resonates across the centuries with such power and brilliance that one can't believe it to have been other than meant. To Mozart, consciously or not, it must – you feel – have come in answer to deep creative if not personal instincts. For whatever reasons – and the theory that it was guilt aroused by the death of his father is quite unprovable – he was waiting for it. For evidence – indirect at best, but compelling once it has struck you – listen to the Prague symphony. Written before there was any question of an opera commission, it contains anticipations of the opera that are uncanny. One of Mozart's grandest symphonic works, it reverts to the non-Viennese, Italian-derived three-movement tradition, though the old formula is transformed with a vengeance. The finale, apparently (the paper-type indicates) composed about six months before the other two movements, at about the time of the first *Figaro* performances, begins with a rapid four-note figure identical to the opening of the duet sung by Susanna and Cherubino just before the page jumps out of the window. But the opera that this effervescent movement evokes even more forcibly is *Don Giovanni*. It is as if the still unborn, still unthought-of drama were exerting an invisible influence. The second part of the finale, with its dramatic alternation of violent tuttis and half-skittish, half-hectic fragments of the Cherubino theme, is a presage of the peremptory motif for unison strings, followed by playful violin figure, in the overture – a likeness emphasized when the finale's second repeat is observed.

Don Giovanni casts its shadow over the first movement as well. The parallels between the opening bars of the symphony's allegro and the overture's – quiet, tense string theme followed by wind fanfares and then, at its repetition, accompanied by a similar woodwind counter-theme – are only the most obvious examples. The monumental but troubled introduction has more than a touch of the colour and atmosphere of the opera: wailing chromatic lines for the flute, change from regal D major to ominous D minor (the opera's supernatural key), stealthy bassoon arpeggios, darkly gleaming trumpets – gestures and sonorities that establish from the outset the ambiguous character of both works. The allegro has a driven quality that again looks forward to the opera, not least in the long, magical dominant preparation for the reprise and the manic intensity of the movement's final pages. The symphony sounds at moments like a rehearsal for the opera.

Da Ponte says that Mozart accepted the idea with enthusiasm when it was put to him. But could he not have already been thinking of an opera on the subject? Alternatively, did the inner impulses that produced the Prague symphony prompt *him* to propose Don Juan when he was offered the commission, whereon Guardasoni responded by giving him the Bertati libretto?

Whatever the truth of the matter, it was probably spring or early summer before Da Ponte and Mozart got down to serious work on the libretto, and summer or autumn before Mozart began composing the score. Very few letters survive from the seven and a half months between Mozart's and Constanze's return to Vienna on 12 February and their departure for Prague on 1 October; those that do – the famous one to the ailing Leopold (quoted in Chapter 2), a couple to Nannerl about their father's death and the disposal of his estate, and one or two other fragments – say next to nothing about his public life or compositional activities during this period, and nothing at all about *Don Giovanni*. Da Ponte's bravura account of writing the libretto in tandem with librettos for Salieri's *Axur* and Martín y Soler's *L'arbore di Diana* cuts a histrionic dash appropriate to this most myth-encrusted of operas but doesn't really tell us anything either:

Having found these subjects, I went to the Emperor, revealed my thoughts to him, and informed him that my intention was to write these three operas simultaneously. "You won't succeed," he replied. "Perhaps not," I answered, "but I shall try. For Mozzart [sic] I shall write at night and shall account it reading Dante's *Inferno*. I shall write during the morning for Martini, and that will be like studying Petrarch, [and] in the evening for Salieri, and he shall be my Tasso." He found the parallel very good, and scarcely had I got home than I began to write. I went to my writing table and sat there twelve hours on end, a small bottle of Tokay on my right, my inkstand in the middle, and a box of Seville snuff on my left. A beautiful sixteen-year-old girl, whom I had meant to love only as a daughter, but . . ., was staying in my house with her mother, who looked after the housekeeping; she came to my room at the sound of the bell, which in sooth I rang rather often, when it seemed to me that my inspiration was beginning to cool . . . [. . .] On the first day, however, between the Tokay, the Seville snuff, the coffee, the bell, and my young Muse, I wrote the first two scenes of *Don Giovanni*, two others of *L'arbore di Diana*, and more than half of the first act of *Tarar*, a title I changed to *Assur*.

We can be certain that, as before, Mozart was intimately involved in the shaping and wording of the libretto, perhaps even more than with *Figaro* – plenty of internal evidence points to it. (His, not Da Ponte's, is certainly the hand behind the great dance scene in the finale of Act 1, modelled on the typical Viennese ball that Mozart, who loved dancing, knew so well.) He had time to lavish on it, being less hectically busy in 1787 than two years before.

1787 is a watershed in Mozart's career in Vienna. Even if musical events take place for which no documentary evidence survives, the great popularity of his concerts, public and private, is a thing of the past. The C major, K503, will be his last piano concerto for well over a year: there is apparently no further occasion for new concertos with which to dazzle and, increasingly, puzzle the Viennese. It is not so much that the novelty of his playing has worn off as that his new compositions have left the public too far behind. He continues, as performer or composer, to take part in events put on by others: in Nancy Storace's farewell concert given on 23 February at the Kärntnertortheater; at other concerts there during March, when friends and colleagues – the oboist Friedrich Ramm, Fischer the first

Osmin, and the pianist Walburga Willmann – perform music of his. But he puts on few if any of his own; the four Advent concerts mentioned in a letter of Leopold's to Nannerl as being planned for the previous December (perhaps to include K503 and the new symphony, No. 38) are the last of which there is any word till the summer of 1788. Mozart has no need now of a central apartment, near the main concert halls, from which his piano can be easily transported, as it was "at least a dozen times" during Leopold's visit in the winter of 1785.

No doubt that was one reason why, that spring, he and Constanze left Grosse Schulerstrasse and moved to the Landstrasse suburb in the south-east of the city. Another may have been that Mozart had again been ill, perhaps dangerously so (his doctor, Sigmund Barisani, quoted above, had "served" and "saved" him a second time). Their new rooms looked out on a garden and the surroundings were peaceful. Little Carl was two and a half and Constanze was pregnant. The low rent – about a tenth of what it was in the city – could also have been a factor in the decision to move ("I can guess the reason," was Leopold Mozart's sardonic comment), though we can't be sure: calculating Mozart's income, or for that matter his expenditure, at any given moment is rarely more than guesswork. If he borrowed money, he also lent it, with more generosity than prudence: 500 gulden to Stadler and 300 to Franz Anton Gilowsky, neither of whom ever repaid him.*
He had come back from Prague with a good lot of money – if Nancy Storace is to be believed – and had the prospect of more from the new commission. On the other hand he seems no longer to have had a steady income from teaching. His publisher, Artaria, was bringing out works of his in some profusion: symphonies (Nos. 31 and 35), piano concertos (K413–415), quartets (the six dedicated to Haydn), seven violin sonatas, piano sonatas (including the fantasia and sonata in C minor). Yet when Mozart advertised the three string quintets K406 (516b), 515 and 516 for sale in the spring of 1788, in manuscript copies "finely and correctly written", there was so little response that he postponed publication, and they were eventually sold to Artaria.

---

* Mozart seems to have been the not uncommon type of artist who, though by no means feckless and improvident, is not deeply interested in money or in the mechanics of making it. More than one account of the concert he gave in Leipzig in 1789 shows him handing out tickets to fellow-musicians, though the paying audience was small.

Dissatisfaction with his status in Vienna was clearly behind the plan, much discussed through the winter of 1786–7, to go to England and try his fortune there. Even after Leopold Mozart had, not unreasonably, put his foot down at the "brilliant idea" that he should look after Carl and the new-born Johann Thomas Leopold while his parents stayed in London and perhaps even settled there – "not at all a bad arrangement!" – there was talk of it. "I am still receiving reports from Vienna, Prague and Munich which confirm that your brother is going to England," wrote Leopold to Nannerl on 12 January. Three days later Mozart was lamenting to Gottfried von Jaquin that on his return to Vienna from Prague he would be able to enjoy his friend's company only for a short while and would then have to "forgo this happiness for a long time, perhaps for ever". Later in February Nancy Storace and her entourage, passing through Salzburg on their way to London, told Leopold – who showed them the sights – that his son and daughter-in-law had first thought of travelling with them, before it was agreed that Thomas Attwood should "procure a definite engagement for him". Nothing came of it. By the time of the move to Landstrasse the plan had apparently been dropped. But it was by no means the last time Mozart would think seriously of leaving Vienna and finding a city that offered better employment for his talents. Between the Six German Dances of February 1787 and *Don Giovanni*, completed in October, every item entered in the thematic catalogue is a private work or, if a public one, on a small scale: six songs with piano, the scena for Fischer, an aria for Jaquin, the Rondo in A minor for piano, K511, a sonata for four hands, K521, the madcap *Musical Joke* (perhaps composed for some convivial occasion that has left no trace), the exquisite serenade *Eine kleine Nachtmusik*, and the string quintets in C major and G minor, K515 and 516.*

Whether the G minor quintet's passionate desolation and the sadness of the elegiac A minor Rondo (intensified when it turns to the major, as happens in Schubert's A minor quartet and in Dido's "Va, ma soeur, l'implorer" in *The Trojans*, in the same key) represent

* The two quintets, and also the *Musical Joke* and the serenade, are examples of the pairs of sharply contrasting works, composed at the same time, which recur in Mozart's oeuvre: e.g. the piano concertos K466 and 467, and K488 and 491, and the G minor and Jupiter symphonies.

Mozart's response to the death of his close friend and exact contemporary Count August Hatzfeld we cannot say. Mozart loved him dearly, as well as greatly admiring his violin playing: Hatzfeld was given the obbligato part in Idamante's aria composed for the revival of *Idomeneo* in March 1786 and, though an amateur, was said to play Mozart's chamber music with greater understanding than anyone. But no connection can be established, any more than it can between the death of Leopold Mozart and the music inspired by the killing of the Commendatore in *Don Giovanni* and the vengeance he exacts. Rushton may be right when he speculates that his father's death "tapped a dark force in Mozart's creativity which welled up" in the opera. But it is only speculation. Though 1787 was a grievous year for Mozart – Hatzfeld died on 30 January, Leopold Mozart on 28 May, Sigmund Barisani, his saviour, on 3 September – and though *Don Giovanni* is a death-haunted score, he would surely have shaped the drama and exploited its expressive possibilities no differently if none of them had died. The dramatist in him would not have done otherwise.

What we can say is that the Prague symphony is not the only work of this period that looks forward to the opera. So, indirectly, do the quintets. It is not so much a change of style that comes over the music written that winter and spring as a deepening, a greater density and weight and expansiveness and fullness of sonority, an ever greater richness of part-writing. *Don Giovanni* is the culmination of that development. It comes at the perfect moment in his artistic career.

One of the most implausible of all Da Ponte's recollections is that Mozart had to be persuaded to make the work a comedy. The coexistence of serious and comic is of the essence of Mozartian opera. In *Don Giovanni* the two elements are so deeply interfused as not to be separable. They are of one substance. The "comic" characters no less than the "serious" are subject to the same overmastering force. (Only the duet for Leporello and Zerlina, added for the Vienna production in 1788, lacks this driven quality.) To the end there is no letting up. At the final curtain, when the actors have stepped chorus-like out of the action to proclaim the conventional moral – "This is the fate of all evil-doers" – the brief orchestral epilogue surges unstoppably on to the violent final chords, while oboe and bassoons repeat the descending chromatic phrase associated all through the opera with the anti-hero and his fatal influence. A moment before, a dazzling trumpet arpeggio strides down the notes of the common chord, a last reminder of the imperious personality that divine retribution had rid them of. At the same time the inimitable duality of the work holds sway to the last. Even as the woodwind recall that wailing chromatic motif, the violins' exuberant trills, as Andrew Steptoe remarks, "suggest the bustle of everyday life and the return to normality".

I shall never forget the experience I had the first time I heard Mozart's C minor Mass. Suddenly I was transported to another world by the passage near the end of the Quoniam where solo voices, accompanied by sustained woodwind, softly repeat "altissimus" in a panting rhythm against offbeat string chords – an almost identical pattern of melody, harmony and orchestral colour as at the end of the duet for Donna Anna and Don Ottavio in the opening scene of the opera. For a moment the Mass was forgotten in the enveloping frisson of *Don Giovanni*.

Is there any other opera that has this spellbinding effect, the almost palpable emanation that rises before you like a physical presence and takes you over body and soul when you hear a passage from it? E. T. A. Hoffmann called it "the opera of all operas". Rossini, when asked which of his own works he preferred, replied, "*Don Giovanni*." It is a matter not simply of the power, undimmed after more than two centuries, of the scene where the Statue, whose voice has already chilled us in the graveyard, comes to supper and the unrepentant libertine is dragged down to hell. Nor is it just because of the music of Giovanni himself, the mania which Mozart makes unmistakably clear in the obsessive repetitions that are so characteristic of his role: the touch of hysteria in the Ds and E flats in the so-called champagne aria, "Fin ch'han dal vino", the relentless "Io mi voglio divertir" and "Vivan le femmine" in the supper scene. The whole score has a demonic quality. Every emotion seems raised beyond normal pitch. The most apparently light-hearted music sounds in the grip of uncontrollable powers. It is not only the Don whose music is obsessive. All who come within his orbit are like creatures under an enchantment they cannot shake off. In the Act 1 finale the masked guests are drawn into his triumphal invocation to liberty as though helpless to resist. Or listen to the writhing chromatic lines of the voice parts in the epilogue, just before the final cadences. The pious words say one thing – "The death of the wicked matches the life they led", we are free of him at last – the music says another. Such rich chromaticisms are all over the score, in its fabric and being, to an extent no other score by Mozart matches: not only in a highly charged piece like the sextet but also – to cite one example – in Zerlina's coquettishly pleading aria "Batti, batti". They are an integral part of the melodic, harmonic, textural and sonic substance that makes *Don Giovanni* unique in Mozart's output or anyone else's.

No other opera equals its sense of headlong momentum, of moving in a single continuous impulse from first note to last. That is why, for anyone who has come under its spell, the criticisms often heard of the work's ill-conceived mixing of genres or defective structure are meaningless. You do not question a torrent in spate. "How can anyone say that Mozart 'composed' *Don Giovanni*?" exclaimed Goethe. "It is a spiritual creation, the detail, like the whole, made by one mind in one mould, and shot through with the breath of life"; the author was "bidden by the daemon of his genius to do what he did". Of course Mozart very much did compose the work, bringing to it his highest intelligence. But, with all its ingenious craftsmanship, the opera is a force of nature.

Da Ponte may well not have expected anything so extreme even from a composer he had got to know intimately while working on *Figaro* two years before. It was no doubt Mozart who insisted on their taking the intellectually discredited supernatural element and the traditional pantomime devilry of the protagonist seriously. The overture makes his intentions clear, not only by its eerie, monumental introduction (beginning with what Ernest Newman called "the most magically evocative chord in the history of music") but by its main, allegro section (in strict sonata style), whose vehemence bears no trace of the buffo manner of the overtures to *Figaro* and, later, *Così*.

To that extent Da Ponte's recollection quoted above was correct. But Mozart, as we have said, needed no persuasion to cast the work as a comedy. Comedy, in the broadest sense, was his natural environment. Just as in *Figaro*, he can be seen adding comic touches of his own, in the supper scene for instance – touches not present in the libretto that was printed shortly before the first night. Some of the most spine-chilling moments in the score occur in a musical context that is unabashedly buffo, like the modulation that cuts the ground from under Leporello's feet, and ours, at the Statue's elemental "Sì!" in the graveyard duet. In the first scene, even after Anna and the Don (masked and therefore unidentifiable in the darkness) have rushed in and the music, though with no change of tempo, has moved into an entirely different mode, Leporello's interjections maintain the buffo character of his opening soliloquy. The same is true, even more strikingly, of the great confrontation between Giovanni and the Stone Guest in the final scene, where Leporello's terrified comments continue in pure buffo style, paradoxically strengthening the musical and dramatic effect. The expansion of the role of Leporello, as compared with that of his counterpart in Bertati's libretto, must have been at least as much Mozart's choice as Da Ponte's; the dramatist who couldn't resist developing Osmin into a central character can only have relished the opportunity it gave him.

None of this should surprise us. Mozart, as many contemporary accounts and his own letters testify, loved jokes, charades, masquerades, mystifications. Not only the "supernatural solicitings" of the story stimulated his imagination: he responded with equal alacrity to the scope for comedy, even farce. But only he could have mixed them, each intensifying the other.

Even if Mozart's spectacular musical fusion went far beyond anything Da Ponte had envisaged, there is absolutely no doubt that the libretto, and its conception, was their joint work. It was what he wanted. Such a text, making no attempt to rationalize the story, as Goldoni had in his play, might not do for the sophisticates who directed and attended the court theatre in Vienna, but the provincial city of Prague – looked down on by the Viennese for centuries, and without a court theatre – had broader tastes as well as a more serious musical culture. Prague would not object to an opera on a subject the *bien pensants* regarded as reeking of the fairground and the improvised buffoonery of the commedia dell'arte – an entertainment popular in the worst sense of the word, fit only for the lower orders, as the right people considered it. Goethe, who was in Rome this same year,

1787, later recalled his amazement that a crude Don Juan opera ("not the Mozartian one!") could be packed out night after night for a month: "Life was not worth living if they hadn't seen Don Juan roasting in hell." (The second act of Janáček's *From the House of the Dead*, where the convicts watch a pantomime Don Juan fending off devils with his dagger while he flirts with a succession of blowsy women, shows the depths to which the old tale could sink.) Bertati himself, in the dramatic prologue to his *Don Giovanni Tenorio*, has the theatre company, desperate for a hit, reluctantly agree to put on this "*stupenda porcheria*" because the common people always flock to see it. And Gazzaniga's setting, with few exceptions, treats it in the same one-dimensionally comic spirit. But Mozart, and Da Ponte, had different ideas. Da Ponte himself would not have forgotten the improvised Don Juan shows he had seen in Venice and elsewhere, which have left their mark on one or two incidents and ideas in his libretto (especially in the second act). And when he sat down at his writing table to draft it, he had other things at his elbow beside Tokay and snuff and the bell to summon his muse: Molière's *Dom Juan*, for one, probably Tirso de Molina's play *El burlador di Sevilla* (*The Trickster of Seville*) as well, perhaps the seventeenth-century *Il convitato di pietra* of Giacinto Andrea Cicognini, and not least Bertati's libretto.

Da Ponte's borrowings from Bertati have long been held against him – as if an eighteenth-century librettist, devising a text on a subject as hoary as Don Juan, was expected to proceed in any other way. We do not blame Shakespeare for similar thefts, nor think less of Juliet's magnificent "Gallop apace, ye fiery-footed steeds" because it incorporates a phrase of Marlowe's – any more than we regard annexations and improvements of other composers' ideas as anything but further proof of Mozart's genius; the main theme of the C minor piano concerto's opening movement is not the less inspired and characteristic for being derived from a symphony by J. C. Bach. Da Ponte's failure to mention Bertati in his *Memoirs* is the only thing truly reprehensible. His deeds are better than his words.*

---

* When Da Ponte was ousted by Leopold II in 1791, Bertati replaced him as court theatre poet.

In fact the debt to Bertati is smaller than is often stated. Where Da Ponte's libretto takes his as its model it is superior in every respect. The actual verbal borrowings are few – usually the words are different even where the situation and the sentiments are similar – and almost always they are improved. To cite a small example, Bertati's Pasquarello, after the killing of the Commendatore, answers his master's "Son io" ('It is I') with "Vivo o morto?" Da Ponte's whispered exchange is based on Bertati's but makes more of the situation:

DON GIOVANNI Leporello, ove sei?
LEPORELLO Son qui per mia disgrazia. E voi?
DON GIOVANNI Son qui.
LEPORELLO Chi è morto, voi, o il vecchio?

"Who's dead, you or the old man?" is funnier than the mere "Alive or dead?"

Generally, where Da Ponte follows Bertati he comes out of the comparison wittier, more stylish, more concise and more effective. How evocative are the words that begin Anna's narration: "Era già aliquanto avanzata la notte" – "It was already quite late at night" (but an English translation gives no idea of the vividness of the words). Mozart's setting creates an extraordinary tension as the forte G minor of the strings, entering at that moment, gives way to a sudden hushed, motionless E flat minor; but it was Da Ponte's text that inspired it.

It is the same with the structural changes. Da Ponte's reshaping and trimming and tightening of the opening numbers of the opera provided Mozart with the means for one of the most electrifying first scenes in all music-drama. By postponing Anna's account of the attempted rape, which in Bertati comes immediately after the murder, till later in the act (where its effect, following straight after the quartet, is incomparably greater), and replacing it with the vengeance duet, "Fuggi, crudele, fuggi", he gave Mozart the opportunity to round off the whole opening sequence in the ideal way, with the result that the first twenty minutes of the opera move in a single hurtling trajectory, and in a tonal arch that spans D minor/D major, F, B flat, G minor, D minor and F minor, returning to a feverish D minor as Anna and Ottavio reaffirm their oath.

Of course, when we examine what Da Ponte did with Bertati's looser, inconsequential sequence of scenes we have what Mozart made of it in our heads as we do so. Yet the improvement is incontestable – as it is in the supper scene, which in Da Ponte's version is better in every way, both large and small: the placing of Elvira's entry after the serving of the dishes and the concert by the Don's private band, not before, and the case of the stolen pheasant leg. Not only is the latter a meat ball (polpetta) in Bertati: the incident, as written by Da Ponte, is altogether more amusing.

The whole first part of the graveyard scene in *Don Giovanni*, with its skilful pacing and characteristic mixture of the buffo and the macabre, is Da Ponte's invention, or rather Da Ponte's and Mozart's: the introducing of trombones, as the Statue's voice speaks out of the darkness, breaking in on the simple (secco) recitative with an effect that no amount of familiarity can ever dim, must have been the composer's idea. He remembered the first act of Gluck's *Alceste*, where the harmonies of the Oracle's last four bars are identical to those of the Commendatore's "Before the dawn you will have ceased to laugh": a sepulchral sound which moved a contemporary German critic to exclaim that Mozart seemed "to have learned the language of ghosts from Shakespeare".

Equally, though it is through Mozart's music that the characters become as real as people we know, Da Ponte's craft and art made the alchemy possible; his libretto, in contrast to Bertati's, breathes life into them and gives them substance. And by reducing the number of characters and reordering and tightening the plot, so that Giovanni's adversaries are no longer separate but are brought together and interact, he provided Mozart with the wealth of ensembles that he craved and that singles him out from nearly all the other opera composers of his day; ensembles account for over half the duration of the opera.

For professional critics of Da Ponte, however, it is not enough to demonstrate that he transformed out of recognition the scenes he lifted from Bertati, or that in every instance where a comparison can be made his versification is more elegant and more incisive. It is in the passages where he could not borrow but had to fend for himself that they find him wanting. Bertati's *Don Giovanni* cut straight from the peasants' scene to the graveyard. Everything in between except Donna Anna's narration – the quartet, "Fin ch'han dal vino", the finale of Act 1 and the whole of the first half of Act 2 – is Da Ponte's invention; and, in this view, his invention, in Act 2 at least, was insufficient: pressed for time, he resorted to the hack devices of countless comic dramas, the swapping of hats and cloaks and consequent mistaken identities, and in so doing fatally weakened the dramatic structure. The Act 1 finale is grudgingly allowed to be good; but Act 2, from the beginning right up to the end of the sextet, is wasted on tomfoolery.

That the opera has been criticized so wildly and irrationally, in terms that say more about the critics than about the work, is a mark of its disturbing power. The simplicity of *The Magic Flute* may still baffle and irritate the over-intellectual; *Così fan tutte*, now so admired, was for long a sad case of divine strains dragged down by a silly, squalid fable. But the discomfort caused by *Don Giovanni* goes deeper. Most of the commonly heard objections spring from that. Partly it is, as in the eighteenth century, dislike of the supernatural, or fear of it masquerading as disbelief. Partly it is revulsion from the character of the anti-hero – for just as some are temperamentally attracted by the rebel who defies society and who claims dominion over the sensual world, so there are others who are repelled and who react by attempting to belittle him. Partly it is the discomfort of offended good taste, which cannot stomach a work embracing such extremes of high seriousness and farce or cope with the sharply conflicting emotions it simultaneously provokes. The normally level-headed Dent, author of the pioneering and still indispensable *Mozart's Operas*, is a case in point. The work, he says, had to be set as an opera buffa because, apart from the fact that the Prague people wanted one, "a really serious treatment of the whole story would have been too utterly repulsive for stage presentation". Dent takes particular exception to the trio in the opening scene of Act 2. Donna Elvira, on her balcony, wooed from the shadows below by the ingenious Don, is again prey to the fondest love, while Leporello in his master's hat and cloak stifles his laughter and gestures extravagantly. This, "perhaps the most beautiful [number] of the whole opera", brutally wedded to "the most repulsive" dramatic situation, is "endurable only if one takes a completely frivolous view of the whole play".

Quite apart from the certainty that Mozart was involved every step of the way and therefore is as much to blame as Da Ponte (if it is a question of blame), I do not see Da Ponte in this condescending light. His is surely an altogether more substantial and inventive mind than that would suggest: not slavishly dependent on Bertati and lost when he is no longer there to help, but annexing what is useful and transforming it, and ignoring the rest. The first-act finale – "a masterpiece of construction" (Dent) – is entirely his work. Or, compare his graveyard scene with Bertati's if you think him a mere opportunist. The so-called clichés of the first half of Act 2 are no different in kind from those in scenes which no one thinks to disparage: the graveyard, where we laugh even while our hair stands on end, or the supper scene, where the comedy descends even lower, to comic-strip level:

LEPORELLO What huge mouthfuls – I'm almost fainting with hunger.
GIOVANNI Watching my mouthfuls he's almost fainting with hunger.

You can see the balloons coming out of their mouths. Yet the design and balance and pacing of the whole scene are rightly regarded as masterly. Leporello filching a piece of pheasant and being forced to speak before he can swallow it is followed immediately by Elvira's heartrending intervention (placed, as we have seen, later than in Bertati, where it could have nothing like the same effect). Next, the comical terror of Leporello's description of "l'uom di sasso", the stone man, leads directly to the awe-inspiring actuality. And the elemental drama of the Statue's confrontation with the unflinching Don Giovanni is continually undercut by Leporello's farcical interjections from beneath the table.

Da Ponte's invented scenes are in the same vein – comedy, farce if you like, constantly interfused with danger and violence. They culminate in one of opera's supreme numbers, the sinister comic-tragic sextet, the acme of the work's strange combination of opposites, where the disguised Leporello is mistaken for his master and nearly killed for it, a movement in which only "Mozart could have achieved so many dramatic shades, from low comedy to high tragedy and within the same ensemble" (Heartz). It goes without saying that Mozart's setting is the crucial element in this wonderful piece; but Da Ponte's text made it possible. Whether he fully realized what Mozart's response would be does not signify. The librettist is required not to be a creator on the same level as the composer but to serve the composer's genius well, which he did.

Nor does it seem to me weak dramaturgy to follow the sextet with Leporello's blustering escape aria (beginning with a phrase taken from the final section of the sextet) – a number which intensifies the sense of destructiveness and confusion that the Don spreads even in his absence. In practice, sung and played for all it is worth, it comes as an anti-climax only if one is over-influenced by the notion that the sextet was originally the third-act finale of a putative four-act opera. For the same imagined reason Ottavio's "Il mio tesoro", which followed it in the Prague score, is often judged out of place. Yet, far from being mere marking time and superfluous filling-in until the real business of the drama can be resumed, all these scenes in the second act have a positive function: they prepare for the drama's climax. As Rushton says, "the first half of Act II shows the futility of merely human endeavour against Giovanni, and thus leads naturally to the graveyard scene". It also adds something important: it enlarges our perception of the Don and uncovers deeper layers in the psychology of his complex relationship with his servant and alter ego, Leporello. The scenes Da Ponte devised and Mozart set do not hold up the drama: they extend and enhance it. Since Don Giovanni is the central figure, to an extent matched by few protagonists of other operas – the magnet to which all are drawn helplessly, like moths to a flame – anything more that we can find out about his elusive nature is relevant. I will return to that in a moment.

At no point in the score does the music convey anything but total conviction, total commitment to the drama as conceived and presented. The composer, no less than his characters, is in its grip. When the work was given in Vienna the following year, some regretted that so lofty a talent had stooped to such base gross matter, thus drawing the distinction between score and libretto that has been a feature of Mozart commentary ever since. But Mozart's identification with every element in the text is manifest from the start. The completeness with which the music takes possession of it extends to the simple (secco) recitative, which even more than in *Figaro* is an integral and characteristic part of the score.

He wastes no time in making his position, and the Shakespearean diversity of the work, clear. The opening establishes it, and covers most of the ground of the opera in one sure, swift sequence, from Leporello's grumbling, boastful patter, through the struggle of his master and Donna Anna, the intervention of the Commendatore, his fatal duel with the Don and the awestruck, muttered trio, to Leporello's "Who's dead, you or the old man?", the discovery of the body and the oath of vengeance. Nothing that happens thereafter, not the most extreme juxtaposition of terror and buffoonery, should surprise us. Base gross matter is fundamental to the work. To object to it is, logically, to object to the whole opera. The comic and the serious – fused in the sextet and the final Statue scene – are systematically juxtaposed, each throwing the other into relief, throughout the work. But so skilfully is it done, so fine and precise is the balance, that questions of style, of what kind of opera it is, dissolve and vanish. It is what it is.

Whatever the situations they are subjected to, the reality and integrity of the characters, as the music portrays them, is never undermined. Even Ottavio, even Elvira, are not the figures of fun they are often said to be. Ottavio may be powerless against Don Giovanni, but that is the point. No power on earth can stop him. If, as some maintain, Ottavio is cuckolded at the beginning of the opera, and his "respiro" ("I breathe again") when Anna tells him she struggled free of the Don's embrace is a tragic irony (for which there is no evidence in the music), that doesn't make him a laughing stock.* Mozart didn't lavish the strange, luminous modulation to which Ottavio and Anna enter the courtyard in the sextet, nor Ottavio's grand heroic phrases, punctuated by quiet but momentous trumpets and drums, on a character he expected us to snigger at. The last of Ottavio's wide spans of melody begins with two bars that are identical

---

* The theory that Anna *was* seduced, first advanced by E. T. A. Hoffmann and strongly espoused by Einstein and others, is attractive to the prurient side of our natures, but is not necessary in order to account for her insistence on revenge: the assault on her virginity and the killing of her father which results from it are enough.

to the opening six notes of the overture's molto allegro theme. The man is no ninny.

Elvira, for her part, *is* a victim-figure, and her music depicts her obsessiveness, her continued sexual fascination with Don Giovanni, her lack of control; but, unlike the Don, it doesn't deride her. Even without the great scene that was added for the Vienna production, she rises above the indignities callously heaped on her, and earns our respect. Her denunciation of Giovanni to the willingly unsuspecting Zerlina – the splendidly overwrought aria "Ah, fuggi il traditor" – may have a touch of hysteria and even jealousy about it; but her intervention succeeds in rattling him, and her music, in particular the motif, sung to Anna, "Te vuol tradir ancor" ("He will betray you too"), dominates the quartet

and is adopted by Anna; and her instrument, the B flat clarinet, gives the ensemble its particular colour – for, as in Mozart's other major operas, instrumental colour is a vital means of characterization. (Oboes figure in none of Elvira's solo numbers, nor in the quartet, which is her piece.) In the brief but fraught development section of this modified sonata-form movement (the quartet), where the three other participants voice their perplexities to themselves, successively in F major, C minor and G minor, Elvira's concluding phrase is the most beautiful, the one that reasserts both the home key, B flat, and the essential question of Don Giovanni's trustworthiness. The effect of her passionate words is to sow doubts in Anna's mind. At the same time they cause the Don to overplay his hand as, a moment later, he offers his services to "bellissima Donn'Anna", so that she recognizes him as her father's killer. The quartet – a small dramatic masterpiece and a movement as haunting as anything in the score, and a turning point of the drama – establishes Elvira as a leading player, with all her eccentricities (which her erratic vocal lines reflect). It is a mark of her softening influence on Donna Anna that clarinets replace the usual oboes in the aria Anna sings towards the end of the opera, "Non mi dir". Elvira embodies half of the prescription for a good comic opera that Mozart set out four years before in the much-quoted letter of May 1783, when he was toying with the project which became briefly *The Goose of Cairo*: "two equally good female roles, one of them must be seria, the other mezzo carattere – the roles must be equal in quality"; Elvira – the in-between role, between seria and buffa – is equal in quality and in importance to Anna. At the end, after the heartbreak and humiliation, her resigned, infinitely weary decision to abandon the world and its deceptions and withdraw to a cloister has its own triste dignity.

Don Giovanni may be, as Einstein says, sui generis, but it is decked with the trappings of opera buffa. Yet, for Mozart above all, that was never exclusive. "One of the roles [in a good comic opera] must be seria." That is Donna Anna. She is the descendant of Elettra and all the other *donne furiose* whose torments he had known how to simulate from almost his earliest years: not so neurotic as they are, nobler, more poised, still mistress of herself, but inwardly seething. Listen to the serpentine bassoon and viola phrases as she pictures the gaping wound in her father's breast and relives the horror of that moment, in the great vengeance aria "Or sai chi l'onore" ("Now you know who sought to rob me of my honour"). When she begins to sing, in the sextet, the harmony twists and veers. The power of her music – the steely, implacable high A's in "Or sai chi l'onore", the magnificent passage where she reveals the identity of the murderer (introduced by those quiet, hair-raising cello and bass notes, and with the trumpets blazing out for the first time since the overture), the poignant beauty of the recitative "Crudele! Ah no, mio bene" – is such that otherwise temperate commentators are lured into reckless fantasies. Mozart and Da Ponte have endowed all the characters with such abundant and disturbing life that, as with many of Shakespeare's, we cannot help thinking of them and discussing them as real people. But Anna's motives need no psychological probing. They are clear. *Pace* Hoffmann, Einstein and the rest, neither her account of her nocturnal adventure nor her stated reason for postponing her marriage is a lie. Mozart's art is steeped in irony; but there is no hint of it here.

It is characteristic of the dual nature of the work that Anna's fiery aria, in high seria style, should be followed almost without a break (in the Prague score) by Giovanni's "Fin ch'han dal vino", and that explosive outburst by Zerlina's "Batti, batti, o bel Masetto", the bewitching song with which she twines her lover round her little finger. As Mozart's letter said, "the third female role must be entirely buffa – and so can all the men's, if need be". Ottavio is the exception here, a true opera seria nobleman (though his relations with Anna have a vividness and an ambiguity that transcend the conventional limits of the genre). Leporello, Masetto, the Don himself are buffo characters – with a difference, but still recognizably in the tradition. The difference is what counts. Da Ponte and Mozart made Leporello a richer, more ambivalent figure than any of his ancestors in the sources, and more closely linked to the protagonist. His voyeuristic relish, half disgusted, half lip-smacking, is new. The furtive bassoon arpeggios at "his chief passion is the young beginner" and "you know what happens then" in the catalogue aria are as lewd as anything in music.

There had been and would be other catalogue arias, but none like this. The wit of the orchestral writing, starting with light repeated notes and a rising arpeggio that set the tone with expert sleight of hand, is needle-sharp and irresistibly graphic: the chortling oboes and horns; the innocent descending violins answered with wicked insinuation by rising cellos and basses; the unholy glee of the doubly emphasized "but in Spain . . ."; the woodwind which at "among them country girls, serving-maids, baronesses", etc. pant with their tongues hanging out like dogs copulating in a park, watched by scandalized matrons; and a dozen other touches. In the slower second half, a kind of parody minuet, Leporello has almost become what he longed to be as he kept sentry duty in the opening scene of the opera and cried: "I want to play the gentleman"; he leers and struts as he fancies a practised seducer would. Though, at the end of the opera, he proposes to find himself "a better master", you wonder what kind of life he can ever have without Don Giovanni. Like the others, he is helplessly in thrall to the Don's demonic personality.

It is a kind of tribute to the magnetic force of the man and the chaos he spreads round him that he continues to stir up such extreme reactions from commentators and still more from opera directors, in whom he brings out the beast; they have to parade their interpretations, however fantastical and absurd – to be the one to drag him down and pluck out the heart of his mystery, and in pursuit of it to encumber with elaborate, tendentious decor a work that needs practically none. This is partly Mozart's fault, for composing a score so hypnotic that it turns brains and breeds obsessions, but also for leaving his protagonist "in such a questionable shape", so enigmatic. "Who I am you shall not know": the masked assailant's reply to Donna Anna in the opening trio is like an epigraph to the work. Who is he? He can take any part. With effortless cunning he adapts himself to the musical style of whoever he has set out to seduce or dominate. His "Là ci darem la mano" is in Zerlina's artless vein and in 3/8, then 6/8, metre, so that she is compelled all the more readily to yield, singing his music even while her words pretend to hesitate. In the Act 2 trio he courts Elvira in her own tones; though his impassioned protestations of love and penitence begin with the same melodic phrase as the serenade he will shortly sing to Elvira's maid, they end, cynically, with a cadential turn taken from the quartet, where Elvira said she would proclaim his faithlessness to the world. Disguised as Leporello, and taking charge of Masetto and his gang, he adopts Leporello's garrulous patter and clipped phrasing, so as ostensibly to become one of them; the key of his "Metà di voi", F, is that of Leporello's "Notte e giorno faticar" and the arias of Masetto and of Zerlina in Act 1. Even when he is, so to speak, himself, in his two duets with his servant, his idiom is Leporello's rather than his own. And in the final scene, where he confronts his destiny, the Commendatore sets the tone and the Don, in part at least, follows it.

Nonetheless, we can make too much of his "lack of character", the supposed blankness which has enabled people, from the Romantic age to the present, to fill the void with their own ideas and see in him everything from fallen Lucifer or Faustian super-hero to suppressed homosexual. He has his own voice, when he is not playing a part. We should be in no doubt of that; he is himself often enough for us to make no mistake. His superhuman vigour and appetite are abundantly clear. That he achieves no new conquests during the twenty-four hours of the action is of no significance. That is essential to the buffo plot, maybe, but certainly not to the man, as Mozart has written his music: music of thrusting virility, and of reckless daring and arrogance, of aristocratic hauteur, with the phrases striding over the notes of the common chord – a persistent feature of his musical characterization: "Fin ch'han dal vino"; "Ma non manca in me coraggio", as he faces his accusers at the end of Act 1; "Ho fermo il cor", as he fearlessly accepts the Stone Guest's invitation.

In the aria "Metà di voi", where he impersonates Leporello for the benefit of the peasants, his enjoyment of the situation and his sadistic humour get the better of him and the mask slips, as he revels in describing how they will recognize Don Giovanni, "a white plume on his hat, clad in a great cloak" (more common-chord phrases), "with a sword at his side", and – to put the wind up the peasants – a meaning emphasis on the sword, repeated four times, complete with nasty gleaming trills, made more insistent still by flutes and oboes. In the coda of the aria the smoothly menacing phrases addressed to the mesmerized Masetto, with stabbing accents in the orchestra (sadistic again), are pure Don Giovanni.

So is the opening of the Act 2 finale, introduced by two gunshot chords for the full orchestra. His opening phrase, "Già la mensa è preparata" (D major, on the notes of the common chord), works up to a manic intensity at "Io mi voglio divertir" ("I intend to enjoy myself"). It has the same touch of madness as the syncopated Ds and obsessive E flats in "Fin ch'han dal vino", mentioned above. But then immediately afterwards comes the deliberately farcical scene where his musicians play popular tunes and master and servant, as if oblivious of who they invited to dinner, indulge in comic byplay and comic-strip asides.

Such dichotomy is the essence of the work. Every listener, every performer has to come to terms with what has been a stumbling block for so many: how to present, how to perceive a work expressly compounded of such antithetical elements and a central figure whose preternatural charm and destructive energy the authors have placed in an unashamedly opera buffa context. An opera buffa with a difference, naturally: that Masetto should spend his wedding night roaming the streets, armed with a blunderbuss, is both comical and deadly serious, proof of the tension and angry fascination Don Giovanni arouses in all who come into contact with him. But Don Giovanni too is a comic character. Listen to the way the orchestra mocks him while he mocks Masetto in the scene in the finale of Act 1 when Masetto steps out of the arbour just as the Don is steering Zerlina into it. The situations are constantly making fun of him. Shakespeare's Falstaff is a comparable case of a stock figure – the Lord of Misrule – who grows into a personality of mythic dimensions; but he does so by going further in the same direction. Don Giovanni achieves it in the teeth of serious or rather comic obstacles and in spite of what happens to him for three-quarters of the action. And then comes the encounter with the Statue, and music which after all the developments in the art in the past two hundred years still harrows us with fear and wonder.

Don Giovanni is, even by the standards of Mozart opera, a fabulously rich score. In its development of music as a dramatic language it goes even beyond *Figaro*. Dent exaggerates the similarities between *Figaro* and *Don Giovanni*, which he says was planned to be as like *Figaro* in layout and detail as possible. But it is the experience of composing *Figaro* and working with Da Ponte that makes *Don Giovanni* possible. The sudden change in colour, rhythm and mode which conveys the general astonishment at the Countess's entry in the final scene of the earlier opera is justly admired; but as a musical expression of stupefaction the totally unexpected sotto voce modulation (from G minor to the dominant seventh of A flat) when Leporello throws off his borrowed hat and cloak in the sextet is something else, imagined at a pitch of intensity exceptional even for Mozart. The subject, everything about it, has seized his imagination. Listening to the opera, we feel that every bar is loaded with meaning. The composer cannot help himself, he is himself possessed. He is like his hero, driven by a force he is powerless to arrest. Yet at the same time no score is more tightly organized, more unified, more aware of what it is doing.

In no opera, either, is the orchestra a more active, committed participant, itself a player, an extra personage, abetting, questioning, deepening. Its sounds and colours reverberate in the memory: the long, quiet trumpet notes in the andante of the overture, the woodwind's chromatic wail as the Commendatore's life ebbs away (a motif that recurs to the end of the work), the baleful entry of the horns at the conclusion of Ottavio's and Anna's D minor duet, sealing the oath of vengeance, the intertwining chromatics in violins and violas in the Zerlina–Giovanni duet, the heaving phrase in the violins over a descending bass as Anna describes twisting free of her attacker's embrace, the distant strains of the F major minuet floating out into the night in answer to Anna's tense D minor as Leporello opens a window, the insolent horn arpeggio that punctuates the reprise of the strings' caressingly beautiful melody in the A major trio, the magical, erotic effect of the strings' still chord after two bars of chirpy woodwind in Zerlina's "Vedrai, carino", the soft trumpet notes and timpani roll as light floods the courtyard in the sextet, the sinister, gliding movement of Mozart's favourite violas in the same number, the pale, enchanted tones of the flute at so many points (how can it be true that Mozart disliked the flute, given the way it colours so much of the score?). Nothing escapes him. He lives every moment of the characters' griefs and joys and crimes. But he never judges them, even his totally callous and amoral anti-hero, who treats women like commodities and is simply not interested in the consequences, however dire, of what he does. Mozart allows, encourages, helps everyone to be themselves. He sympathizes and identifies with them all, the Don included. At the end, faced with damnation, his Don Giovanni rises to heroic heights. He is offered forgiveness, a seat at his victim's table where he will eat "cibo celeste", the bread of heaven. But the price, repentance, is impossible; though for the first time in his life he knows fear, he stays true to his principles.

His last scene inspires Mozart's most magnificent and harmonically audacious music. The late-eighteenth-century idiom is pushed to its limits and beyond. As Rushton says, not melody but "the mysteries of harmony, tremendous and beautiful, are Mozart's answer to the tragic and supernatural elements of *Don Giovanni*" in this climactic scene where, "as the Statue refuses mortal food his modulation

from D to A minor seems to travel the tonal universe". The rising
harmonic progressions in the succeeding allegro, as subterranean
voices with brass and drums hammer out their inexorable unisons,
thrill us to the core every time. Yet, viscerally exciting as the music is,
it is not just that. The Don *is* damned. Mozart does not shirk it.
The opera, with all its prodigious comic verve, was always coursing
towards that end. Its title, *Il dissoluto punito, o sia il Don Giovanni*,
says as much.

How should we respond to it? Nicholas Till, in *Mozart and the
Enlightenment*, argues that *Don Giovanni* represents a conscious
decision on Mozart's part to treat the subject as a parable of contemporary life and to reassert the belief in divine retribution rejected by
the Enlightenment, because the Don's crimes are so bad "that only
the ultimate punishment can serve". There is no protection against
his fundamentally destructive energies, which attack not, as with
Molière's Don Juan, religion, which is of no interest to him, but
society. He is the logical consequence of the Enlightenment's cult of
individualism and unrestrained liberty. He has to be stopped, but
cannot be by any human agency. Hence the denouement and hence,
in the finale of the first act, two remarkable passages which show
which way the wind is blowing. The first is the celebration, with
trumpets and drums, imperious dotted rhythm and the full woodwind
band (otherwise reserved for final scenes, the overture and the end of
the sextet), of "libertà" – liberty, which for Giovanni means licence
to do as he pleases without restraint from any once-sacred moral or
legal sanction; the words "Viva la libertà" are repeated, fortissimo,
with fanatical insistence.* The second is the scene that follows it,
where separate instrumental groups play socially distinct dances, minuet, contredanse and German dance, not in sequence and in different
rooms or different parts of a large ballroom but simultaneously, as
Don Giovanni had commanded when, in his instructions to Leporello
before the party, he called for "a minuet, a follia, an allemana", to be
danced *without order*". "The dances that had underpinned the
orderly intertwining of individuals in the classic vision of society are

---

* The political implications it also carried could not have been lost on contemporary
audiences.

1. Leopold Mozart, c.1765, when he was forty-six, by an unknown artist, possibly Pietro Antonio Lorenzoni. Wolfgang was then nine.

2. The Mozart family in 1780, by Johann Nepomuk della Croce, with Leopold standing and Nannerl and Wolfgang at the keyboard. Behind them is Lorenzoni's portrait of their mother, Anna Maria Mozart, who had died two years earlier.

3. View of Salzburg, in an eighteenth-century engraving.

4. Interior of the Cuvilliés-Theater (Residenztheater), Munich, where *Idomeneo* was first performed in 1781, watercolour by Gustav Seeberger, 1867.

5. Elisabeth (Lisel) Wendling, the first Elettra in *Idomeneo*, pastel portrait by an unknown artist.

6. Dorothea Wendling, the first Ilia, miniature on ivory by an unknown artist.

7. A page of the autograph full score of *Idomeneo*, the Act 2 finale: the people of Crete recoil in horror at the violent storm unleashed by the angry Neptune.

8. Emperor Joseph II and (left) his brother Leopold, Grand Duke of Tuscany (later Emperor Leopold II), Rome, 1769, by Pompeo Batoni. On the table beside them is a copy of Montesquieu's *L'esprit des lois*, one of the central documents of the Enlightenment.

9. Announcement of the premiere of *Die Entführung aus dem Serail* (*The Abduction from the Seraglio*), Burgtheater, 16 July 1782.

10. Johann Ignaz Ludwig (Karl) Fischer, Osmin in the first production of *The Abduction*, lithograph by an unknown artist.

11. Silhouette of Caterina Cavalieri, Constanze in the first *Abduction* and Donna Elvira in the Vienna *Don Giovanni*, by Hieronymus Löschenkohl.

12. Constanze Mozart, née Weber, *c.* 1782, painted by her brother-in-law
Joseph Lange not long after her marriage.

13. Vienna, Michaelerplatz, with St Michael's church, left, and the Burgtheater, right, coloured etching by Karl Schütz, 1783.

14. Vienna, view of the Graben, looking towards the Kohlmarkt, coloured etching by Karl Schütz, 1781. Immediately on the right is the Trattnerhof, where Mozart gave subscription concerts and where he and Constanze lodged in 1784.

Den 24th: März.

Ein Clavier Concert - Begleitung. 2 violini, 2 viole, 1 flauto, 2 oboi, 2 clarinetti, 2 fagotti, 2 corni, 2 clarini, timpany e Basso.

Den 29th April.

Le Nozze di figaro. opera buffa in 4 Atti. ♦ Pezzi di Musica. 34. Attori. Signore. Storace † Laschi, mandini, Bussani, e nannina gottlieb. — Sig:ri Benucci mandini, occhely e Bussani. —

den 3th: Juny.

Ein Quartett für Clavier, violin, viola und Violoncello.

den 10th:

Ein kleines Rondò für das Clavier allein.

den 26th:

Ein Waldhorn Concert für den Leitgeb. Begleitung. 2 violini, 2 viole, 2 oboe, 2 Corni e Basso.

15. Two pages of the 'Catalogue of all my works' kept by Mozart from 1784 till his death, from spring and early summer of 1786. The five works whose 'incipits' (opening bars)

figure here are, in order, the C minor piano concerto K491, *Figaro* K492, the E flat piano quartet K493, the piano rondo in F K494, and the horn concerto K495.

16. Lorenzo Da Ponte, librettist of *Figaro*, *Don Giovanni* and *Così fan tutte*. Engraving by Michele Pekenino after a miniature by Nathaniel Rogers, *c.*1820.

17. Antonio Salieri, engraving by Johann Gottfried Scheffner, *c.* 1800.

19. Baron Gottfried van Swieten, engraving by Johann Ernst Mansfeld after J.C. Lakner, *c.* 1780. Van Swieten, diplomat, civil servant and keen amateur musician, was an important patron of Mozart, and of Haydn, the texts of whose *Creation* and *Seasons* were largely his work.

18. Joseph Haydn, painted by Thomas Hardy in 1791 during Haydn's first visit to England, not long after his last meeting with his friend Mozart.

20. The entry of the Stone Guest, from the autograph full score of *Don Giovanni*, the Act 2 finale, showing the double-bass, cello and viola prolonged beyond the rest of the orchestra in the second and fourth bars. See note on page x.

21. Set design for the graveyard scene in Act 2 of *Don Giovanni*, Mannheim, 1789, by Giulio III Quaglio.

22. Mozart, Dresden, 1789, after the silverpoint drawing by Doris
Stock (the original disappeared during the Second World War).

23. Preparations backstage for a performance of *The Magic Flute* at the Weimar court theatre, watercolour by Georg Melchior Kraus, 1794.

24. Frontispiece, rich in Masonic symbols, of the 1791 libretto of *The Magic Flute*, engraved by Mozart's fellow-mason Ignaz Alberti.

25. Papageno the bird-catcher, the role taken by Emanuel Schikaneder, etching by Alberti, from the first printed libretto of the opera. Though the example given by the densely feathered image is commonly ignored in modern productions, it explains why Monostatos thought that Papageno was an 'unusual bird', not a human being.

26. Photograph of a Maquiritare Indian of northern Brazil in the 1950s, listening to a gramophone record of Mozart's music played by the French explorer Alain Gheerbrant during an expedition to the Amazon. (See p. 15.)

superimposed in a scene of steadily mounting rhythmic tension and confusion." The Don may have a particular reason for wanting to promote confusion: it will help him lure Zerlina away unnoticed; the Teutsche or allemana, a kind of proto-waltz, which Leporello forces Masetto to dance with him, involves the couple clasping each other in a close embrace – Masetto will be physically prevented from intervening. But Mozart's metrical tour de force has also a symbolic meaning: "it demonstrates the social chaos to which libertarian egalitarianism gives rise". Giovanni is "a harbinger of chaos".

The world of the opera, Till argues, is the negative of that of *Figaro*. It is a world "in which the stable values of hierarchy and status are persistently undermined", and in which "the unyielding hierarchies of heaven and earth, optimistically abolished in *Figaro*, have in the end to be restored". Mozart being the person he was, Don Giovanni, unlike the hero of Tirso's *El burlador de Sevilla*, is not denied the possibility of repentance. The Stone Guest comes not to drag him down to hell but to offer him salvation. But he refuses it, and is duly damned. This damnation, "commonly brushed aside [by commentators] as an aberration", is "central to our understanding of the whole opera".

Yes . . . but, even while damning him, Mozart continues to respond to his magnetic appeal and enjoy every aspect of him, every moment, to the hilt. The fascination that compels the other characters, and not only Leporello, is also "central to our understanding of the whole opera". It is much more marked in Mozart's telling of the tale than in any of the sources. Da Ponte played his part; but it was the composer-dramatist who brought it so enthrallingly to life. We really have no idea if Mozart was the womanizer some legends claim he was. Luigi Bassi, the Prague Don Giovanni, told Stendhal, many years later, that he "was very popular with the ladies, in spite of his small size; [. . .] he had a most unusual face, and he could cast a spell on any woman with his eyes". But who can say whether or not he made use of it? All we know for sure is that he was devoted to his wife. Someone as highly sexed as Mozart seems to have been can, without actually being a womanizer, easily imagine himself one. The music of *Don Giovanni* clearly shows his fascination with the idea, if not with the reality.

We hear it still in the final scene, the notorious *scena ultima* which, true to the spirit of the work, follows straight after the vision of hell and the sulphurous, engulfing D minor, and which has provoked and still provokes so much disapproval and dissent. Whether or not the scene was removed when the opera was produced in Vienna in 1788 – the evidence is contradictory, though it probably was – it was part of the original conception of the work and fundamental to it; and its music is on the same exalted level and in the same style. Leaving it out may not be quite as heinous as omitting the first scene of *Hamlet* (and the offence springs from a diametrically opposite point: the *Hamlet* director rejects the supernatural, the director of Mozart's opera, impressed by the power of its supernatural strains, cannot bear to come back to earth afterwards). Nonetheless it betrays a profound misunderstanding of the work.

The parallel, in another sense, is apt. The *scena ultima* is Shakespearean. It has Shakespeare's balancing irony. The surviving characters, like Ottavio in Act 1, breathe again: they are free of that monster at last. But they are not. His fiery fingerprints are all over the last six or seven minutes of the opera. The survivors may tell each other that he's down there with Proserpine and Pluto. In fact, just as in the sextet, he is still here in spirit and they are still in thrall; the final pages, as I said above, make that clear. Anna and Ottavio, as they circle one another in a kind of ritualistic courtship dance, have not escaped. She must mourn and he must wait for a year more before her grief can be healed. Zerlina and Masetto, the least scarred, will go and have supper together; but Elvira will do the only thing left for her – retreat into a convent. Leporello will look for a less strenuous master and no doubt lead a less dangerous existence from now on, but he will certainly not find one half as fascinating. None of their lives will ever be the same again.

At the end of David Pountney's Opera North production of 1981, as they all sang the moral, a linkman stepped forward and set light to Leporello's inventory of his master's conquests. It burned cheerfully. But a moment later something made them turn round, aghast. There, looking down from the gallery above them, defiantly silhouetted against a pale sky, was the man they thought divine retribution had neatly rid them of. It is a nice conceit. At the very least the Don, maybe, is completing his supper in more interesting company, teaching Pluto to grow bigger horns and getting off with Proserpine.

When Mozart arrived in Prague, on 4 October, with Constanze, he still had a good deal of music to complete, notably the Act 2 finale and the overture but also other pieces including Masetto's aria, and most of the simple recitative. The premiere had been scheduled for the 14th, to coincide with the visit of the newly married Archduchess Maria Theresa, the Emperor's niece, and her husband Anton Clemens, Prince of Saxony. Da Ponte came on the 8th for a few days, to rehearse the performers and no doubt to work with Mozart and agree final details of the libretto; his room at the inn Zum Platteis looked straight across a narrow space to Mozart's at the Three Lions (though Mozart was often at the Duscheks' house, the Villa Bertramka in the suburbs, where some at least of the missing numbers were composed). In the event the opera was not ready in time. As Mozart explained to his friend Jaquin,

In the first place, the stage personnel here are not as clever as those in Vienna when it comes to getting up an opera of this kind in a short time. Secondly, I found on my arrival that so little had been prepared and arranged that it would have been impossible to produce it on the 14th – i.e. yesterday. So *Figaro* was performed, in a fully lighted theatre, and I myself conducted. In this connection I have a good joke to tell you. A few of the leading ladies here, and in particular one very high and mighty one, were kind enough to find it very ridiculous, unsuitable and heaven knows what else that the Princess should be entertained with a performance of *Figaro*, the "Crazy Day", as the management were pleased to call it. It never occurred to them that no opera in the world, unless it is written specially for it, can be exactly suitable for such an occasion, and that therefore it was of absolutely no consequence whether this or that opera was given, provided that it was a good opera and one the Princess didn't know – and *Figaro* at least fulfilled this last condition. In short by her persuasive tongue the ringleader brought things to such a pitch that the government forbade the impresario to produce this opera on that night. So she was triumphant! "Ho vinto," she called out one evening from her box. No doubt she never suspected that the "ho" might change to a "sono". But next day Le Noble appeared, bearing a command from His Majesty that if the new opera could not be given, *Figaro* was to be performed! My friend, if only you had seen the handsome, magnificent nose of this lady! Oh, it would have amused you as much as it did me. *Don Giovanni* has now been fixed for the 24th.

Once again it was postponed, this time because of the illness of one of the female singers. Bondini's troupe was small, so the impresario had to tread carefully. Mozart had had plenty of opportunity to get to know them – only the Ottavio, Baglioni, had been away (singing the title role in Gazzaniga's opera) when he visited Prague in January, but probably he was aware that the tenor had a good florid technique when he wrote "Il mio tesoro" for him. The others he was familiar with. Two of them, Luigi Bassi (Don Giovanni) and Felice Ponziani (Leporello), were noted for their skill as actors and improvisers. Comparison of the final libretto, printed in Prague, and the autograph score suggests that the supper-music scene was worked out with the performers in rehearsal: Leporello's remarks identifying and commenting on the three tunes that the band plays are in the score but not in the libretto. It was probably Mozart too who was responsible for the two puns which the scene contains. "Ah che piatto saporito!" – "What a tasty dish!" – says Don Giovanni. The singer who took the role of Donna Anna was called Teresa Saporiti. Mozart makes him repeat the word "saporito" three times. (Does this mean we are meant to believe that the Don did possess Anna after all?) The emphasis on the excellence of Giovanni's cook was another in-joke, inspired by the harpsichord player Jan Kritel Kuchar. Kuchar – "cook" in Czech – had made a piano reduction of *Figaro* (advertised in the *Wiener Zeitung* in June) and was busy making one for the new opera. As Daniel Heartz says, "as arranger of Mozart's two operas, Kuchar was a 'cook' in a very special sense". Mozart makes a point of emphasizing "Sì eccellente è il vostro cuoco/il cuoco mio", sung to the tune of "Non più andrai". No doubt, in addition, a good deal of adlibbing went on in the performances. Luigi Bassi later recalled that "we never sang this number the same way twice". Such practices have largely died out, though Bruno Walter said that he never knew what his Don Giovanni, Ezio Pinza, was going to do from one performance to the next: it was different every time, and always good.* (But basses, even the greatest of them, should be forbidden by law from singing the Don, a gentlemanly baritone role lighter, if anything, than the Count.)

Heartz also argues, ingeniously, that the three tunes played by the wind band were chosen partly because of the aptness of their original texts to the larger dramatic context: the one from Martín y Soler's *Una cosa rara* because it concerned the foiling of the lascivious designs of a nobleman actually called Don Giovanni; Sarti's *Fra i due litiganti* because it refers to a rival lover "going like a lamb *to the slaughter*" (which Don Giovanni will shortly do, if in anything but a lamblike manner); and "Non più andrai" because its "amorous butterfly" will soon cease "disturbing the peace of the ladies". Leporello's comment, "I know that one all too well," combined with the huge popularity of the tune, here embellished with captivating clarinet variations, must have brought the house down.

How well prepared was the opera when it finally reached performance on 29 October? The story of Mozart sitting up all night to compose the overture, kept awake by Constanze who cut him fresh pens and nudged him when he nodded off, was confirmed by Constanze herself when the Novellos visited her years later. Another account claims that the parts of the overture were handed to the players with the proverbial ink still wet, and that Mozart commented that "a good many notes fell under the desks" but it had gone well enough. Others say that that was at the dress rehearsal, not at the premiere, and Mozart wrote the overture on the night of 27–28 October, which seems more likely. In any case the opera was a success from the first. The *Prager Oberpostamtszeitung* of 3 November reported "connoisseurs and musicians" as saying that "nothing like it" had "ever been seen in Prague".

Herr Mozard conducted in person. When he entered the orchestra he was received with threefold cheers, which happened again when he left. The opera is, moreover, extremely difficult, and everyone admired the fine performance

---

* When the original version of Strauss's *Ariadne* was given at the Edinburgh Festival in 1950, Miles Malleson (Monsieur Jourdain), sitting cross-legged at the side of the stage during the opera and asking plaintively, "Aren't there going to be any bugles?", was answered from the pit by Sir Thomas Beecham with a different reply each night ("Bugles on the *Third Programme*?", "Not on this particular occasion", with a glance at the box occupied by the Queen, "They've gone to the castle for the Tattoo", etc.).

given after such a short rehearsal period. Everybody, on the stage and in the orchestra, strained every nerve to thank Mozard by rewarding him with a good performance.

Guardasoni sent Da Ponte a jubilant note: "Long live Da Ponte, long live Mozart! All managers, all musicians, should bless them. As long as they live we will never know what theatrical dearth is."

Prague's immediate enthusiasm for *Don Giovanni* is shown by the fact that it had four performances in the first six days (the fourth given as the composer's benefit), and no doubt many others during the rest of November. On the 4th Mozart wrote to Jaquin: "How I wish my friends could be here just for one evening, to share my delight. But perhaps my opera will be given in Vienna. I hope so." People, he added, were trying to persuade him to "stay on for a couple of months and write another one. But I can't accept the proposal, flattering though it is."

He was in Prague for the next ten days or so. His friends remembered the visit as a happy time. The scena for Josepha Duschek, "Bella mia fiamma", K528 – music of an intensity appropriate to a piece that came into being in the orbit of *Don Giovanni* – was composed in her summerhouse. It was said he had promised it to her but not yet delivered it, so she locked him in till he finished it, and he retorted that she would only have it if she sang it correctly at sight – which if she did, she was a formidable musician, given its audacious chromaticisms. Another anecdote recalls how, on his return to the Duscheks' from the theatre or some other function, he would drink a cup of black coffee at the Steinitz coffee house. "Sometimes the place was already closed; so Mozart would knock at the window and the landlord would make the coffee himself, which had to be very strong. [Mozart] wore a blue tailcoat with gilt buttons, nankeen [pale yellow] knee breeches and stockings, with buckled shoes."

Don Giovanni continued to draw the crowds. No wonder Guardasoni wanted another opera. But by the third week of November 1787 the travellers were back in Vienna. Perhaps Mozart should have stayed on. *Don Giovanni* was given in Vienna, as he hoped. But it would be nearly two years before he received another commission.

6

Catechisms of love

Così fan tutte

performed
x
oct 29   performed
JAN 26
1987 + 1790

In the Mozart mythology the two years between *Don Giovanni* and *myth*
Così fan tutte were the beginning of the end. By 1788 he was on the
treacherous slope that led inexorably to the tragic end of the career
that had begun so brightly seven years before. Count Arco's prophecy
– "a man's reputation here lasts only a short time" – was cruelly
vindicated. The great trilogy of symphonies composed in a few brief
weeks that summer (so the theory has it) was written for himself
alone, out of an inner necessity, with no prospect of performance and
no thought of the world – the Viennese were no longer interested.
Mozart's journey to Berlin in the spring of 1789 failed to yield the
results he had hoped for. He came back with empty pockets. His
Leipzig concert of 12 May was poorly attended. The one tangible gain
– the commission for string quartets from the King of Prussia – taxed
his powers to the utmost; he managed in the end to compose three
quartets but, in order to get started on what he called "this exhausting
labour", was reduced to using a quartet draft from a good fifteen
years earlier, so weakened had the creative impulse become; the third
quartet, K590, was not completed till more than a year later. Shortly
after the return from Berlin came the first in the long series of desperate
begging letters to his friend and fellow-mason, Michael Puchberg.
Mozart could no longer make ends meet. He was becoming a back
number.

This picture of genius spurned has had to be radically revised and *Tyson*
in many respects discarded. Alan Tyson's study of the paper-types of
Mozart's manuscripts has shown that the three symphonies, Nos. 39,
40 and 41, were not an isolated eruption of creativity but part of a
richly productive period of composition. Moreover they were intended

Don G. x Vienna 5/88 Vienna p.175

for concerts which, though they have left no record, nevertheless probably took place. By no means all musical events were announced or reported in the Viennese press. (We know of Mozart's three subscription concerts of December 1786 only from a letter of Leopold's.) Mozart in one of his letters to Michael Puchberg, probably written not long after the composition of the three symphonies, speaks of concerts that are due to begin the following week, and sends him two tickets. To this same period belong not only the great divertimento in E flat for string trio, K563, but the first two movements of the so-called "late" piano concerto, K595 in B flat, and nearly two hundred bars of the first movement of the clarinet concerto (a work completed three years later). Mozart, Tyson's researches revealed, would sometimes get quite far with a new composition before breaking off and putting it on one side for as long as several years, and turning to something else. Tyson also dated to 1788 several fragments of masses, thus showing that Mozart did not after all forsake church music between the C minor Mass of 1783 and the Requiem and the motet "Ave, verum corpus" of 1791 – a supposition that is confirmed by Joachim Daniel Preiser, an actor from the Theatre Royal in Copenhagen, who spent an afternoon with him in August 1788 and reported that Mozart "is writing church music". Preiser's account of the visit and the picture it gives of the Mozart family come from the same period as the first of the begging letters to Puchberg:

In the afternoon [of 24 August 1788] Jünger, Lange and Werner came to fetch us to go to Kapellmeister Mozardt's. There I had the happiest hour of music that has ever fallen to my lot. This small man and great master twice extemporized on a pedal pianoforte, so wonderfully, so wonderfully! that I quite lost myself. He intertwined the most difficult passages with the most lovely themes. His wife cut quill pens for the copyist [?copying orchestral parts of the new symphonies], a pupil composed, a little boy aged four walked about in the garden and sang recitatives – in short, everything that surrounded this splendid man was musical!

As for the "Prussian" quartets, far from dragging his heels (or, for that matter, disinterring a fifteen-year-old draft for the opening movement of the first of them) Mozart was so keen to get started that he began composing on the way home, buying manuscript paper for

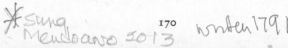

the purpose immediately after he left Berlin, in Dresden or in Prague, and writing the whole of the first quartet, K575, and part of the second, K589, on it – paper which because it had ten staves, not the normal twelve (three × four), was not ideal for quartet-writing, since it meant leaving two staves blank on each page, but which was presumably all he could find at the time. The expression "exhausting labour" is no different from the "long and laborious toil" he had earlier used to describe the composition of the quartets dedicated to Haydn – works not generally thought to betray weakened creative impulse, though they took over two years to complete. As Tyson says, "the string quartet was never an easy means of expression for the mature Mozart".

It is true that 1790 was an unproductive year, the only major works being the second and third quartets (the second completed in May, the third in June), the string quintet K593 and the Adagio and Allegro for mechanical organ, and otherwise nothing more substantial than the two Handel arrangements, *Alexander's Feast* and the *Ode for St Cecilia's Day* (though it is now thought that the imposing Kyrie in D minor, K341, long ascribed to 1781, may in fact belong to 1790). But it was followed by a year of abundant creativity, including both 1791 *The Magic Flute* and *La clemenza di Tito*, the E flat string quintet K614, the choral works already mentioned, the masonic cantata K623, the completion of the clarinet concerto, and more than thirty orchestral dances for the court. At his death, Tyson reckons, Mozart was working not only on the Requiem but also on a horn concerto, a violin sonata, a string trio, a string quintet, a mass and several other pieces. He could not have been further from the burnt-out case of legend.

It is possible that the journey to Berlin in April–June 1789, for whose apparent lack of planning Mozart has been reproached by commentators, was undertaken not with the aim of earning money and making profitable contacts but for a quite other purpose. Nicholas Till puts forward the intriguing notion that Mozart and his travelling companion and friend Count Lichnowsky, son-in-law of Mozart's patron Countess Thun, went to Berlin at the invitation of Frederick William II, as emissaries of Viennese Freemasonry, to discuss masonic matters with the king and in particular to explore the idea of Mozart's writing an opera to promote the cause. The king was a fervent believer in the esoteric Rosicrucian–Christian doctrines of the masons. Mozart, since the amalgamation of the Viennese lodges in 1786, had belonged not to True Concord, with which his former lodge, Beneficence, was merged, but to Crowned Hope, known for its Rosicrucian activities.

If that is true – and though there is no way of proving it, it cannot be disproved either – the journey was not the botched attempt it is often said to have been: Mozart had not come to fill his pockets with gulden. According to Constanze's later testimony, the King offered him a post at court, but he declined it, preferring to live in Vienna. It is documented fact that in the spring of 1792, a few months after Mozart's death, Frederick William twice tried to have *The Magic Flute* put on at the Berlin National Theatre (against the opposition of the directors) and at about the same time bought eight unpublished manuscripts from the Mozart estate. Though there was no instant opera commission in 1789, it is not impossible that (as Till surmises) the King's words planted "the seeds of the idea that eventually flowered in *Die Zauberflöte*".

Seen in this light, the journey to Berlin, and to Prague, Dresden and Leipzig, takes on a different character. Mozart's surviving letters to Constanze (some went astray, as did some of hers) don't give the impression of a tour that is going wrong nor of someone who is putting a brave face on adversity. Though he misses her and is anxious about her health and her behaviour in society, he is otherwise in high spirits:

Yesterday I went to the Neumanns, where Madame Duschek is staying, to deliver her husband's letter. Her room is on the third floor, beside the corridor, and from it you can see everyone who is coming to the house. When I arrived at the door, Herr Neumann was already there. He asked me to whom he had the honour to speak. "I shall tell you in a moment," I replied, "but please be so kind as to call Madame Duschek, so that my joke won't be spoiled." But at the same moment Madame Duschek was standing there before me – she had recognized me from the window – and said immediately, "Here is someone who is very like Mozart." Well, we were all delighted. There was a large party, with lots of ugly women, who by their charm, however, made up for their lack of beauty. [. . .] If I were to tell you all the things I do with your dear portrait, I think you would laugh. For instance, when I take it out of its case I say, "Good-day, Stanzerl – Good-day, little rascal, pussy-pussy, little turned-up nose, little bagatelle, Schluck and Druck," and when I put it away again I let it slip in very slowly, saying all the time "Nu-Nu-Nu-Nu" with the peculiar *emphasis* this word so full of meaning demands, and then just at the last, quickly, "Good night, little mouse, sleep well."

In Prague Mozart sees Guardasoni, who still wants another opera and negotiates with him for one for the autumn season. His concert in Leipzig, he admits, reaps "meagre reward" but is loudly applauded (for a programme that includes two piano concertos, K456 and K503, two unidentified symphonies, and the scenas "Ch'io mi scordi di te" and "Bella mia fiamma", sung by Madame Duschek); Mozart lets many musicians in without paying, "distributing", a report says, "free tickets to impecunious friends of music". Rochlitz's account says that Mozart "could not have been in better humour, even if the room had been crowded with paying customers"; when members of the chorus ask about free tickets and are referred by the box-office to "the Herr Kapellmeister", Mozart answers: "Oh, let them in, let them in! Who wants to be pedantic in such matters?"

In Leipzig "his fortepiano playing enchant[s] private gatherings". At Bach's church, the Thomaskirche, he gives an organ recital ("without payment") which makes the organist, Doles, exclaim that Johann Sebastian is alive again. Doles has the choir perform Bach's *Singet dem Herrn* for his benefit, which causes Mozart in his turn to say, "This is music one can learn something from!" Afterwards Doles shows him the separate voice parts of other Bach motets, and Mozart spreads them out in front of him on a table (one account says on the floor) and immerses himself in them. The story is often dismissed as apocryphal; but there is evidence that Mozart did learn from at least one Bach motet: the rising five-note figure of the fugato theme which surrounds the Armed Men's chorale in the second act of *The Magic Flute* is surely traceable to the chorale prelude "Gute Nacht, o Wesen" which forms the ninth section of *Jesu, meine Freude*, a movement whose words – the soul putting the cares and corruptions of worldly life behind it – have the same sentiment as the *Magic Flute* text.

In Dresden news of his arrival spreads so fast that a concert of his music is improvised the very next day in one of the large rooms of the Hôtel de Pologne where he and Lichnowsky are lodging, at which one of his recent trios (either K542 or K563) is played and Josepha Duschek sings arias from *Figaro* and *Don Giovanni* to Mozart's accompaniment. He is hastily added to the programme of a concert already arranged in the salon of the Electress, and during his five-day stay in Dresden plays (a newspaper reports) "in many noble and private houses, with boundless success". (In one of them, the home of Schiller's friend and musical amanuensis Christian Körner, whose idealistic view of music is similar to Mozart's, Körner's sister-in-law Doris Stock makes the famous silverpoint drawing of the composer as he improvises for the household.)

In short, he is a celebrity: perhaps more in Germany, where his operas are frequently given (*The Abduction* is being performed in Berlin while he is there), than in Austria – Mozart tells Puchberg that he expects to find more subscribers for his quintets "abroad than here"; but he is a celebrity in Austria too. Even if many Viennese consider his music self-defeatingly complicated and overwrought, few if any deny his genius. In that respect an item in a Viennese almanach commenting on his appointment as chamber composer to the court is significant: "All lovers of music will doubtless feel the most lively satisfaction at this promotion, this excellent musician having for so long been misjudged and not valued according to his merits." He is not appreciated as much as he deserves to be; but there are those who recognize this and deplore it, and some of them are men of influence. We cannot assume that when noble and merchant patronage of music declined in the late 1780s as a result of inflation and the Turkish War, Mozart was no longer invited to their palaces and houses just because the (scanty) correspondence for those years contains no mention of the fact. There is no word of the Trattners in Mozart's letters after 1785. But they did not stop being his friends. The Trattners were godparents of the Mozarts' youngest child, born in 1791.

One of his aristocratic patrons who continues to promote him is Baron van Swieten. Mozart may now give far fewer concerts on his own account (though that is not certain, given the paucity of letters compared with the mid-1780s), but he is still active in Viennese concert life, directing a series of oratorio performances sponsored by Swieten and the Society of Noblemen and arranging the scores in accordance with modern practice (for which he is no doubt paid): C. P. E. Bach's *The Resurrection and Ascension of Jesus Christ*, with a well-rehearsed orchestra of eighty-six, at Count Esterházy's and then at the Burgtheater in 1788; Handel's *Acis and Galatea* the same year; *Messiah* in 1789, and *Alexander's Feast* and *Ode for St Cecilia's Day* in 1790.

The remaining seven months of 1789, after Mozart's return from North Germany, are undeniably a difficult and often unhappy period for him and Constanze: pregnant again, she falls seriously ill (at one point he fears for her life) and has to take an expensive cure at Baden, the health resort fifteen miles south of Vienna; he is forced once more to borrow heavily from Puchberg; in November their fifth child, Anna Maria, dies within an hour of her birth; he himself is ill for several weeks. For a time he is unable to compose. Yet these months also see the completion of the first Prussian quartet and the composition of the piano sonata K576, the celestial clarinet quintet, and the last of the three Da Ponte operas, or at any rate a sizeable part of it.

Above all, there is opera. Admittedly, the promised commission for Prague fails to materialize: Guardasoni moves to Warsaw before that can happen and does not return till 1791 (when the Mozart work he stages is the opera seria *La clemenza di Tito*). But in May 1788 *Don Giovanni* is put on in Vienna, with three of the same singers who sang in *Figaro* two years before – Benucci, Bussani and Laschi – and with the blessing of the Emperor, who corresponds about it with Count Rosenberg from the tented field and keeps in touch with the progress of rehearsals (Rosenberg has evidently come round to Mozart's music – "I am pleased to see your taste is becoming reasonable," writes Joseph). The opera divides opinion but it has twelve performances that summer and a further three in the autumn and early winter.

In 1789 *Figaro* is revived, with a new Countess, Caterina Cavalieri (Constanze in the first *Abduction*), and a new Susanna, Da Ponte's mistress Adriana Ferrarese del Bene, "la Ferrarese", for whom Mozart replaces the two original arias with new ones in keeping with her style and pretensions. It is hard for us to imagine the work without

Susanna's "Deh vieni" and her enchanting "Venite, inginocchiatevi"; but the revival (on 29 August) is a success. The opera has ten further performances that year and fifteen the next. It may well have been on the strength of it that the Emperor instructed his officials to commission another Mozart/Da Ponte opera for the court theatre.

Così

Surprisingly little is known of the origins of *Così fan tutte*. We have stories but few facts. Da Ponte's *Memoirs* mention it only briefly, as "*La scola degli amanti* [The School for (male) Lovers], with music by Mozzart, a drama which holds third place among the sisters born of that most celebrated father of harmony". According to Constanze, as reported by the Novellos, Salieri began setting the libretto, then gave up, and it was passed to Mozart. Salieri did indeed make a start, composing one of the three male-voice trios that form the first scene of the opera – the one (No. 2) where Don Alfonso compares women's constancy to the mythical phoenix, which everyone talks about but no one has ever seen – and drafting another, "La mia Dorabella capace non è" (No. 1); his autograph manuscript – much revised in the case of No. 2 – is in the Austrian National Library.

This seems to suggest that Da Ponte wrote the libretto for Salieri and only handed it to Mozart when Salieri, for whatever reason, decided not to go on with it. But it is not impossible that *Così fan tutte* was in origin a Da Ponte–Mozart project, and Salieri, envious of Mozart's superiority (of which the revival of *Figaro* provided a painful reminder) and invoking his authority as director of the court opera, annexed it for his own use before renouncing it – or perhaps being forced to by the Emperor – when he had got no further than the first two numbers. Joseph II was a sick man and would have only a few months to live; but he continued to take an interest in what went on at the court theatre and, ambivalent as he was about Mozart's music, certainly did not want to lose him; Mozart, he must have been aware, was receiving offers from abroad and might be tempted to leave Vienna. Mozart's appointment as Kammer-musikus to the court in 1787 was made – an official later confirmed – "expressly to prevent an artist of such outstanding genius from being obliged to seek his livelihood abroad". Mozart's remark about "Salieri's plots, which have, however, completely failed already" (in a letter to Michael

Puchberg inviting him to a rehearsal of the opera), is often discounted, on the grounds that the Society of Musicians, of which Salieri was director, gave a public performance of Mozart's new clarinet quintet that same autumn, and because Salieri would conduct a Mozart symphony (possibly the G minor) at another of the society's concerts a year or so later, and direct several Mozart masses at the Frankfurt and Prague coronation ceremonies in 1790 and 1791. But that proves nothing. If anything, it points to the opposite conclusion. It was after all in the interests of Salieri, jealous of a gifted operatic rival, to foster that rival's reputation as a composer of non-operatic music. He could also afford, two years later, to be generous in his praise of *The Magic Flute*, a German opera performed at a suburban theatre: it was in Italian opera, at the court theatre, that Mozart was a competitor to be feared.

What part the growing enmity between Salieri and Da Ponte played – exacerbated as it was by the mutual antagonism of their mistresses, the rival sopranos Caterina Cavalieri and La Ferrarese – and whether (as Mozart's letter to Puchberg implies) Salieri continued to try to block the opera even after it was accepted, there is no means of telling. That Da Ponte originally intended it for Mozart is no more than conjecture. But the text of the opera as we have it bears the mark of Mozart's close and vigilant participation. It is not just a matter of that Mozartian hallmark, the large proportion of ensembles – greater even than in *Figaro* or *Don Giovanni* – nor of Mozart's addition of the words of the opera's title, "Così fan tutte" ("That is what all women do"), to the arioso in which Don Alfonso explains to the outraged officers the philosophy behind his stratagem (the words are not in the libretto), nor the text of the recitative before the "phoenix" trio, which is completely different from the one in the Salieri manuscript, nor his changing Despina the doctor's "Salvate amabiles, bonae puellae", in Da Ponte's text, to the dog Latin that we know. His touch is recognizable all over the drama. It was he who knew Mesmer, whose fashionable invention is caricatured in the finale of Act 1, and he, not Da Ponte, who had been to Naples and could recall its sites, referred to in the libretto, and the soft airs and silky sea of the fabled bay which his music evokes.

True, Salieri, whom Da Ponte thought unusually well read for a musician, would have appreciated the literary allusions which pepper the text: allusions to Ariosto's *Orlando furioso*, to Boccaccio, to Beaumarchais, to the sixteenth-century novelist Jacopo Sannazaro, to Ovid's *Metamorphoses* and *Ars amatoria*, to Metastasio (all concerned with the central theme of the testing of the lover's or the spouse's fidelity), which sprang from Da Ponte's passion for Italian and Latin verse; allusions to his own librettos for Martín y Soler's *Una cosa rara* and the pastoral *L'arbore di Diana*; references to other literatures too: Don Alfonso's "Arabian phoenix", and Fiordiligi's "basilisk", echo Shakespeare's *Cymbeline* as well. But Mozart, though posterity liked to picture him as a genius with no artistic interests outside music, was a keen reader and an avid playgoer. (He had seen *Cymbeline* in Salzburg in 1783, and very possibly in Vienna the year before, and he was no doubt familiar with Marivaux's *Les fausses confidences*, which was given at the Burgtheater, in German, in 1785.) Da Ponte's poetic reminiscences would not have been lost on him either. And, to an extent that Salieri could never have equalled, the libretto's web of allusion is paralleled by the music's. Mozart's score teems with quotations from other operas, his own included, and at the same time with references to itself. The quotations begin with the flute's laughing motif in the twenty-first and twenty-second bars of the overture's main, presto section, which is taken from the Act 1 trio of *Figaro*, where the cynical Basilio sings "Così fan tutte le belle". The self-references, as Daniel Heartz has demonstrated, constantly reflect and emphasize the ironies and ambiguities of the dramatic situation. Mozartian comedy is a commentary on contemporary opera, his as well as others', but none so much as this.

Così fan tutte has clear links with the favourite eighteenth-century genre of "demonstration comedy", of which Marivaux's plays were popular examples, and in which human nature, and human beings purportedly in love, are examined as though under laboratory conditions, and psychological equations are proposed and proved. The text of the opera postulates characters cut off from the real world, inhabiting an artificial and enclosed environment, an Arcadia where they give themselves to the business of love. Nothing exists outside it. The war to which the two officers are summoned is imaginary (however much Despina's identifying the disguised lovers as "Turks" or "Wallachians" may have struck topical chords in a city preoccupied with the Turkish War and in a theatre much frequented by officers). The soldiers and sailors and musicians who execute Don Alfonso's orders are shadowy figures, called into being solely to do his bidding. The sisters the young men are betrothed to come from Ferrara and are living or staying in Naples, but otherwise no information is given. They are alone (except for their maid and, in the second act, an anonymous chorus of servants), but men are free to walk in as and when they please. In this social, moral and economic vacuum Don Alfonso and his ally Despina conduct an experiment whose result is known from the beginning.

Yet, with all its artifice and its apparent unreality, Da Ponte's scenario gave Mozart the ironist and compassionate anatomist of the human heart a perfect field for his gifts. For the first time in their collaboration, however, one senses a divergence. Before, Mozart had not so much contradicted Da Ponte as enhanced him, realized him on a higher level of poetic feeling; it was a difference of degree more than of kind. The librettist may not quite have expected what the composer made of the *Don Giovanni* sextet or of the final duel between the Libertine and the Stone Guest, nor have imagined an Elvira redeemed from her folly by the beauty and sincerity of her music; but what his words provoked was an intensification, not an alteration or a transformation. They were at one. The score fulfilled the text's potential; it gave what it was music's role to give. But now there is a crack between them. Da Ponte's brilliant *Così fan tutte*, if one reads it without the music in mind, is determinedly misogynistic. This is what women are like. The poor dears can't help it – it's their nature, for them it's simply an imperative, and we have to accept the fact. If men are deluded, it's their own fault; hence the elaborate lesson that has been set up to puncture their fond illusions and educate them in the realities of life. They are very angry, understandably, but they will be the better for it in the long run.

This is different from Marivaux's *La dispute*, where the question is even-handed: which sex is more inconstant in love? With Da Ponte, the answer – women – is so obvious that it doesn't need asking. We could not be further from the revised denouement of Jane Austen's

Persuasion and Anne Elliot's sublime "All the privilege I claim for my own sex (it is not a very enviable one, you need not covet it), is that of loving longest, when existence or when hope is gone." Mozart's *Così fan tutte* is nearer in spirit to Jane Austen than to Da Ponte. His music frequently undercuts the plot and the words. Feminists are often scandalized by the work, but they might not be if they gave closer attention to the score. As so often in his operas – in *Figaro* most strikingly, but in others too – the women in *Così* feel more deeply than the men. (Even Despina, the hard-bitten serving maid so sure of her own worldliness, is shocked by the revelation of male trickery.) Mozart's music, even as it mocks them, loves them. In the duet at the beginning of the Act 1 finale the flutes and bassoons may chuckle knowingly, but at the same time the sisters' distress and confusion of mind is conveyed with touching sympathy. The long allegro section which follows, beginning with the entry of the "Albanians" brandishing their phials of arsenic and ending with the arrival of Despina dressed as a doctor and armed with her Mesmer apparatus – dramatic invention as fine as anything in the great finales of *Figaro* and *Don Giovanni* – is similarly poised. Utterly farcical the situation may be; but Mozart lavishes on it some of his strangest and most original music. The passage where the Albanians lie "dying" on the ground and the ladies touch their foreheads and feel their pulses sounds a new note, comic but mysterious, absurd yet almost exotically beautiful; as Rosen says, "the surprising combination of baroque contrapuntal movement and the thinnest of *opera buffa* textures [. . .] holds the finest of balances between seriousness and comedy". Mozart continually dives below the surface, to come up with yet more contradictory meanings. The conventional images of the farewell trio, "Soave sia il vento", as Fiordiligi and Dorabella, with Don Alfonso, watch the boat disappearing into the distance, are transformed by the luminous sounds and soft pulsations of voices and orchestra into a spellbound beauty that lifts the work into a different realm of being. A moment later, Don Alfonso, alone, explodes in derision, and Mozart faithfully portrays it in a testy D minor, with stamping bass, syncopated first-violin arpeggios and irritable second-violin figurations. But the tenderness of the trio still hangs on the air, its implications not forgotten.

Much later, the musical depiction of Fiordiligi's growing love for

Ferrando and of Ferrando's response to it practically turns the drama on its head. This, the music surely makes clear beyond irony, is no longer play-acting by either of them; if there is irony in their recall of the music to which Ferrando celebrated his love for Dorabella in the opening scene of the opera, it is a heartbreaking irony. And though the final ensemble matches, outwardly, the moralizing sentiments of the text, Mozart interrupts the allegro molto at several points by enigmatic pauses.

In a recent production by English National Opera these pauses were seized on by the director Samuel West and the conductor Mark Wigglesworth and prolonged so as to show the lovers, traumatized by what they have been subjected to, unable to go on. Don Alfonso, self-appointed principal of his school for lovers, has to wave them on impatiently and then, the second time, stamp his foot on the next downbeat to make them continue. That was by no means the first production to end the opera with Alfonso's clever experiment in ruins and the lovers cruelly disoriented. As is often pointed out, there is absolutely no sanction in the libretto or even, except indirectly, in the music for such an interpretation. But it is a measure of the ambiguity of Mozart's score that for many listeners the opera, by the end, refuses to be confined within its neatly ordered category: the drama has burst its bounds. There are more things in *Così fan tutte* than are dreamt of in Da Ponte's philosophy.

For a work that is outwardly so clear it is remarkable how differently it has been thought of – by its admirers, that is, not by those who once thought of it only with distaste. The following is a random sample of opinions.

Così fan tutte is the best of all Da Ponte's librettos and the most exquisite work of art among Mozart's operas. It is as perfect a libretto as any composer could desire, though no composer but Mozart could ever do it justice. [. . .] It is artificial comedy of the best, and the unity of time helps to heighten the artificiality which makes its charm. Don Alfonso is a real person [. . .]; Despina too has a certain reality [. . .] But the four lovers are utterly unreal; they are more like marionettes than human beings. Yet, as the opera develops, we see them explore an amazingly wide range of emotions; indeed, it is only because they are marionettes that they are capable of such emotions, for they are themselves playing parts all the time. *Così fan tutte* is the apotheosis of insincerity – the only moment when anybody speaks the truth is when Don Alfonso utters the statement which forms the title of the opera. [. . .] Whether the ladies pair off with their original lovers or their new ones is not clear from the libretto, but [. . .] it will not make any difference to speak of. (Edward J. Dent)

This is not a pleasant little comedy of intrigue but great theatre, forthright and provocative, diametrically opposed to all the little buffo operas that present the illusion of an ideal world where everything returns to normal at the end. (Volkmar Braunbehrens)

Da Ponte poked fun at the emotions and situations and sentiments of serious opera; and Mozart (much as he loved *opera seria*) was delighted to further his librettist's designs with clever musical parody. As a result [the opera] emerges as an uneasy and unsettlingly mixed artistic experience, in which some of the truest and tenderest music Mozart ever wrote coexists with such dangerously empty pieces as the allegro of "Come scoglio" [. . .] or the (for Mozart) merely *routinier* funny music of the Act One finale, so empty and meaningless when compared with the Act Two finale of *Figaro*. (Brian Trowell)

"Mozart [said Stendhal], with his overwhelmingly sensitive nature, has transformed into real persons the superficial inclinations which amuse the easygoing inhabitants of Aguas Frescas in Beaumarchais." Stendhal is right. Mozart made the same transformation in *Così fan tutte*: where the libretto suggests irony, he offers us deep feeling; where the story might be expected to leave the audience chuckling drily, we experience as deep an emotion as music is able to give. (Erik Smith)

A current of violence and unpredictability begins to wrinkle the sunlit surface almost as soon as the conductor raises his baton. We should be warned that what is to follow is [. . .] a tragicomedy in which disaster is only narrowly averted, perhaps not averted at all [. . .] what is averted is not the unhappy ending but the happy one. It is, rather, a comitragedy. (Germaine Greer)

The opera is a bitter-sweet tale of lost innocence. [...] The true moral experiment of *Così fan tutte* is conducted beyond the blinkered gaze of Don Alfonso (and perhaps, by implication, of Da Ponte). (Nicholas Till)

Romantic critics dismissed *Così fan tutte* as an amoral clinical experiment, rigged by the heartless scientist Don Alfonso aided by his venal laboratory assistant, Despina. [...] [But] Don Alfonso is an "old philosopher", not a scientist, and one need only put oneself into the frame of the Josephinian Enlightenment to realize that he was a force working for good and truth – like Sarastro, who also used rather harsh teaching devices. Ferrando and Guglielmo [...] need to be cured of their ridiculous notions about love just as much as their shallow and stagestruck sweethearts [...]. Don Alfonso's "School of Lovers" is thus compulsory for both sexes, and this is a major difference with *Figaro*, where only the men need to be taught a lesson. [...] Callow youths have to be put to the test and come to know themselves before they are worthy or capable of true love. (Daniel Heartz)

Yet Heartz, as though exemplifying the uncertainty the opera engenders, can also point out that "what Fiordiligi's gradual melodic symbiosis with Ferrando" throughout the opera tells us is that they were destined to become lovers from the beginning:

No wonder Mozart chose this very same melodic figure for the oboe solo at the beginning of the overture: it was his way of saying that romantic, idealistic love figures in the opera just as importantly as the schooling of lovers, no matter what Da Ponte wanted.

It is not surprising that stage productions of an opera superficially so simple but in reality (if one can use the word) so elusive differ so widely; I am thinking not of those which come with ready-made theories and impose them on the work but of those that illuminate it by drawing their ideas from within its multiple layers of meaning. Each, if it is well done, can seem right. But, in one, Don Alfonso will be a shrewd Rousseauist counsellor wisely and humanely leading his ignorant young charges away from their dangerous illusions, in another a blinkered cynic bent on enforcing his limited and offensive convictions on his unfortunate quartet of guinea-pigs, in another a jovial clubman revelling in every moment of the intrigue.

We love *Così fan tutte* in different ways and see different things in it.

It is also an opera one can have different ideas about at different times in one's life. I used to think the enigma of *Così* could be quite easily and simply resolved. My theory was a reaction to the highly mannered style of production then fashionable, in which the story of the two young officers who for a bet pretend to go off to war and return in disguise to seduce each other's fiancées was pictured as a mere diversion, a beautiful game to take us out of life's neuroses and imperfections; the characters going through their preordained motions were so many figures on a glorified musical box, for which Mozart had devised the most exquisite sounds, playfully to mock their puppet passions. Such an interpretation simply inverted the nineteenth-century view; it relished the work for the very thing our ancestors detested, its artificiality – whereas the farcical trappings of the plot, the symmetry, the absurd disguises, the limitation of the action to a single day, were no more than a convention within which human psychology was observed as penetratingly and ironically, and human situations developed that were as true to life, as in *Figaro* or *Don Giovanni*. Dent's statement that it would "not make any difference to speak of" how the couples pair off at the end was manifestly untrue. The real irony was that they failed to acknowledge the truth which the play-acting had unwittingly revealed. For what was Mozart saying but that the false situation, in which the officers, fantastically disguised, made love to each other's women, was the true one and the unreality was in the original pairings? Under the influence of their assumed personalities Guglielmo and Ferrando became fully realized people. Before, and after, they were indeed puppets, hardly differentiated, singing shoulder to shoulder in thirds and sixths (a symbolism that was underlined when the rarely heard Act 1 duettino was included). In the "false" situation, on the other hand, each expressed his nature – the one down-to-earth, quick-witted, sensual, egotistical, the other romantic, idealistic, a dreamer – and each found his real partner. Their self-discovery worked a similar change in the two sisters: Dorabella and Fiordiligi, too, developed into the women they never were when they sat and sighed, also in thirds and sixths, over the portraits of their gilded imaginary lovers. Between the parodied indignation of Fiordiligi's "Come scoglio", with its pompous dotted notes and Handelian paradings up and down the scale, and the genuine distress and passion of her second-act aria (whose extravagant vocal leaps were no longer merely parodistic) was the difference between sham and reality, a green girl and a woman of deep feeling. So with Dorabella's arias: the first protested too much, the second was the joyous expression of one who had discovered her true nature. It was no accident that the most heartfelt music in the opera occurred at the point where cynicism was supposed to achieve its greatest triumph, the scene where Ferrando finally broke down Fiordiligi's resistance. Don Alfonso, the seaside Mephistopheles, had conjured a situation he could neither control nor comprehend.

This no doubt partial argument (Ferrando and Guglielmo are clearly differentiated, from the very opening scene) was influenced by a production staged at Aachen in the late 1950s by the German director Georg Philip. The production had the couples returning to their original pairings, but only after experiences whose genuineness should have showed them the truth: it was a denouement, Philip said, that "would lead straight to the divorce courts". The idea was presented in more subtle form by Anthony Besch's perceptive Scottish Opera production in the 60s. In John Stoddart's designs the sterile white of the opening scenes became gradually suffused with warmth as the opera proceeded, only to be drained of colour again at the end. Profoundly persuasive though it was, however, it was a suggestion, not a statement. That is the most we can hope for. Così fan tutte eternally eludes generalization.

It was this fathomless ambiguity of gesture and meaning, as much as its immoral plot and the unthinkability of the divine Mozart being associated with it, that made the work so problematic for nineteenth-century taste. *Don Giovanni* too posed grave problems of morals. But at least the hero-villain got his just deserts. And its other problem, the mixture of genres, could be easily accommodated to Romantic values. Romanticism, regarding contrast as the lifeblood of art, relished Mozart's juxtaposition of the sublime and the grotesque. A number like the graveyard duet presented no difficulty to minds which admired the gravedigger's scene in *Hamlet* and which could accept the even more bizarre contradictions of Hamlet's dialogue with the Ghost in the cellarage ("Swear!" "Well said, old mole! Can'st work i'the earth so fast?"). But the ambiguities of *Così* bit too deep even for Romanticism. In an obvious sense it was an un-Romantic, even a profoundly anti-Romantic work. Quite apart from its plot and the dedicated life-illusion-destroying philosophy of Don Alfonso which, outwardly at least, carried the day, the music went about its debunking task with a most distressing energy.

It should shock us too. Dorabella's extravagant recitative in Act 1 apes the musical language both of Ilia's poignant utterances in *Idomeneo* and of Elvira's moving "In quali eccessi" in Act 2 of the Vienna *Don Giovanni*: there are the same or similar anguished gestures, the same sighs. It is the context that has changed. Or listen to the accompanied recitative for the disguised officers which provokes Fiordiligi's first outburst. The incisive melodic lines and pungent harmony have a cynical verve and at the same time a hint of genuine sexual threat that are breathtaking. It is a parody of passion so vivid that even at this early and still uncomplicated stage of the intrigue we are caught unawares by the intensity of it and already begin to doubt how much is appearance and how much reality. Parody is present in the two earlier Mozart–Da Ponte operas. But here it is central, and the effect is continually to throw us into uncertainty as to what is actually meant.

Interestingly, side by side with the nineteenth century's rejection of *Così fan tutte* as a serious work of art, its music had a marked influence on Mozart's operatic successors. Moral disapproval did not prevent Beethoven from borrowing from it: Leonore's "Ich folg' dem innern Triebe" in *Fidelio* shares with Fiordiligi's "Per pietà" the key of E major, the obbligato horns, the proud arpeggios and the huge downward leap from a high G sharp, as well as the exalted sentiments. It is as if Beethoven could not ignore such music, had to save it by reincarnating it in a worthy setting. Echoes of *Così* turn up in many others operas: in Rossini's *Comte Ory*, in Meyerbeer's *Crociato in Egitto*, in Liszt's *Don Sanche*. Weber borrowed the ominous, obsessive rhythmic figure of Max's scena in *Der Freischütz* from the Act 1 finale of *Così*, and clearly had the beautiful canon of the second-act finale fresh in his mind when he wrote the trio in the same key in Act 2 (where Despina's music in the denouement of Mozart's opera is also recalled). Berlioz took the violins' rhythmic pulsations and the wailing woodwind octaves of Dorabella's mock-heroic "Smanie implacabili" and, like Beethoven, transforming them to a genuinely heroic context, used them in *Les Troyens* to express the despair of Cassandra as fate closes its grip on Troy. Mendelssohn reproduced in his *Midsummer Night's Dream* overture the soft, mysterious dissonant harmony near the end of the trio "Soave sia il vento", where the music hangs for a moment in throbbing suspense.

As in much of Mozart's most beautiful music, that sudden harmonic darkening creates an unsuspected sense of unease; it opens up for an instant, in the midst of the serenities of a summer's day magically evoked, another world of reality where things are not as we imagined. Yet it was this trio and one or two other movements such as the serenade in Act 2 that provided admirers of the work with a way out of their discomfort by enabling them, as they thought, to remove it on to an ideal, timeless plane of existence where a golden idyll is enacted for our pure enjoyment, and laughter "gives delight and hurts not". The French historian Hippolyte Taine was the leading exponent of this evasive if understandable attitude. His interpretation was echoed by Beecham (the first British conductor to perform the work unadapted and uncut) when he described *Così fan tutte* as "a long summer day spent in a cloudless land by a Southern sea [. . .] its motto might be that of Hazlitt's sundial: 'Horas non numero nisi serenas' – 'I count only the hours that are serene.'"

We, with our no doubt superior understanding, may marvel that so misguided a view could be seriously entertained. For us *Così fan tutte*, with all its charm, is an unconsoling work. There is no character with whom an audience can comfortably identify. It leaves all the main questions unanswered. What have the lovers really learnt about each other or themselves? Which feelings, if any, were real? How deeply are they changed? Do they go back to their first lovers? ("Marry them," Don Alfonso says. Yet the wedding Despina immediately sets up is the opposite of what he meant.) The logic of the text suggests that they do go back, but nothing is specified. The end of the opera, we cannot help feeling, is not an end at all.

This deliberate incompleteness, this refusal to tie everything up in a neat solution which settles all problems for ever after, is of the essence of *Così*, whatever Da Ponte's original intentions were and whatever the final ensemble may say. The most artificial of all operas is also – as Mozart has composed it – one of the truest to life. It exploits extreme convention in an unconventional way. Disguise, the archetypal machinery of comic opera and pantomime, becomes a principle which is used to explore, with Shakespearean curiosity, the difference between appearance and reality. And it is not just the characters on stage whom the unanswered questions are addressed to but the audience watching them. *Così fan tutte* has implications far beyond the "School for Lovers" and the "All women do it" of its titles. It speaks, existentially, of the randomness of life, the fickleness of affection, the brevity of happiness. Continually stimulating though it is, it is not a work that sends you out of the theatre in a glow of contentment with the world.

How then to account for its great popularity, a popularity that now rivals or even exceeds that of *Figaro*? The change in its status is part of the general acceptance of Mozart, the willingness to let him be as he is in all his Protean diversity. But one particular factor, obviously, has been the disappearance of many of the moral attitudes and prejudices which used to militate against it. (Whereas the Victorians thought it implausible that the girls should give in so soon, we are more likely to be surprised at their not doing so sooner.) Another is the revolution brought about by psychology and the new attitude to and interest in the complexities of human personality that have resulted from it. Till then, *Così* had been at least partly impenetrable. Science found out by enquiry what art understood by instinct. Perhaps more than anything, though, the cause is the simple if circular one, of its being more appreciated because it is more often performed. The accumulated effect has been to enable us to get to know thoroughly a score which in richness, aptness and individuality of invention is the equal of any Mozart wrote but which perhaps reveals itself less immediately. No great Mozart opera is quickly mastered, however dazzling the first moment of discovery; but none takes so much knowing as *Così*. Partly this is because of its terse economy of composition, which contains many more riches than are at first apparent, but also because of its dual nature – that duality which reflects the ambiguity at its core. It has us continually in two minds. It is entirely typical of *Così fan tutte* and its unrelenting irony that in the most sincere and heartfelt aria in the work, Fiordiligi's "Per pietà", the singer's avowals of fidelity should be shadowed by those time-honoured emblems of cuckoldry, horns, at their most rampant.

The opera's duality is expressed, among other things, in the systematic contrast of different kinds of orchestral texture which runs through the score. On the one hand, the smooth, mellifluous sonority of clarinets, horns, muted violins, and women's voices entwined in long, lingering phrases full of half-suppressed longing: nothing in music is more blissfully sensuous, more meltingly beautiful as sheer sound than the trio "Soave sia il vento", the two quintets of farewell, Ferrando's "Un'aura amorosa", the duet in which the sisters choose their men, the serenade, the duet where Dorabella surrenders to Guglielmo. On the other hand, the extraordinary asperity and astringency of texture in other scenes or parts of scenes.

Each of the great Mozart operas is scored with such resourcefulness and such mastery of colour used for dramatic ends that it is pointless to single out the orchestration of one at the expense of the others. In *Così* we may note the prominence of the bassoon, as a kind of droll, sceptical questioner of high-flown sentiments, and the even-for-Mozart unusually important role of the violas, whose long, sustained lines amid the animation of the rest of the orchestra seem to speak of a different world of feeling. But what is particularly notable is the lean, wry, sharp-eyed sound that is associated with Don Alfonso's stratagem. It does not specifically belong to Alfonso himself (he has his own characteristic music, of whimsically shaped phrase-lengths and brusque, sometimes rasping harmonies). Rather, it occurs at moments when the mechanics of pretence are most fully in operation or feelings are being openly mocked; and it is summed up, in instrumental terms, in the replacement of horns, as the normal brass members of the orchestral ensemble, by the keener-edged sound of trumpets. In no other opera of Mozart's do trumpets play so large a part. It is a remarkable fact that in no fewer than eight numbers or sections of the work – nine, if we count the elaborate aria that Mozart wrote for Guglielmo in Act 1 and later discarded – trumpets take the role conventionally played by horns (and in four of them trumpets without drums, as independent voices): the C major trio in scene 1, the march, the sextet, Fiordiligi's first aria, the passage in the Act 1 finale where Ferrando and Guglielmo pretend to drink poison, the one where, on being restored to life by Despina's magnet, they mistake the sisters for goddesses, the quartet in Act 2 in which Don Alfonso and Despina formally introduce the new lovers to each other, and the allegro in E flat in the Act 2 finale, where Ferrando and Guglielmo feign anger at the discovery of the marriage contract. I cannot think of another major orchestral piece from that period, by Mozart or anyone else, that is scored in this way.

It is also significant that this leaner, sparer sound is much less in evidence in the second act, where what started as a jape has begun to turn unexpectedly serious. We sense the change from the first scene of the act. Not only is the sisters' "Prenderò quel brunettino" quite different from their opening duet in Act 1, more individual, more genuinely playful, arousing in us both pleasure and pity: Despina's aria, "Una donna a quindici anni", beginning with a lovely casual suavity, whereas her "In uomini, in soldati" in Act 1 was perky and spiky, has caught the new relaxed atmosphere. (Dorabella's Act 2 aria, in its turn, reflects the influence of Despina and her teaching, with its carefree 6/8 metre and teasing pauses, though the prominent clarinets preserve the class divide.) But the scoring of those eight movements is enough of itself to refute the summer-idyll interpretation of the work. The sound is symptomatic. *Così fan tutte* has rightly been called "a deadly experiment in human nature".

And yet ... The locale of the opera may be a laboratory where human emotion is probed and personal identity questioned; but at the same time it is a dream place, a sea-coast "full of sounds and sweet airs". There is, after all, an idyllic aspect to *Così*. The cloudless sky school of criticism was wrong in seeing the work solely or largely in those terms, but it was not wrong in responding to the unique beauty that laps these strange, disturbing happenings. In this opera Arcadian beauty and the clinical investigation of human frailty coexist. *Così fan tutte* breathes a Cytherean air. Its deadly experiment is carried on in an atmosphere like the August afternoon evoked by John Cowper Powys in *Weymouth Sands*, shining with "a marvellous heathen glamour that seemed to take it out of time altogether and lift it into some ideal region of everlasting holiday, where the burden of human toil and the weight of human responsibility no more lay heavy upon the heart".

It is also an extremely amusing work. I have never forgotten the zest of the great Mariano Stabile's performance as Don Alfonso at Edinburgh in 1948, the immense chuckling glee with which he advanced across the stage, lace-wreathed hands thrust forward, dewlap wobbling, to take his position behind the screen and survey through quivering lorgnette the latest move in the game. He was responding to something that is there in the music, along with the cruelty and the heartbreak – its enjoyment of absurdity, its sheer high spirits. There has never been a composer who knows how to make us laugh as Mozart does, not only through comic situations expressed in apt music but through music itself, and Così is no different in this respect. Don Alfonso's mock-tragic announcement of calamity, Despina dressed as doctor and notary, the officers twitching rhythmically to the pull of the magnet, the endless comic asides, are as funny as anything in the other operas.

Does all this mean that Così fan tutte is too many different things to be a satisfactory whole? Does it follow that "the most exquisite work of art among Mozart's operas" is, in fact, flawed by its dual if not triple nature, by the "crack" between what Da Ponte provided and what Mozart did with it? Did Mozart dislocate the drama irretrievably when he was lured into making Fiordiligi's love for Ferrando and Ferrando's response to it – an affinity hinted at from the beginning – the central moral truth of the opera, an imperative from which, emotionally speaking, there is no going back, but which the exigencies of the plot insist on brutally reversing? If we are honest, must we concede that, in Joseph Kerman's words, "the confusion is in the piece as well as in the minds of the audience"? The volte-face of the ending, "witty enough in Da Ponte's scheme", is in Mozart's "simply an anticlimax", and actually "immoral", even unbearable at face value, as "emotion is eradicated in Lorenzo da Ponte's final jest" as though it had never been, and "Fiordiligi's experience goes up in smoke as she turns blankly back to Guglielmo".

There are times when I feel forced to agree – in theory, at any rate – and to seek solace in those productions which either maintain the new pairings (in defiance of the libretto and Don Alfonso) or at least conclude by showing the four lovers in helpless emotional disarray. Yet, as Kerman also says, the composer is the dramatist. In Così fan *tutte*, as in all great operas, the music that the words generated is the drama; the libretto is subsumed in it. Perhaps that is something easier to say than to prove; the discrepancies pointed out by hard-nosed commentators remain. But at other times the music seems miraculously to resolve all contradictions and to transcend, in a way that can only be felt, not put into words, the defects in the drama that analysis is obliged to identify. A profound sense of balance is one of the qualities by which Mozart, among music-dramatists, comes nearest to Shakespeare. By the power of his music he can reconcile opposites, or rather hold them in equipoise. Fiordiligi's experience is still there, uncontradicted by Da Ponte's volte-face. What happens afterwards, when the curtain has fallen, is not relevant. And if Mozart, while creating his Watteau-like radiance, is able, simultaneously, to conduct an examination of the human personality which leaves us disoriented and unsure of everything, such mysteries are at the centre of his art. He always refuses to be pinned down, but nowhere more than in his last Italian comedy. We cannot explain it; we can only recognize the power of *Così fan tutte* to perplex as well as enchant.

The opera was rehearsed at the Burgtheater during January 1790 and given for the first time on the 26th (with Haydn in the audience), to a packed house – the biggest recorded in the theatre's archives for that season. Four more well-attended performances followed in the next couple of weeks. Mozart, who directed from the keyboard, had a good cast, whose capabilities and styles he knew well. His Don Alfonso, Francesco Bussani, an excellent actor-singer, had doubled Bartolo and Antonio in the original *Figaro* and Masetto and the Commendatore in the Vienna *Don Giovanni*. Guglielmo was the great Benucci; his comic genius, which had shone as Figaro and the Vienna Leporello, had splendid scope in the two arias, the one in the first act where Guglielmo enumerates the Albanians' charms (culminating in their superb moustaches, "triumphs of manliness, the plumage of love"), and the long and brilliantly varied attack on feminine wiles and caprices in Act 2, "Donne mie, la fate a tanti", with its repeated "ma" and "perchè" and "a tanti e tanti e tanti", a gift for a clever comedian. The tenor, Vincenzo Calvesi, who had been singing at the Burgtheater since 1785, was renowned for the fluency and attractiveness of his voice, qualities which no doubt like those of Adamberger – Belmonte in *The Abduction* eight years before – inspired the lyrical music Mozart wrote for Ferrando: Ferrando's ardent, idealistic nature is suggested even before he sings his A major aria, "Un'aura amorosa", indeed from the opening scene, and again in the first quintet, where his vocal line follows the flowing phrases of the ladies rather than the clipped dotted rhythms of the other men's. Adriana Ferrarese, Fiordiligi, had sung Susanna in the recent revival of *Figaro*, so Mozart was familiar with her strengths, which included agility and a powerful lower register. The Dorabella, Louise Villeneuve, who like La Ferrarese came from the northern Italian town of Ferrara (as, inevitably, do the sisters in Da Ponte's libretto), had only been singing in Vienna since 1788, but Mozart had been able to test her abilities in three arias that he composed for insertion in operas by Martín y Soler and Cimarosa. The sixth and last member of the cast, Dorotea Bussani, Francesco's wife, who took the role of Despina, had sung Cherubino in the original *Figaro* in 1786.

It looks as if the opera won the approval of the Burgtheater public not only by the wit of its text and the humour and suggestiveness of its situations, but also by the tunefulness of a score which, despite all its sophistication and subtlety and its intricate web of cross-references, appeared less complicated and challenging, more approachable, than *Don Giovanni*. Count Zinzendorf, the music-loving government official whose diary entries generally show him rather bored when a piece of Mozart's comes his way, decided that the music was "charming" and the subject "rather amusing"; he was at the theatre every night. *Così fan tutte* seemed set to run for weeks, when the death of the Emperor, on 20 February, brought it to an abrupt halt.

7

Mozart the visionary

The Magic Flute

Joseph II may not have been an ideal patron for Mozart or an unequivocal admirer, but he had recognized his worth and taken a fatherly, or at least avuncular, interest in his career. He respected his music, even if he found it a bit above him and had to acknowledge that it was "too strong meat for the teeth of my Viennese" (as he is said to have remarked of *Don Giovanni*). It was his doing that *The Abduction*, *Figaro* and *Così fan tutte* were commissioned for the court theatre and *Don Giovanni* put on there not long after its Prague premiere, and his doing that Mozart was appointed Kammer-musikus on the death of Gluck.

All that now changed, or most of it. For the first few months of his reign the new emperor, Leopold II, was too busy taking steps to calm the seething unrest of his kingdoms to bother with music. It was September before he set foot in the Burgtheater. But in any case Leopold was not a man of the theatre as his brother Joseph had been. He and the Empress Maria Luisa favoured opera seria, but were hardly passionate about it. Music, for the moment at least, was not a priority. There had, naturally, to be changes. In due course Count Rosenberg would be replaced as director of the court theatres by Count Ugarte, Da Ponte himself would be dismissed, and even Salieri, Joseph's admired protégé, obliged to make way temporarily for Cimarosa. Though Mozart's court appointment was allowed to stand, there would be no more commissions.

At first he had been optimistic about his prospects under the new regime. Leopold knew him, after all, and could not have forgotten him: Mozart had played to him as a boy of six, in Vienna, and again, as a teenager, in Florence, by which time Leopold was Grand Duke of Tuscany, in the early days of what came to be regarded as an impeccably enlightened rule. Furthermore, one of the many decrees rescinded by Leopold concerned the performance of orchestras in church, restricted under the puritanical Joseph. Mozart saw an opening. With van Swieten's encouragement he petitioned for the post of second court kapellmeister, with responsibility for church music (it was not, he pointed out, a speciality of Salieri's). At the same time he offered himself as keyboard instructor to the royal family.

Nothing came of either démarche. Leopold and his consort do not seem to have liked Mozart's music (an official report refers to their prejudice and even their "strong aversion" to La clemenza di Tito). From now on his function at court was limited to providing dance music for the lavish balls given in the Redoutensaal during Carnival and on saints' days. Otherwise he was ignored. Figaro was still in the repertory but Così, though it was revived for a few performances when the theatres reopened, never regained its impetus. When the King and Queen of Naples visited Vienna in September Mozart was not invited to play for them, as he would certainly have been if Joseph had been alive. Nor was he assigned the smallest role in Leopold's coronation as Holy Roman Emperor in Frankfurt that autumn; he went there not as a member of the delegation of court musicians led by Salieri but on his own initiative, in the hope – vain, as it turned out – of attracting the Emperor's attention. It was in Munich, at the Elector Carl Theodor's command, that he finally got to play to the King and Queen of Naples. "What a credit to the Viennese Court that the king has to hear me in a foreign country!" was Mozart's sarcastic comment.

Though this second German tour seems not to have been particularly, or even at all, profitable, it again showed him how highly regarded he was outside Vienna. It was not just old friends like the Cannabichs and the Wendlings who welcomed him: altogether he was "made a great fuss of". His last letter before his return to Vienna talks of coming back to Germany next summer, this time with Constanze, so that she can try the effect of other waters on her health but also presumably with some unnamed musical project or projects in mind. The idea of his leaving Vienna is now in the air. There are so few practical, professional arguments for staying. Composing has practically shrunk to providing minuets and German dances for the court, writing the occasional piece for mechanical organ or glass harmonica and the odd chamber work, and bringing Handel up to date for Viennese taste. Apart from the four performances of *Così* in the summer of 1790 (at least one of which is conducted by Mozart), his sole musical activities to have left a trace are quartet and quintet sessions at home or at friends'. One of them, if old Abbé Stadler's recollection is correct, involves Haydn and Johann Tost (former leader of the second violins in the orchestra at Eszterháza); they play Mozart's three string quintets, K515, K516 and K593, Mozart and Haydn alternating the two viola parts.

Haydn was in Vienna that December, the month when Mozart entered K593 in his thematic catalogue. The death of his employer Prince Nicolaus Esterházy in September had left him free to travel. The London impresario Johann Peter Salomon arrived in November, apparently with the intention of engaging both Haydn and Mozart. According to one report it was agreed between them that Haydn should go to London first and Mozart should follow a year later. Haydn and Salomon set off on 15 December, after a "merry meal" with Mozart.

Would Mozart have gone had he lived? Salomon's approach was not the first. As we have seen, the possibility of moving to London had been raised as early as 1787, when Thomas Attwood and the Storaces were encouraging him to try his luck there and the newspapers carried reports to that effect. Though he didn't go, the idea simmered on. The music publisher John Bland, who was in Austria in 1789, made contact with him and may well have tried to lure him to England. On his return from Germany that November Mozart found a letter from another London impresario, Robert May O'Reilly, who on learning "through a person attached to H.R.H. the Prince of Wales" (i.e. Attwood) of Mozart's "desire to undertake a journey to England" offered to commission him to compose two operas for the coming Italian season for the large fee of three hundred pounds, with the option of also writing "for the professional concerts or any other concert-hall with the exception only of other theatres". Salomon's terms were no doubt equally good. Mozart, after another year of financial strain (with further calls on Puchberg's generosity), due partly to Constanze's continued illnesses and many weeks of expensive treatment at Baden, had recently succeeded in negotiating a substantial loan, and the family had moved to a commodious first-floor apartment in the Rauhensteingasse, not far from the Kärntnertor, the south-western gate of the city. Nevertheless he might well have taken up one or other of the offers but for Constanze's poor health – the thought of going without her was more than he could bear. Though he loved Vienna and felt thoroughly at home there and, other things being equal, had no wish to leave, there was less and less to keep him.

Several sources suggest he was ready for a move. In January 1791 he advertised his chamber organ for sale in the *Wiener Zeitung*. In the spring, one of a group of writers interested in getting him to compose an opera on *The Tempest* reported that he was "in very straitened circumstances and [supporting] himself by teaching". As late as September 1791, when his talents and energies were fully occupied with *The Magic Flute* and *La clemenza di Tito*, Countess Thun's son-in-law, the Russian diplomat Count Rasumovsky, writing to Prince Potemkin, could describe Mozart as "somewhat discontented here" and quite possibly "disposed to undertake such a journey" (to St Petersburg) with a view to being employed by the Prince.

A month later Potemkin was dead; we have no means of knowing whether Mozart was seriously considering it. But it is no accident that his last Viennese opera is written not for the court but for a suburban company, beyond the jurisdiction of the Hofburg. Da Ponte's dismissal in March and his departure in April severs Mozart's links with the imperial theatre. The Emperor thinks of him, if he thinks of him at all, as the fellow who supplies his dance music. The thirty-five minuets, Teutsche and contredanses that pour from his pen in the early months of 1791 – K599, 600, 601, 602, 603, 604, 605, 607, 610, 611 – are much more than hackwork; they are often bizarre, experimental, with colours and textures not found elsewhere in Mozart, as if he is not so much not troubling to take the job seriously as chancing his arm and trying something quite new without caring what people think (in fact they are very popular and published in large numbers). But this is hardly what he came into the world to do. His orchestral music is heard occasionally, but apparently not in concerts put on by him: a piano concerto, perhaps the B flat, K595, with Mozart as soloist, in Jahn the restaurateur's rooms (a few yards from Mozart's house) on 4 March, at a concert given by the clarinettist Joseph Beer; K595 also, possibly, at a concert in the Auersperg Palace on 9 January, when the pianist was Barbara Ployer; and a symphony, very probably the G minor K550, at the Society of Musicians' Burgtheater concert on 16 April, repeated next day. About the same time Mozart petitions the Vienna City Council, successfully, for the post of assistant to the kapellmeister of St Stephen's Cathedral, Leopold Hoffmann, who is in poor health; the post is unpaid but the holder is guaranteed the (salaried) kapellmeistership when it falls vacant. A new outlet for his creative powers is opening. But Mozart the dramatist must go outside the city walls.

We have several eyewitness descriptions from around this time. The first is by his hairdresser:

As I was doing Mozart's hair one morning and was just completing his pigtail, M. suddenly jumped up and, despite the fact that I was holding him by his pigtail, he went into the next room, dragging me along with him, and started to play the piano. Full of admiration for his playing and for the lovely tone of the instrument – it was the first time I had ever heard such a one – I let go of the pigtail and didn't dress it again until M. got up again. One day when I was rounding the corner from the Kärntnerstrasse into the Himmelpfortgasse in order to see M., he arrived on horseback, stopped, then as he rode on a few steps took out a little board and wrote some music. I spoke to him again and asked if I could come to him now, and he said yes.

The second is by Count Ludwig von Bentheim, who was at Mozart's Frankfurt concert on 15 October 1790 and, in his diary, described him as

a little man, of rather pleasant appearance, wearing a navy-blue satin coat, richly embroidered. [. . .] He played a concerto of his composition [?K459] of extraordinary gentillesse and charm, [on] a fortepiano by Stein of Augsburg belonging to Baronesse de Frantz, apparently the best of its kind, costing from 90 to 100 ducats. [He also played] a Fantasy, without the music, enchanting, in which he was quite dazzling, displaying the full force of his genius.

About a week later Mozart was in Mannheim, where *Figaro* was in preparation. According to a hand-written note on a playbill for the opera, Mozart directed the premiere (24 October). "The reason I am still here", he wrote to Constanze on the 23rd, "is that the whole cast begged me to stay on and help them with the rehearsals. *Figaro* too is the reason why I can't write as much as I should like – it's time for the dress rehearsal. In fact the first act at least will already be over." He seems not to have been looking his best when he arrived at the rehearsal, to judge by the diary of the actor Wilhelm Backhaus:

Kapellmeister Motzard here on the 23rd, he gave numerous tempos at the rehearsal of *Figaro*. Embarrassing situation. I took him for a journeyman tailor. During the rehearsal I was standing at the door. He came up and asked if it was all right to listen to the rehearsal. I told him to clear off. "But surely you would let Kapellmeister Mozart listen?" he said.

From Haydn's biographer Dies, in a book based on conversations with the composer, we have an account of Mozart at their last meeting, in December 1790. Mozart is at pains to warn the fifty-seven-year-old Haydn about the hazards of what he is letting himself in for:

"Papa" (as he generally called him), "you are not prepared for the great world, and you speak so few languages." "Ah," Haydn replied, "my language is understood all over the world." [. . .] Mozart that day could not leave his friend. He dined with him and at the moment of parting said, "We are probably saying our last farewell in this life." Tears welled in both their eyes. Haydn was deeply moved; he applied Mozart's words to himself, it never occurred to him that the fates would cut the thread of Mozart's life the very next year.

The last of these pictures of Mozart is his own. It comes from early June 1791, when Constanze was again in Baden and he was in Vienna, deep in the composition of *The Magic Flute*, staying with his friend the cheesemonger and horn player Joseph Leutgeb and writing to Constanze in the garden room of their house:

I've just this moment received your dear letter and am delighted to see that you are well and in good spirits. Madame Leutgeb did my cravat for me today. My God, you should see it! I kept on telling her, "she [Constanze] does it like this", but it was no use. I am pleased you have a good appetite –

but whoever gorges a lot must also sh- – I mean, walk a lot. But I shouldn't like you to take long walks without me [Constanze was seven months pregnant]. I entreat you to follow my advice, it comes from the heart. Adieu, my love, my only one. Catch them in the air – those 2999½ little kisses from me that are flying about, waiting for someone to snap them up. Listen, I want to whisper something in your ear – now you in mine – now we open and close our mouths – again – again, and again. Finally we say: "It's all because of Plumpi-Strumpi . . ." You can imagine what you like – that's what's so nice about it! Adieu. A thousand tender kisses. Ever your Mozart.

The notion that Mozart composed *The Magic Flute* only because of poverty and neglect by the court – that he was driven to the expedient of slumming it at a suburban theatre in a working-class district for want of anything more worthy of his genius – dies hard. It was always an insufferably condescending idea, and a snobbish one – a sort of musical equivalent of the disapproval commentators expressed at Mozart the man's unfortunate penchant for low company. As it happens, his contacts with the actor-manager-playwright Emanuel Schikaneder's theatre, for which *The Magic Flute* was written, went back at least two years, to 1789, when he supplied an aria for his sister-in-law Josepha Hofer, who was a member of the company, to sing in a projected German-language production of Paisiello's *Barber of Seville*.

It was natural that he should do so. Schikaneder was an old friend of the Mozart family. His troupe had been in residence in Salzburg for five months in 1780–81 (and possibly earlier as well), with a large repertory of singspiels, ballets and plays (including *Hamlet* and works by Beaumarchais, Gozzi, Voltaire and Lessing), during which time he was a regular visitor at the Tanzmeisterhaus and a member of the jovial group, including the Mozarts, which met regularly for *Bölzlschiessen*, an outdoor game of target-shooting (in December 1780 Leopold Mozart writes to tell his son – by then in Munich for *Idomeneo* – that Schikaneder "has bought a very fine popgun which we are going to christen at our shooting tomorrow"). Schikaneder provided the family with free passes for his performances. When Mozart left for Munich in November Nannerl was instructed to write and tell her brother about the shows they saw in his absence; his replies, written in the midst of all his preoccupations with his opera, make it clear how interested he was. The correspondence is also much concerned with an aria that Wolfgang had agreed to provide for a production of Schikaneder's, based on one of Gozzi's plays, but which, understandably in view of the demands of *Idomeneo*, he was slow in sending, though in the end he did.

When, after more touring, Schikaneder was offered the lease of the Kärntnertortheater by Joseph II, late in 1783, one of his first productions was a revival of *Die Entführung*. And when, following further wanderings including another season in Salzburg and a period as theatre manager in Regensburg, he returned to Vienna to take over management of the Theater auf der Wieden in the summer of 1789, it is no surprise to find Mozart involved with the company almost from the first. The aria for Josepha Hofer was entered in the thematic catalogue on 17 September. A year later a document shows Mozart taking part in a collaborative enterprise for Schikaneder's company, the magic opera *Der Stein der Weisen oder Die Zauberinsel* (*The Philosophers' Stone, or The Magic Island*); he is named as one of five composers who contributed to the work: Schikaneder himself, the company's young kapellmeister J. B. Henneberg, Mozart (a duet and two sections of the Act 2 finale), and the singers Benedikt Schack and Franz Xaver Gerl, both of whom Schikaneder had brought with him from Germany. Twelve months later Schack will sing Tamino in *The Magic Flute* and Gerl, Sarastro.

That is not the end of the connection in the months leading up to *The Magic Flute*. In March 1791 the catalogue records an aria, "Per questa bella mano" (K612) with double bass obbligato, written for Gerl and Friedrich Pischelberger, the company's principal bass player. The next entry is a set of piano variations on "Ein Weib ist das herrlichste Ding auf der Welt" ("A woman is the finest thing in the world"), a song which figured in the popular series of singspiels featuring the comic gardener Anton, played by Schikaneder – no doubt with many nods and winks at the audience, for Schikaneder was a famous womanizer. *The Stupid Gardener from the Mountains, or The Two Antons*, libretto by Schikaneder and music by Schack and Gerl, had six sequels over the years.

All this strongly suggests that Mozart was not drawn into Viennese popular theatre against his will, and that the collaboration with Schikaneder on *The Magic Flute* was no mere marriage of convenience, let alone of desperate necessity. He surely did not consider himself demeaned by it. He was at home in that world; he judged it by the same exacting standards as he judged everything else. (Wenzel Müller's *Der Fagottist oder Die Zauberzither*, which was creating a sensation at the rival Leopoldstadt establishment in the northern suburb, struck him as having "nothing to it", but he enjoyed Schack's *Anton bei Hofe*, the fifth of the Gardener series.) Popular theatre, with its mixture of magic, streetwise humour, mystery, farce, spectacle and didactic sentiment, was an enduring and quintessential part of the culture of Vienna, and Mozart, as a thoroughgoing Viennese, embraced it wholeheartedly. *The Magic Flute* was a natural consequence of the interest he took in it. He raised it to a different plane, no doubt; but that was what he usually did: *The Abduction*, the Da Ponte operas, the Vienna piano concertos, leave their models almost invisibly far below. Here was a chance to do what he had long desired, to create a specifically German opera, a new genre, different in spirit and structure from his Italian comedies, mixing playfulness and solemnity, the vernacular and the lofty.

Nor should we think of it as a drastic step down in standards from the Burgtheater or from the Estates Theatre in Prague. Schikaneder did not operate on the cheap. He employed capable singers, and his orchestra, with thirty-five players, was as large as the Burgtheater's – three fewer strings, but trombones, three of them, on the strength. Mozart, evidently, was not writing for a second-rate band: the obbligato double-bass part in K612 presupposes an accomplished musician.

As stage director, Schikaneder was renowned for the splendour and ingenuity of his productions; they made use of the latest technological innovations: flying machines, lifts, swift transformations, special lighting effects including impressively lifelike waterfalls and infernos. Nor were magic plays (most of them written by himself) the only kind of entertainment he offered his public. Contemporary playwrights of the order of Lessing, Goethe and Schiller figured on the bills (in 1791, for example, *Don Carlos* was given). Schikaneder's audience was by no means exclusively local and artisan. The upper classes also came. The Emperor conferred on the house the title "Imperial and Royal" in 1790, and in August 1791, with his son and heir Francis, attended the first night of the revival of one of Schikaneder's plays, a few days after the author had been received at court. The theatre was easily accessible from the city, and the previous manager had planted lamps along the route from the Kärntnertor to the Wieden. Late in 1791 a new entrance was created so that carriages could drive up to the door.

The Theater auf der Wieden or Freihaustheater was part of a large complex of buildings, just beyond the walls to the south, belonging to the Counts Starhemberg – "free house" because it had been granted exemption from taxes as a mark of imperial favour when the family acquired the property in the mid-seventeenth century. It was like a little city, with its own church and inn, its own shops and factories, its resident apothecary, six large courtyards, a garden, vineyards, and over 300 apartments, many of them occupied by members of the company (Josepha Hofer among them). The stone- and brick-built theatre, with wooden interior, which opened in 1787, had room for nearly 1,000 spectators. This was where *The Magic Flute* saw the light, on 30 September 1791, proving so popular that by early December, nine weeks later, it had had thirty-five performances.

It is likely that Mozart and Schikaneder were at work on the libretto by the spring of 1791. The genesis of the opera has given rise to endless stories and much speculation but remains obscure. One thing, though, is certain. Whoever first thought of it – whether it was Schikaneder, or whether, as Nicholas Till suggests, the conception went back to Mozart's visit to Leipzig and Berlin in the spring of 1789 – the composer-dramatist was involved in it from the beginning. That was his practice. Even if we did not have Schikaneder's own testimony – that *The Magic Flute* was an opera that he "planned and worked out carefully with the late Mozart" – we can be sure of it. Schikaneder's verse has been the object of a good deal of scorn, but the drama is well constructed. As Peter Branscombe has shown, the libretto's superiority to what he produced for other composers, in coherence and depth of characterization as well as in the exceptionally wide range of source materials it drew on, points to an obvious conclusion: that the dramaturgy of *The Magic Flute* was the joint work of librettist and composer.

Unravelling the complex origins of the plot has developed into a minor industry. (The genealogy of Papageno the bird-man has alone provoked pages of explication.) The identified sources are numerous. Abbé Terrasson's early eighteenth-century masonic novel, *Sethos, histoire ou Vie tirée des monumens anecdotes de l'ancienne Egypte*, where the princely hero is attacked by a serpent and is later admitted to a temple after passing trials by fire and water – a book that places great emphasis on the number three, and whose German translation (1777) shows verbal parallels with Schikaneder's text; the magic fables of Carlo Gozzi, popular in Vienna in the 1780s (one of which has a clownish character dressed as a bird-catcher); Chrétien de Troyes' twelfth-century Arthurian romance *Yvain* (translated by Mozart's fellow-mason Karl Joseph Michaeler), where the hero, as he lies unconscious, is rescued by three ladies and then meets a strange figure, dressed in hides, whom he questions, whereupon the creature replies, "I'm a man, as you see," and boasts of his power to overcome animals with his bare hands; Wieland's verse epic *Oberon*, of which Mozart owned a copy, and which features a magic instrument and the trials of two pairs of lovers; Wranitzky's opera *Oberon, King of the Elves*, staged at the Freihaustheater in December 1789; perhaps Goethe's fragment *Die Geheimnisse* (*The Secrets*), published in Vienna two years before, in which a knight seeks admission to a mysterious brotherhood, hears a flute uttering music of sublime beauty, and sees three boys with girdles of roses encircling their waists; *The Philosophers' Stone* (September 1790), the magic opera with two pairs of lovers, serious and comic, and two magicians, one good and one evil, to which Mozart contributed; *The Beneficent Dervish*, the third in the series of magic operas given at Schikaneder's theatre (in March 1791), with a plot which like that of *The Philosophers' Stone* is derived from one of Wieland's stories in *Dschinnistan*; and not least *Dschinnistan* itself, Wieland's three-volume collection of quasi-oriental fairy tales, which began appearing in 1786 and in whose stories can be found characters and incidents familiar from *The Magic Flute*, including a young man falling in love with a young woman's portrait and setting out to rescue her, a black slave who spies on the heroine, a "starblazing queen", a temple of Friendship and Benevolence (Wohltätigkeit – the name of the lodge Mozart joined when he became a Freemason), three wise boys who advise the hero and later descend from the sky to avert a tragedy, and a hero who is presented with a flute which has the power to move all who hear it to love – even all these do not exhaust the list of possible origins.

A further likely source was the long essay "On the Mysteries of the Egyptians" by Ignaz von Born, which appeared in the *Freemasons' Journal* in 1784 (the year Mozart joined the order), the final section of which compared the Egyptian mysteries and their ceremonies with those of Freemasonry. Mozart knew the great mineralogist, then Master of True Concord, in whose honour he composed the masonic cantata *Die Mauerfreude* when Born was created Knight of the Empire in April 1785.

How systematically masonic the opera is remains a matter of dispute. Opinion ranges all the way from Branscombe's cautious "the surviving evidence is incomplete and to some extent contradictory" to Jacques Chailley's exuberant detection of masonic symbolism in every compositional detail of the work, in what Rodney Milnes has called his "massively indiscreet" study, *The Magic Flute, Masonic Opera* (1972) – the book which revealed secrets of ritual till then known only to the brotherhood. But wherever the truth is to be found in this wide spectrum of interpretation – and it probably never will be – what is not in dispute is the general intention of both authors, Schikaneder and Mozart. As Heartz says, the libretto "testifies to an intimate knowledge of the order's initiation rites and symbolism". Mozart was an active member of the brotherhood. Schikaneder had been expelled by the Regensburg lodge for immorality but would have retained a working knowledge of the Craft.* The illustrated frontispiece to the printed libretto, engraved by Ignaz Alberti, a member of Crowned Hope, is made up of symbols of Freemasonry, and in particular of Rosicrucianism. They would have been recognized instantly by initiates. (Thomas Bauman points out that in the 1790s "Masons in north Germany saw at once in the opera an allegory of the brotherhood's secrets".) So – at least by musically literate masons – would the number symbolism that permeates the score as well as the libretto: the knocking triple figure heard at the beginning of the

---

* The claim, advanced nearly sixty years later, that the real author was Carl Ludwig Gieseke, librettist of Wranitzky's *Oberon* and a member of Schikaneder's troupe (he played the speaking role of First Slave in *The Magic Flute*), is now generally discredited.

overture and repeatedly thereafter, the key of E flat, with its three flats, the three-fold wind chords (each one a group of three) which interrupt the overture halfway through and later summon the postulants at various stages of their initiation; also the five-note figures which are prominent in scenes that take place in or under the influence of the feminine domain, five representing woman in masonic numerology. Freemasons in the audience may also have seen in the character of the wise, authoritative Sarastro a portrait of Ignaz von Born himself, the former Master who had died only a few weeks before, and perhaps also, in the despotic Queen of Night, an identification with the Empress Maria Theresa, a dedicated enemy of Freemasonry.

What decided Mozart and Schikaneder to make the opera a vehicle for specifically masonic ideas we cannot say. Robbins Landon sees it as a response to the crisis facing the order in the climate of fear precipitated by the French Revolution, when Freemasonry was suspected of Jacobinism and no one was sure how the order would be treated by the new emperor and his chief of police Count Pergen: "Mozart and Schikaneder risked a long shot – to save the Craft by an allegorical opera, *The Magic Flute*." Till, on the other hand, interprets it as Mozart seizing "the opportunity to communicate his spiritual ideals to a wider audience"; Mozart wrote it "not as a secret work for initiates only" but for all who were willing to hear.

The "wisdom, beauty and strength" celebrated in the concluding words of the work are precisely the goals to be aspired to in Freemasonry. But the opera's masonic affiliations and its central theme of initiation are already manifest long before the final chorus of rejoicing; they are there from the beginning. The old idea which still lingers on, that *The Magic Flute* becomes a masonic opera only halfway through the action, and that this represents a late change of plan forced on the authors by circumstance, is untenable. The circumstance in question was the accident of another rescue opera, *Kaspar der Fagottist* – featuring a malevolent sorcerer, a captive maiden, a prince and his comic servant, and two magic instruments – appearing at the rival Leopoldstadt theatre early in June 1791 and pre-empting Schikaneder's plans. Until then (the theory goes) Sarastro had been the wicked magician and the Queen of Night and her abducted daughter the innocent victims of his machinations. But this is moonshine. Mozart was never going to be content with composing a simple romance of quest and rescue like so many of the other plays with music in the repertory of Viennese popular theatre; *The Magic Flute* was always going to be different. And quite apart from the fact that, given the large number of magic operas, all deriving from a common stock and sharing plot details, plagiarism would not have been an issue nor accusations of it something to wish to escape, the main lines of *The Magic Flute* were in place by the time *Kaspar* came on. On 11 June, three days after the premiere of Müller's opera but before he had seen it, Mozart could quote a line from the priests' Act 2 duet in a letter to Constanze: "Tod und Verzweiflung war sein Lohn" ("Death and destruction were his reward"). The masonic symbolism of three in the overture cannot of course be cited in evidence – the overture was not written till September – but there is no need to: such symbols abound from the start of the action.

Above all we need only to hear the Queen's music in the fourth number of the work to understand that she is not the good fairy she makes herself out to be and Tamino believes she is – the "unhappy woman weighed down by grief and lamentation" that he will speak of to the Priest in the first-act finale. There is more than a hint of self-pity in her opening recitative (as well as of overweening self-esteem in the allegro maestoso orchestral introduction, with its insistent violin chords in cross-rhythm and portentous bass), and the G minor larghetto confirms it. Halfway through, the combination of agitated string accompaniment and sinuous bassoon and viola recalls Donna Anna's "Or sai chi l'onore", creating a comparable sense of suppressed hysteria. Mozart also makes a clear distinction between the first phrase of the larghetto and the similarly shaped opening of her daughter Pamina's aria in the same key: the one, contrived in its pathos, the other, music of genuine and spontaneous distress:

Even without such pointers, it hardly seems likely that an emblematic figure of Night and Darkness could ever have been chosen to represent the good, least of all in the Age of Enlightenment. We see her at first through the unenlightened eyes of Tamino, and then, like him, are disabused. There is no inconsistency in the fact that the flute and the bells are the gifts of the Queen. Magical objects in fairy stories are by tradition morally neutral. The pious homilies uttered during the first quintet – "If all liars could have a padlock placed on their mouths, instead of hatred, bitterness and black rancour, love and brotherhood would prevail" – are no more than conventional moralizing. In due course we learn that the flute is in the Queen's possession for the simple reason that it belonged to her late husband, the leader of Sarastro's priesthood, who made it. All that is "inconsistent" about the opening scenes is that the story is presented from the limited and distorted viewpoint of the Queen and her creatures. To them Sarastro is an enchanter and the changes he works in people mere magic. (Similarly, the Pamina of the first scenes, being still subject to her mother's view, believes that Papageno will be tortured and killed if Sarastro catches him.) They see the flute likewise as a purely magical piece of property and not, as in reality it is, symbol of music's Orphic power and of the spiritual power of man and woman united. Tamino and Pamina attain their goal by suffering and love, not by supernatural means.

As for the Three Boys, to object that, being on the side of the good, they should not be in any way associated with, let alone recommended by, the enemy, that is again to be too literal and also to mistake the nature of the allegory. It is a question not so much of good versus evil as of the progress of the human soul from the darkness of ignorance to the light of understanding, in which state its former contradictions are reconciled and all its parts, having shed their negative aspects, are joined in a single harmonious whole. The Three Ladies stand for human development at its lowest. They have no imagination. The strict limit to their understanding is shown by their inability to do more than set Tamino on the first stage of his journey (which they see only in materialistic terms). They can take him no further; it is the Boys – higher beings – who will do that.

The truly significant change, the new direction the opera took, was in the role of the heroine. This must have been Mozart's doing.

Schikaneder appreciated women, no doubt of that, but not exactly in a spirit of emancipation. He was very well satisfied with the old decrees: women's place – their "duty", as Papageno puts it in his duet with Pamina – was to serve and please men. The libretto of *The Magic Flute* is full of condescending or disparaging comments fit to raise the hackles not simply of feminists but of anyone with the most elementary sense of justice. "A woman told you that?" says the Priest to Tamino; "a woman chatters a great deal but does little [of importance]." "Beware women's wiles," the priests warn in their oddly and surely deliberately stilted duet (as Mozart has written it); "that is the first commandment of our order." "She is a woman, she thinks as a woman," says Tamino a moment later, like the good pupil he is. (Though he has started on the road to wisdom, he has much to learn.) Pamina will be his "reward" for passing the trials.

Mozart changed that. Significantly, he did not set the passage in the libretto where the Boys tell Papagena that she will be her husband's "property". The masonic doctrines and rituals were, for him, without doubt deeply serious matters; he was furious when an acquaintance in the audience kept on laughing during the long deliberations of Sarastro and the priests in the opening scene of Act 2. But he would not be confined by them. The crucial text is: "a woman who does not fear night and death is worthy *and will be initiated*". With Pamina's sudden entry at the end of the Armed Men's chorale – turning Tamino's tense, austere F minor to warm D flat, and shaking the three men out of their solemnity – the opera abandons orthodox Masonry. The final tableau, the stage directions state, reveal "Tamino and Pamina in priestly raiment". No wonder the assembly is struck dumb ("Silence reigns over all the priests") when Sarastro orders Pamina to be brought into the pyramid's sacred vault just after they have been singing of the "noble youth" through whose advent gloomy darkness will yield to glorious light. But that is only the beginning. A woman, a representative of the unreasoning, instinctive, "inferior" half of humanity, will not only achieve full initiation – unheard of, unthinkable in Viennese masonic doctrine – but will take command, will lead the man on the last and most hazardous stage of the journey. "A man must direct your heart," Sarastro himself had told her, sententiously, in the finale of Act 1, "for without him a woman tends to stray from her proper sphere of activity." By the middle of the second act Pamina and her progress have become the central issue of the drama and the inspiration of the most intensely charged music in the score: her desolate aria, the trio of farewell, which she dominates, and her scene with the Three Boys, perhaps the most beautiful section of the whole opera. Not only are her trials more terrible than Tamino's: unlike him she has no idea that they are trials, imposed on her for a specific purpose; Tamino's refusal to speak to her can only mean total rejection. Her sufferings bring her to an understanding beyond his. In the scene of the ordeals, the heart of the work, after their first exchange of greetings it is she who gives the lead – "I myself guide you, love guides me" – and takes him by the hand, telling him the true meaning and numinous power of the flute and how it will protect them on their way. This is now very much her sphere of activity. The printed libretto assigned the crucial lines "Nun komm und spiel' die Flöte an", etc. to both Pamina and Tamino. In the score they are sung by Pamina alone.

How could Mozart have done otherwise? Pamina's continuous development throughout the drama, from naïve, unthinking girl to fully evolved woman, is one more example of the thread that runs through the operas – what Daniel Heartz has called Mozart's "infinite care to create strong and deeply moving female characters in [. . .] all his operas". Although the musical characterization in *The Magic Flute* is often said to be two-dimensional, far less vivid and complex than that of the great Italian operas, Pamina's is quite as richly imagined and consistently realized as Elvira's or Ilia's or the Countess's. From the beginning her melodic line aspires outwards and upwards. When we first see her, threatened by Monostatos with rape, her phrases, as she pleads for mercy, are soon taking wing, their expansiveness contrasting with the blunt squatness of the moor's. In the duet with Papageno – where, although not understanding the meaning of the love she sings about with such fervour, she commits herself to it instinctively – her part is notably richer than his, as it is when we next see them, excited at the thought of finding Tamino: her music, at first falling in with Papageno's idiom, breaks free at "holder Jüngling". It is the same as they await, in trepidation, the arrival of Sarastro. Here the difference in their natures and destinies, till now partly concealed by their common interests and mutual sympathy, is exposed – his music earthy and fragmented, with nervous unison accompaniment, hers warmly harmonized and exalted even in fear. Her radiant "The truth, the truth" foretells the Pamina of the final scenes.

So it continues. Anguished though it is, her G minor aria flows, above its broken accompaniment; it has the melodic abundance that is natural to her. In the farewell trio the freedom of her vocal line – culminating in the wonderful passage in G minor, "Oh, if you loved as I love you, you would not be so calm" – is in marked contrast to the more formal utterances of the two men; only when Sarastro announces that "the hour has struck, you must part" does it join with Tamino's, in plaintive thirds and sixths.

Even in the scene with the Three Boys, where grief at the separation from Tamino and the struggle within her soul to liberate herself from her mother's destructive influence drive her to the verge of madness, her music never loses its untrammelled melodiousness. Nothing in the score is more beautifully imagined than the increasing wildness of her melodic line – contrasted with the Boys' disciplined, luminous phrases – and the gradual growth of tension by means of syncopated upper strings and a more and more urgent bass, to the moment of truth where G minor, the key of Pamina's grief, yields decisively to E flat major. At first, in the joyful allegro that follows, her phrases remain wayward, as though she still hardly dares believe that Tamino loves her. When she does, her voice combines with the other three, then breaks free again, to soar up to an exultant high B flat, sustained for four bars, then swooping down nearly two octaves, like a bird released from captivity.

Tamino's moment of truth comes much earlier, at the end of his long dialogue with the Priest in Act 1. This is the turning point of the action. The scene – the first of the Act 1 finale – opens with a new sound: trombones, muted trumpets and drums, soft pulsation of bassoons, with gleaming flutes and clarinets, propelling a slow march. Tamino, guided by the Three Boys, has left the realm of the Queen and her acolytes. His initiation can begin. If we have understood the allegory behind the preceding scenes, the more elevated tone that comes over the work is evidence not of any change of intention on the authors' part but, rather, that the drama has entered its second phase (for which there have been clear premonitory signs). It is a shift in perspective. Till now we have been looking through the eyes of the unenlightened Tamino and his earthbound companion. Now it is as though we have passed through a curtain into a different world – a world presaged in the coda of the quintet, where clarinets and high bassoons floating down heralded the coming of the Three Boys, Ariel-like "spirits of another sort". Under the guidance of the patient, kindly Priest, Tamino takes a decisive step away from ignorance and false values, towards enlightenment. He is ceasing to be the callow youth who fell in love with a portrait and believed everything the Queen said. The pleasant grove he finds himself in and, beyond it, the three temples joined by elegant colonnades are nothing like the embattled turrets and frowning walls his chivalrous fancies had pictured; and his first words, in answer to the question "What do you seek here in the sanctuary?", are those of a postulant: "The domain of love and virtue"; the words are sung in a serene E flat major, with clarinet, bassoon and cello accompaniment whose first three notes are perhaps intended to anticipate those of the March of the Priests at the begin-ning of Act 2 (hinting at what he as yet has no inkling of). That is a fleeting glimpse, however. Tamino is still breathing fire against Saras-tro, and much of his music has an angry impetuosity, in contrast to the calm of the Priest's.* By the end of their exchange he has come dimly to recognize his error. His aggressiveness has been disarmed; and his final question, "When will the veil be lifted?", unconsciously looks forward to the moment when he will be received into the brotherhood. The Priest's reply, sung to a glowing but mysterious melody (doubled by the cellos), is hopeful but enigmatic. Tamino is left alone. In a disconsolate A minor – the furthest point from E flat, the home key, the key of enlightenment – the violins repeat the sad, drooping phrase first heard when he discovered that his supposed enemy ruled in the Temple of Wisdom and the certainties of his life crumbled away. "Oh endless night, when will you be gone? When will my eyes find the light?" He has spoken to himself, but distant voices, supported by soft trombones, answer him, still enigmatically: "Soon, or not at all." He asks, this time aloud, "Does Pamina still live?" "Pami-na – Pami-na – still lives," the voices answer.

---

* Mozart emphasizes the contrast by writing "quick" above two of Tamino's phrases and "slow" above the Priest's reply.

The vital step forward in the action is paralleled by the innovatory, prophetic character of the music. From the departure of the Boys till the end of the scene – at which point Tamino, his heart overflowing with thankfulness, takes up the flute and plays it and wild beasts gather round, enchanted by the sound – Mozart writes in a style new to opera, a style which dissolves once-distinct categories of recitative and formal number. Unencumbered by convention, the music moves in easy, perfect response to the ebb and flow of the words: Tamino's by turns indignant, bewildered, chastened, the Priest's courteous, measured, admonitory.

Yet Mozart, having written it, does not then forsake the comedy or the folklike style of the earlier scenes. They too are fundamental to the work. The posturings of the Ladies, whose music he contrives to make both silly and beautiful, Papageno's slapstick encounters with Monostatos, his earthy common sense, simple appetites and constant longing for a mate, are as much part of the plan, the balance of the work, as are the nobility of Sarastro's "O Isis und Osiris", the priests' sonorous D major chorus (full brass but no drums) and the Armed Men's chorale. Papageno's nature may deny him access to the higher mysteries (not that he cares a fig); and it can be argued that the presence of this transfigured but still unregenerate descendant of the Viennese Hanswurst tradition deflates some of the seriousness of the tests the two aspirants are subjected to in the first half of Act 2. His role is nonetheless essential. The fulfilment of his needs will receive as much loving attention as the initiation of the priestly couple. His magic bells are an integral part of the vision of music as the healing force that could redeem the world. They make us dance and laugh; and they unite him with his Papagena no less surely than the flute guides Pamina and Tamino together through the fire and water into the light of a new dawn.

The Magic Flute's combination of high sentiment and pantomime, admired by poets from Goethe to Auden, has always been a stumbling-block for the ultra-sophisticated. But, though there is no arguing over taste, the notion that Mozart cheapened his art and wrote below himself out of deference to his new public is demonstrably false. In creating popular music he "abandons none of the pretensions of high art" (Rosen). It is the product of infinite care. As he nearly always does, he uses the constraints, turning them to fruitful account.

Much has been said, not all of it complimentary, about the neo-classical spareness of Mozart's so-called late style (a perilously subjective question, especially when a work thought to exemplify it, the B flat piano concerto K595, is revealed to have been largely written more than two years earlier, long before Mozart is supposed to have been composing late music). But the score of *The Magic Flute* refutes any notion that his new simplicity is the product either of concessions to a popular audience or of waning creative powers. Its simplicity is a positive simplicity, subtle and purposeful, seemingly uncomplicated in its effect, profoundly artful in the means used to achieve it. It is Mozart's most transparent operatic score, harmonically the most pure and unadorned (its chromatic inflexions contained within a clear diatonic framework), melodically the most direct, in texture the most open; but he wrote it like that not because he was forced to but because he saw it and heard it that way. The subject demanded it. Those who miss the ironies and ambiguities of the Da Ponte operas, their compositional complexity, are not really listening to what *The Magic Flute* offers. Mozart finds other means to realize his vision.

In fact the work has its own sophistication; the musical interrelationships and connections – melodic, harmonic, rhythmic, dynamic – are as subtle as in any of the other more obviously complex scores. It has its ironies too: to take one example, the poignant irony of the accompaniment to Pamina's aria, whose almost unvaried succession of short string chords in groups of two separated by a rest recalls her duet with Papageno, where the identical pattern accompanied her artless declaration of faith in the power of love; the faltering, piteous effect of her disillusionment is made still keener by the reminiscence. The economy and purity of the aria are remarkable – the vocal line, in its rise and fall, its mixture of utter despondency and sharp anguish, is like a distillation of suffering itself – but so is the subtlety: the exquisite first entry of the bassoon, the long-drawn phrases for unison flute and oboe that strike suddenly across the string chords at moments of harmonic intensification, and, when the voice has dwindled to nothing, the strings, contained till then, well out in a flood of compassion which, as Bauman demonstrates, repeats the exact falling intervals of Pamina's passionate "See, Tamino, (these tears fall for you alone, beloved)", thus uniting the silent, listening Tamino with her grief, so that it "becomes Tamino's own as he hears his name die with her last hopes in the final orchestral strains".

Or, at the opposite expressive pole, consider the strutting, skipping figure which recurs at intervals during the first act and here and there in the second, usually in the form of a downbeat followed by a trill and an arpeggio, and with a sense of finger-snapping or indignant assertiveness or, occasionally, of apprehensiveness. We hear it first, on unison strings and bassoons, introducing the padlocked Papageno's "hm"'s at the beginning of the quintet, and again later in the same number when he tries to take his leave.

The violins play it in the next number as Monostatos skips around Pamina, threatening, and ordering his slaves to bind her.

The motif, in fact, belongs to the unenlightened world and particularly to unredeemed Natural Man. But it is significant that the next time we hear it, in particularly assertive, defiant form, it is associated with Tamino: Tamino – still ignorant and confused – advancing impetuously on each of the three temple doors in turn,

only to be stopped at the first two by cries of "Get back!" and at the third by the old Priest (after which we don't hear it again in connection with Tamino, who has started on the road to enlightenment). In the following scene, two variants of the motif appear,

the first introducing the scene, the second as Papageno answers Pamina's ecstatic "holder Jüngling" with "Sh! I know a better way" (i.e. to call Tamino) and plays his panpipes.

(Observe too the five-note figures that punctuate his words, as they will continue to do throughout the opera.) The motif recurs in the Act 2 quintet, when the Three Ladies reveal that the Queen has arrived secretly in the temple – news which makes Papageno blurt out, "What? Where? She's in the temple?", while the violins play

Though it disappears after that, Mozart has not forgotten it. As Papageno and Papagena picture the endless line of little Papagenos and Papagenas that the gods in their goodness will bless them with, we hear it one last time, the trills and arpeggios now innocent and positive, the arpeggios rising instead of falling – their aggressiveness channelled into the begetting of children:

Thematic links constantly make dramatic points, as in the connection between Pamina's aria and the Queen of Night's larghetto already mentioned, or in the dejected Tamino's "Oh endless night" echoing, in a desolate minor key, the Queen's first greeting: "Tremble not, beloved son", which had seemed to promise him a clear career of bold knight errantry:

or in the yearning rising sixth of Tamino's first phrase in the portrait aria – addressed to an idea more than to a person – finding its fulfilment lifetimes later in Pamina's ecstatic "Tamino mein".

The shape of Tamino's aria is typical of the unconventional way Mozart treats form in *The Magic Flute*. Even more than in the Da Ponte operas the melodic repetitions of sonata form (sometimes the harmonic patterns as well) tend to be abandoned in favour of a constant flow of ideas in which every incident finds its apt expression within a seemingly effortless musical continuity. (This of course does not apply to the simple strophic songs, of which the opera, being a singspiel, has more – five – than are found in *Figaro*, *Don Giovanni* or *Così*, three of them, as one would expect, for Papageno.) Tamino's aria preserves the harmonic structure of sonata form but not the melodic. Coloured by the amorous tones of clarinets and horns, this most beautiful of love-songs – a dream of passion, as yet without a real object – is set to a vocal line whose shape, alternately soaring in rapture and hesitating in doubt and wonder, conveys precisely Tamino's love-struck state of mind. The form follows his growing ardour. At the return of the home key the opening idea does not recur; instead, new, yet more rapturous phrases, egged on by the violins, reflect the excited state of his imagination. Only then is the first section recalled, by the repetition of its concluding phrase, now expanded into a great arch of melody, into which the rising sixth of the opening words ("Dies Bildnis" – "This picture"), not otherwise heard again, is absorbed. The developing emotions of the text make regular sonata form out of the question.

In the Queen of Night's Act 2 aria – at first sight a conventional opera seria rage aria – there is again no formal recapitulation, hardly even a vestigial one. There is no time for it; the torrential fury of this prodigious piece sweeps it aside. The opening phrase, set to "The vengeance of hell boils in my heart", is never heard again.* A large part of the aria is in the relative major, F, including much of its vocal pyrotechnics. D minor's return, emphasized by the thrillingly decisive re-entry of trumpets and drums, is marked by no melodic recall. The coloratura, which in her Act 1 aria she turns on as it were to dazzle Tamino, is here shot from her by the force of an uncontrollable fury; the mask the Queen wore in Act 1 is stripped from her and her Medusa gaze glares at us head on. This is music that demands to be sung with maximum vehemence, by a dramatic soprano with an extended top to the voice; no less necessary than a strong high F is the power to project the manic insistence of the repeated Fs and Gs in the middle of the compass, at "be rejected for ever, abandoned for ever, destroyed for ever!", and the splendour of the terrifying sustained B flat at the end.

The subtlety-cum-economy of the characterization in *The Magic Flute* is exemplified in the contrasted but related treatment of Papageno and Monostatos the Moor. Papageno is the archetypal garrulous, boastful, buttonholing comic simpleton of Viennese vernacular com-

---

* The phrase is one more example of the pattern of notes – D-A-F-E-D – found so often in the key of D minor in Mozart's mature music: e.g. the opening movement of the piano concerto K466, the minuet of the string quartet K421 and the penultimate bar of the first movement, and, in *Don Giovanni*, Donna Anna's "Fuggi, crudele, fuggi" and "Lascia, lascia alla mia pena", and Elvira's "Bisogna aver coraggio". One might also cite the D minor phrase in the Act 1 finale of *The Magic Flute*, where Tamino wonders if Pamina has already been done to death, and the notes are (A)-D-A-F-E-D sharp.

edy, raised to immortality by Mozart's genius. His first song (No. 2), in G major, with flowing sixteenth notes alternating with hopping birdlike rhythms and intervals, has the folksong freshness and open-hearted good humour which will typify him throughout the opera. Much of his music is in this same bright G major, including the Act 2 quintet (which begins with a reference to the finale of Mozart's "Haydn" quartet in the same key). Papageno's little duet with Pamina (No. 7) is in the home, masonic key of E flat, but it is Pamina's piece much more than his (as we also know from the presence of clarinets, an instrument otherwise remote from Papageno's world); it is her kindly response to his lament at having no Papagena. After the famous song with glockenspiel, in F, the long scene in the second-act finale which rounds off his character and destiny is again in a bouncy, irrepressible G major, with a passage in a woebegone G minor as he prepares to hang himself, its harmonies and key, tempo, time signature and woodwind scoring only half-humorously recalling those of Pamina's aria – Mozart's characteristic way of reminding us of the affinity that linked the two children of nature before their divergent paths separated them. This is followed by a section in C major, as the Boys once more arrive and, in a musical idiom akin to Papageno's chatter, advise him to play his magic bells (the silly fellow had forgotten them), which brings on the feathered Papagena and a final return to the bird-man's home key, G major.

Monostatos' first appearance is also in G major. His idiom, at first sight, is not so different from Papageno's, only a more brutal version of it. Though each finds the other utterly and appallingly strange (to the end Monostatos believes Papageno to be a huge bird), he is Papageno's darker self, Natural Man corrupted, enslaved to selfish appetites and, as his name suggests, incapable of development. Throughout the opera his music depicts him in a permanent state of sexual arousal and frustration. Yet Papageno, tiptoeing in through the window at the moment when Pamina has fainted and the moor is about to ravish her, can without any change of musical style and with the slightest lightening of touch on Mozart's part take over Monostatos' last phrase and be his own inimitable self. Monostatos' character as *schwarz*-Papageno is reaffirmed in his whispered, lustful soliloquy in Act 2, as he stands over the sleeping Pamina and vows to satisfy his hunger – if the moon will only hide its light (he thus affirms his allegiance to the domain of darkness). Apart from a couple of mezzo-fortepiano accents in each verse, the busy, rapid orchestral accompaniment, topped with glinting piccolo, is pianissimo throughout; yet Mozart has given it a tingling intensity, comic and diabolical, so that the music dances with a priapic frenzy.

What is such a person doing in the Temple of Wisdom? It is a question that bothers the literal-minded, who forget that in becoming an allegory of human enlightenment the opera does not cease to be a fairy story. As a fairy story, it is not required to submit to the test of logical consistency; as a work intended for the theatre it can contain details which may offend the fastidious commentator but which cause no difficulty in performance.*

It was once common to explain Monostatos' presence as a leftover from the ur-*Magic Flute* – the supposed first version of the libretto, in which Sarastro was a wicked magician and therefore a natural employer of the evil moor. In this view the gossipy conversation among the three slaves which comes between the Act 1 quintet and the scene of the attempted rape, and which describes Pamina's escape from the moor's clutches and her recapture, was a careless survival and had no business in the remodelled libretto. One could reply that, though the slaves dislike Monostatos, there is nothing in their dialogue that suggests they regard Sarastro as a tyrant. But the explanation is much simpler. The brotherhood is not perfect. Nor is Sarastro. They are striving towards perfection but have not attained it. That is the purpose of Tamino's initiation. Tamino is the prince from afar, he that shall come, the "noble youth" who (with Pamina – though that

---

* Most of the so-called problems of *The Magic Flute* arise from overlooking these basic premises. One such is the placing of the farewell trio (No. 19), which has provoked reams of unnecessary commentary, according to which the trio should come earlier in the second act: placed where it is, it makes nonsense of Pamina's subsequent despair and attempted suicide and should therefore be moved. In fact there is no problem. The griefs and conflicts under which Pamina's spirit will nearly break have not been resolved; the crucial issue of her mother's influence remains to be settled, and her reunion with Tamino has been tantalizingly brief and overshadowed by doubt. Both the music and the words of the trio breathe a mood of sadness and poignant tenderness that, for Pamina, is only partly qualified by a vague hope; the most vivid reality is her enforced parting from Tamino.

is not yet fully clear even to Sarastro) will bring about the new age that is finally to dispel darkness and banish ignorance and superstition. Sarastro's ideas are still evolving. He tolerates the anomaly of a Caliban-like servant (whom he punishes but does not immediately dismiss), perhaps because Monostatos is part of Pamina's trials. Pamina's loss of consciousness from an attack by animal nature parallels Tamino's symbolic death in the opening scene, when, weaponless, he is attacked by the serpent. For both of them it is the precondition of rebirth into the life of the spirit, which will lead, through trials, to a new world. Meanwhile, however, the order is menaced by hostile forces from without, and there are dissonant notes within. As with the knights in *Parsifal*, by no means all of them are enlightened. Many of the brothers see women as the nemesis of men. Sarastro himself, the text hints, like Hans Sachs with Eva, is half in love with Pamina, the maiden he saved from her mother's grasp to be Tamino's bride. Much remains to be done, and Tamino, with Pamina, will do it.

The character of Sarastro the wise and authoritative leader has aroused oddly negative, even hostile, reactions, particularly in recent years. Anti-authoritarian directors delight in portraying him as a deeply equivocal figure, if not as the "Unmensch" and "Tyrann" of Tamino's outburst in the first-act finale. He has been depicted as a warped egomaniac and even, in one production, as a mad scientist conducting live experiments on his victims and finally blown up by one of his own devices. Yet it seems to me that, though the stage directions for the final scene do not say so, we are meant to imagine him making way for the "edles Paar", the "noble couple" whom the chorus hail at the triumphant conclusion of their ordeals – rather as Idomeneo makes way for Idamante and Ilia, but doing so willingly, in fulfilment of his plan.

In any case, the music Mozart writes for him is quite unequivocal; it shows him as anything but "inhuman". When we first hear him, in the Act 1 finale, in gentle conversation with Pamina – a scene which again combines recitative and flowing arioso in a musical idiom of extraordinary eloquence yet as natural as speech – his phrases have a warmth and dignity, and a shape, that Beethoven remembered when he composed the Minister's statement about human brotherhood (in the same key, C major) in the final scene of *Fidelio*.

A little later, it is true, the chorus respond to Sarastro's punishment of Monostatos in suspiciously regimented, sycophantic tones. But it will become clear that what the priests think and what Sarastro foresees and ordains are different things. (As for the punishment, seventy-seven strokes on the soles of the feet may seem severe, but he *has* tried to rape Pamina, and we learn later that the sentence is commuted.) Sarastro's E major hymn to friendship and forgiveness, "In diesen heil'gen Hallen", with its flowing melodic lines, doubled and echoed in the orchestra, and its flute, bassoon and horn sonority, is the positive counterpart of the Queen's paroxysm of hatred in the previous scene, exorcizing its malevolence. And in the aria with chorus, "O Isis und Osiris" – which Schikaneder designated for chorus alone – Mozart draws a portrait of unambiguously benevolent power (music that demands, but by no means always gets, a true basso cantante of velvety timbre, resonant low notes and ample legato). Nor is the chorus deprived of its opportunity. Its two-fold repetition of Sarastro's final phrase, each time differently distributed among the four parts and the orchestral accompaniment, adds to the mysterious solemnity of the piece, which the three-bar orchestral epilogue seals with a wonderful sense of finality – "the only music yet written", Shaw said, "that would not sound out of place in the mouth of God".

The strange orchestration of the aria – basset-horns, bassoons, trombones, violas in two parts, cellos, and no violins or double basses – is characteristic of a work which we may tend to think of as more plainly scored than its predecessors but which in fact takes the Mozartian principle of particular, dramatically motivated tone colour to its furthest point. Hardly two of the forty-odd separate or linked movements that make up *The Magic Flute* have the same instrumental forces.

This is not just because the orchestra contains exotic instruments: the masonic basset-horns, which appear at Sarastro's first entrance, the glockenspiel which twinkles with (in both senses) enchanting effect when Papageno plays his magic bells: they are used in only a handful of numbers. Nor is it because of the presence of trombones, predominantly ecclesiastical instruments in Mozart's time but used here not just in a scene or two, as they are in *Don Giovanni* and *Idomeneo*, but in fully a quarter of the work, and in nearly half the numbers in Act 2, their glowing, momentous tones at the beginning of the overture telling us that this is not a conventional singspiel but a sacred comedy. (The overture, commonly regarded as a grand but abstract prelude to the action, establishing its seriousness but not directly related to it, is part of the drama: the solemn adagio leading through tension and uncertainty – throbbing syncopations, harmonic darkenings – to the polyphony of the allegro, in which the trials that are to come, and their eventual resolution, are prefigured.) More than these special colours, it is the constantly varied handling of the normal opera band and the peculiar luminosity of the sound that make *The Magic Flute* an orchestral experience fully the equal of the Da Ponte operas and its orchestra a no less active agent in the drama. Restraint is a spur to greater subtlety. The evidence of the changes Mozart made to the autograph score shows him generally reducing the orchestration, not enriching it, as in the opening number, where the tense, rushing C minor music with its sharp dynamic contrasts, stabbing accents and lurid wind chords – Tamino pursued by the serpent – originally included trumpets and drums, later crossed out and reserved for the Three Ladies' arrival in triumphant mock-heroic A flat major. But such economies are always in the interests of greater precision and ever more exact tone colouring.

Or consider the clarinet in *The Magic Flute*. Much as Mozart loved it, his use of it here is sparing. Except for numbers employing virtually the whole orchestra but not using basset-horns or, if so, alternating them with clarinets (the same players) – the overture, No. 1, the Act 1 finale, the priests' duet (No. 11), the Act 2 finale – they play quite rarely and, because of that, with great effect when they do. Clarinets in B flat colour Tamino's portrait aria and punctuate the Pamina–Papageno duet. Their entry at the end of the first quintet, above pizzicato strings – at the point where the Ladies announce the coming of the Three Boys – diffuses a mild, mysterious light over the orchestra, in striking contrast to the sound of the piece up till then (oboes, bassoons, horns, busy strings). In Act 2, after Monostatos' aria (which uses the harder, brighter C clarinets), they are silent for seven numbers. As a result, their reappearance at the beginning of the finale, leading the wind sextet in the small garden as the Boys await the dawning of the day of deliverance, has a healing beauty all the more intense for their absence during the preceding half hour.

Though it would be wrong to single out the Boys' music in *The Magic Flute* for particular praise – Mozart spends his art impartially on all his creatures – no other composer could have created the airy, playful trio (No. 16) as the Boys appear for the second time, floating down in their flying-machine decorated with roses and bringing the Flute and the Bells and a table laid with food and drink. Even by the standards of Mozart's music, which habitually seems to move above the earth as though airborne, touching the ground only momentarily, this A major allegretto – its whimsical flourishes for violins, flutes and bassoons contrasting beautifully with the calm flow of the three-part vocal harmony supported most of the time by cellos without basses – is a minor miracle. There is so little to it yet the delight it gives is beyond words.

Again, nothing on the face of it could be simpler, barer, more obvious than the scoring, and the harmonization, of the music where Pamina and Tamino greet each other before passing through their last ordeals: repeated chords on violins and violas, long horn and woodwind notes, pizzicato cello and bass playing a rising five-note figure (the feminine principle finally vindicated); yet the simplicity of the work here reaches its height. The musical narrative moves with an ease that makes it seem totally natural and unpremeditated; but when, after Pamina (accompanied by an expressive bassoon counter-melody) has recounted the origin of the Flute, the tonality regains F major and the four voices – the lovers and the two men in armour – join in an exalted quartet, we experience a sense of concord and fulfilment that has few parallels in music.

After that there is a quiet modulation to C, a pause, and then – as Pamina and Tamino pass through the fire and the water – the strangest, sparest sound in the whole score, a climax of mysterious stillness. Without raising his voice and by means of a march played by a handful of instruments – an ornate, incantatory melody for solo flute in an undeviating C major punctuated at the end of each phrase by brass chords and by drum notes always on the weak beat – Mozart creates an overwhelming tension, the ordeals of a lifetime compressed into a few bars. In between, Pamina and Tamino, accompanied by strings and woodwind, sing together while the power of music leads them through the fiery furnace and the roaring cataract, and then again as they emerge into a light-filled universe – a love duet lasting two bars. They have become a single soul.*

The balance of the work now demands that Papageno's needs be attended to; his quest too must achieve its appointed end. So we return to the little garden where the Boys saved Pamina, and where Papageno is now searching and calling for his mate and hoping his panpipes will bring her to him. The sound and texture and pulse could not be in greater contrast to what we have just been listening to: bright G major, dancing 6/8, flute, oboes, bassoons, horns, strings alternately skittish and – in the catchy refrain – warmly legato. Mozart's sympathy for the poor fellow's forlorn longing overflows. We do not know exactly when he wrote the piece, but it could well have been when Constanze was in Baden and he was missing her company. At one point he alters the libretto's "Papagena, Herzenstäubchen, Papagena, liebes Weibchen" ("... dove of my heart ... dear little wife") to "... Herzensweibchen ... liebes Täubchen". "Herzensweibchen" – "little wife of my heart" – was one of his favourite ways of addressing Constanze in his letters.

The duet with Papagena – the two of them at first hardly able to believe their good fortune or do anything but stare and mouth the syllables of their names hungrily – is a masterpiece of comic-erotic invention, with orchestration of marvellous freshness and brilliance, full of trilling violins and gurgling bassoons, and with sudden flashing fortes. As they scamper away, the Queen, the Three Ladies and Monostatos rise from the ground, bent on a last attempt to overthrow the order. The orchestral sound is again new, with a combination of wind instruments – flutes, oboes, clarinets and bassoons but no horns – that has not been heard before, and close vocal harmony, stealthy string staccatos and tremolos, and eerie woodwind chords: an effect not so much sinister as dreamlike. The Queen and her creatures, or rather the unredeemed attributes they embody, do not have to be

---

* It is characteristic of this unconventional work that the lovers' first meeting, in the Act 1 finale, should be accomplished almost in parenthesis, in fifteen bars of rapid tempo.

defeated in pitched battle but can be cast off in one final spasm – a blare of brass and syncopated strings in diminished-seventh harmony (prefigured at the end of the second quintet) – to return to the night of illusion to which they belong, for they are now only shadows, faint memories of former discords in the unenlightened soul, fading for ever in the splendour of the rising sun. Sarastro proclaims the passing of night. Then the dark C minor music that introduced the Armed Men returns, transposed to the relative major and transfigured, a solemn brilliant hymn in E flat major hailing the two who brought victory and giving thanks to the gods.

By the end we have no sense that the many different sounds we have heard belong to anything but one work, one comprehensive vision, even though we may not be able to say how Mozart does it: how a score embracing such an extravagant range of sonorities and characteristics – Papageno's peasant patter, the Queen of Night, raging, imperious, the charming frivolity of the Ladies, the hymnlike textures of Sarastro and the priests (which were to have such an influence on Beethoven), Tamino's ardour, Pamina's intensity of feeling and generosity of spirit, the airy purity of the Boys' music – creates a coherent identity, a profound unity-in-diversity symbolized by the healing power of the Flute, the single instrument that in the legends Osiris created out of the shepherd's multiple pipes. The coherence of the *Magic Flute* style – a fusion of Viennese vernacular song, Italian bravura aria and buffo ensemble, German chorale, fugue, Gluckian religious chorus, extended accompanied recitative-cum-arioso, learned and popular, sacred and profane, spirit and earth, the musical analogue of the drama's high theme of reconciliation – is in some ways Mozart's supreme achievement as a music-dramatist.

Though a conscious document of Freemasonry and an affirmation of faith in the beliefs and mysteries of the Craft, *The Magic Flute* reaches out to everyone willing to let it. We do not have to read all the signs in order to receive the message. Its essential meaning is clear (though we may never exhaust its meaningfulness). We have only to rid ourselves of the conviction of our own superior cleverness. We might then discover that we no longer found the no doubt fatuous dialogue between Tamino and Papageno in the opening scene beneath us, and that we so wanted Papageno to find his sweetheart that we could even enjoy his farcical exchanges with the old crone of "achtzig (achtzehn) Jahre" who is Papagena in disguise. "Except ye become as little children . . ." Mozart does not disdain to use the vulgar medium of popular comedy for his parable of the purification of the soul. Like Shakespeare, he sees no incongruity – rather, a fitness.

After all the commentaries that have been expended on this marvellous work, perhaps the wisest words are those of the Three Boys: "Schweige still" – keep quiet, and listen.

It looks as if Mozart was working on the score between late May and mid-July. What little we know about the order of composition comes from his letters to Constanze – she went to Baden on 4 June and was there for five or six weeks – and from study of the autograph and its different inks and watermarks. It was not an easy time for Mozart. He missed Constanze acutely and, though he sometimes joined her and Carl for the weekend, was on his own much of the time and felt restless. He was also distracted by the business of arranging a large loan, apparently with his old friend Baron Wetzlar, and the difficulties and frustrations and interruptions it involved. That may have been why the opera, which seems to have been quite well advanced by early June, was still not quite finished in the middle of July.

The reference to the priests' duet (mentioned above) in a letter written on 11 June – "Tod und Verzweiflung" etc. – suggests that composition of Act 2 was already under way by the first week of June. In the same letter Mozart speaks of composing "an aria for my opera today out of sheer boredom [. . .] I can't tell you what I wouldn't give to be with you at Baden instead of stuck here." By early July his pupil Süssmayr, now in Baden, was copying out the short score of Act 1 and Mozart was urging Constanze to make him hurry up so that he could orchestrate it. The last letter from that period to refer to the opera is dated 7 July. Mozart tells of his longing for her company and of how lonely he feels without her:

When I think how merry we were together at Baden – like children – and what sad, weary hours I am spending here! Even my work gives me no pleasure, because I am accustomed to stop working now and then and exchange a few words with you. Alas! this pleasure is no longer possible. If I go to the piano and sing something from my opera I have to stop at once, it moves me too deeply.

Not long afterwards he brought Constanze, heavily pregnant with their sixth child, home to Vienna, and the correspondence ceased. The next recorded event is an entry in the thematic catalogue: "*Die Zauberflöte*, German opera, by Eman. Schikaneder, containing 22 numbers", given simply as "In July", without precise date. Two numbers, however, the overture and the march which begins Act 2, still remained to be composed: they were entered over two months later, on 28 September, shortly before the first night. Evidence of watermarks and paper-types shows that three others – the Boys' A major allegretto, Pamina's aria, and the farewell trio – were apparently revised at about the same time. *The Magic Flute* had thus still to be completed when Mozart was forced to set it aside and turn his energies to a new commission, from Prague.

8

Propaganda and parable
La clemenza di Tito

Mozart was not first choice for composer of the opera commissioned by the Bohemian Estates to celebrate the crowning of Leopold II as King of Bohemia. The contract drawn up with Domenico Guardasoni, intendant of the Prague company, on 8 July 1791, required him to engage "un cellebre maestro" – a composer of renown – without specifying who it should be. This was common sense. They had left it late. The coronation was scheduled for 6 September, barely two months ahead. In those two months Guardasoni had to find a poet able and willing either to write a new libretto on one of two (unnamed) subjects proposed by Count Rottenhan, Governor of Bohemia, or, if that was impossible in the time available, to adapt Metastasio's *La clemenza di Tito* for the occasion, procure a composer to set it, and engage a top-class prima donna and musico (castrato) for two of the leading roles.

Guardasoni arrived in Vienna in mid-July and secured the services of Caterino Mazzolà, the Dresden court poet who had recently been appointed to Vienna as Da Ponte's replacement. They probably needed very little discussion to decide that an adaptation of Metastasio's well-worn but still admired text, now nearly sixty years old, was the only feasible option. Having got his librettist, Guardasoni then went to see Salieri, but unexpectedly drew a blank. If Salieri is to be believed, Guardasoni asked him five times, brandishing the 200-ducat, 920-gulden fee in his face, but Salieri declined the honour: he was too busy. It was then that Guardasoni turned to Mozart.

By a bizarre twist of fate, Mozart owed this unlooked-for chance to his friend Josef Haydn. Because Haydn was abroad, in London, the task of composing the grand cantata to celebrate the installation of

Prince Anton Esterházy as lord-lieutenant of Oedenburg devolved on Haydn's godson, and Salieri's pupil, Joseph Weigl. Weigl was employed by the Burgtheater. In his absence in Hungary, Salieri had to take on his duties, which – he claimed – left him too little time to accept the Prague commission, "since I alone was attending to the affairs of the court theatre". For once, Mozart had come out on top.

We do not know exactly when Guardasoni concluded arrangements with him (before he set out for Italy in search of his two stars) and therefore how long Mozart had to work on the opera before he left for Prague on 25 August, just under a fortnight before the premiere. But even if all the negotiations took only a few days, that gave him at most six weeks, the first part of which must have been monopolized by joint work on the libretto – for there is no reason to suppose that Mozart left the adaptation entirely to Mazzolà. It was surely a collaborative enterprise, as was his practice. Metastasio's librettos, *Tito* included, had been constantly reused, in shortened form and brought up to date to conform with the new ideas about aria-types and ensembles; but this *Tito* was exceptional in that the text was reshaped to make no fewer than eight ensembles, including the dramatic (and fundamentally anti-Metastasian) finale to Act 1. Mozart's entry in the thematic catalogue, inscribed on 5 September, the eve of the first performance, speaks of "*La clemenza di Tito*, opera seria in two acts" as having been "reduced to a real opera by Sigre Mazzolà" – an operation which, we may be sure, was carried out under the watchful eye and with the active involvement of the composer.

The changes they agreed on – compressing the original's three acts to two, shortening the recitative, simplifying and modifying the plot, reducing the number of arias and rewriting a few of those that remained and, most crucially, removing action from recitative to some of the newly created ensembles – must have been the work of days rather than of hours; it was not a job Mozart would have wished to skimp. Composition may not have begun much before the last week of July. He would then have been free to write the ensembles and choruses and to start on the arias of the one leading singer whose voice he was familiar with, Antonio Baglioni, the tenor for whom he had written Don Ottavio and who was cast as Tito. To compose the obligatory display pieces for the prima donna (Vitellia) and the musico

(Sesto) he must wait till Guardasoni returned from Italy with information about the vocal styles and capabilities of the singers he had
succeeded in engaging.

Tyson's analysis of the paper-types that make up the autograph
score shows that this was, broadly, what happened. The first two
batches (Tyson's Type I and Type II) are concerned almost exclusively
with duets, trios, larger concerted pieces, and arias for Tito. The only
exception is the opening section (adagio) of Sesto's three-part rondo
in Act 2, "Deh per questo istante solo", music of great beauty but
conservative range and style. Type III is mainly taken up with arias
and accompanied recitative for Vitellia and Sesto (including the allegro
and più allegro sections of "Deh per questo") and also with arias for
the supporting characters, Annio, Sesto's sister Servilia, and Publio
the praetorian prefect – by now Mozart knew what he needed to
know about all the singers he was writing for.

From this it is clear that even if Mozart composed *La clemenza di
Tito* in a hurry – as he unquestionably did – he composed it in more
than the eighteen days that Niemetschek claimed was all he had. The
legend persisted, however, and it contributed to the negative image
which dogged the opera through most of the nineteenth century and
a large part of the twentieth. In this view, Mozart did not have the
time to make a satisfactory job of it. Nor, even more fatally, did he
have the will: he took it on not because it appealed to him but
because he needed the money; otherwise he would not have thought
of reverting to a genre as antediluvian and hopelessly limited as opera
seria, which he had last attempted – and transformed – ten years
before, with *Idomeneo*, and had then abandoned for the infinitely
more congenial and artistically rewarding fields of singspiel and opera
buffa. The result was less a drama about living human beings than a
sermon on the responsibilities of enlightened despotism. That was, for
a century and a half, the accepted view.

In retrospect, in the light of the altogether more positive attitude to
the work which followed from the ground-breaking productions by
Jean-Pierre Ponelle and Anthony Besch in the 1960s, 70s and 80s, we
may wonder that Mozart scholars should have been so wrong-headed
– should have allowed their disappointment with what seemed to
them the thinness and frigidity of *Tito* compared to the richness and

abundance of the other mature Mozart operas to blind them to the facts. Opera seria was by no means a dying form in 1791. In Italy especially, its *patria*, but also in many other European centres, it was alive and thriving, as Mozart was well aware: *Tito* shows evidence of a diligent study of recent developments in the serious operas of Sarti, Paisiello and Cimarosa. Mozart wrote none in his first ten Viennese years for the simple reason that he had no opportunity to do so, not because he had lost interest. He thought of performing *Idomeneo* at a concert in the winter of 1783–4, and tried to have it put on at the Burgtheater soon after he arrived in Vienna, but without success. Joseph II largely banished opera seria: it was too formal for his taste and far too expensive, and he liked opera buffa better. Mozart continued to hope for a revival of *Idomeneo*, though in the end he had to be content with performance in a private theatre.

Leopold II, who shared many ideas and policies with his brother, differed from him in this. He was resolved to give serious opera the prominence in Vienna that it had had in Florence during his time as Grand Duke of Tuscany, and in the second year of his imperial reign he took the necessary steps, including the formation of an opera seria company, with (expensive) leading singers brought from Italy. Mozart would have known which way the wind was blowing and would have wanted to go with it, from inclination as well as self-interest. Superficially considered, *Tito* may be a blatant piece of monarchist propaganda; but what attracted Mozart to it, I believe, were its ambiguities and, especially, the idea of forgiveness which, in his treatment of it, is at the heart of the work. The Prague commission was a stroke of luck, to be seized, not merely accepted half-heartedly against his finer artistic judgement. The previous year, Leopold's coronation as Holy Roman Emperor had induced him to go to Frankfurt in the hope – not fulfilled – of commending himself to the imperial attention. Here perhaps was a better chance. The future at the Burgtheater clearly lay with opera seria. By achieving a success in Prague he could become part of it.

Unlike the ultra-rationalist Joseph, Leopold was a firm believer in the political value of elaborate ceremonial as a symbolic gesture of both power and conciliation, at once asserting legitimacy and confirming the alliance with his faithful subjects. He came to the throne only a few months after revolution in France had spread fear and dangerous expectation through Europe, as well as subjecting his sister Marie Antoinette to intolerable indignities and dangers. The Habsburg lands were in disarray – the Austrian Netherlands in revolt, the Hungarian and Bohemian nobility alienated by Joseph's reforms and plotting to recover lost powers and privileges. Leopold hastened to make concessions. At the same time he moved to seal his accession with a series of grand public ceremonies of the kind that Joseph the determined centralizer and puritan had deliberately avoided: his coronations as Holy Roman Emperor and as King of Hungary, both in 1790, and as King of Bohemia in September 1791. The latter involved summoning the Bohemian Estates and taking an oath committing him to uphold their rights. Leopold, whatever his long-term plans, was prepared to do it.* Hence the role of the Estates – the representative assembly of the aristocracy and the Church – in commissioning the opera that would be the centrepiece of the entertainments celebrating the great event, performed on the evening of coronation day itself.

The choice of Metastasio's *Tito* was nicely balanced: a wise and humane ruler who successfully puts down rebellion – by clemency, not by force – but who in so doing overrides the rule of law (Sesto, condemned to death by the Senate, is forgiven and pardoned) and therefore by implication repudiates the Enlightenment doctrine that the law is sovereign, above even the monarch and of course above the nobility. It was a text with reassuring messages for both sides. Every spectator identified Leopold II with the hero of the opera; he had already been called a "latter-day Titus", for his enlightened rule in Tuscany (where he had abolished torture), and a biographer would name him "the German Titus". At the same time, in the context of Joseph's attacks on aristocratic power, Tito's conciliating actions could be seen to carry a sub-text reminding Leopold that he would be well advised (in Nicholas Till's words) to rule "in association with the aristocracy if the new forces of social revolution that were sweeping Europe were to be kept at bay".

*

* Leopold died too soon for it to become clear how far he was intending to continue Joseph's policies.

Given the occasion and the circumstances that led to the work, to what extent if at all was the "neo-classical" simplicity of the music of *La clemenza di Tito* the consequence of the haste with which Mozart composed it? We know that, for want of time, practically all the simple (secco) recitative was delegated to another, in all probability his amanuensis Süssmayr, who was with him in Prague. It is also a reasonable presumption that, with more time, he would not have left the vital opening conversation between Vitellia and Sesto, where the plot to assassinate Tito is broached, as simple recitative. Simple recitative was the prime medium of action in Metastasian but emphatically not in Mozartian drama (where the action is carried on as much in the musical numbers as in the recitatives). For Metastasio its very plainness was the point: it was the text, declaimed by great actor-singers, not the music, that was paramount – the centre of interest, the essential vehicle for the confrontation of the characters and for the working out of their moral and emotional predicaments. Mozart, on the other hand, had from the time of *Idomeneo* onwards, if not before, been master of orchestrally accompanied recitative. In *Idomeneo* accompanied recitative, beginning with Ilia's superb soliloquy, into which the overture leads directly, far outweighs simple recitative in dramatic importance if not in number of bars. It is a basic, but heightened and supremely eloquent, means of communication. *Tito* has its fine accompagnato passages, but far fewer than *Idomeneo*, fewer even than *Così*. Mozart would surely have made the opening dialogue one of them had he not been so hard pressed. Illness may have played a part: Niemetschek's testimony, that "in Prague Mozart fell ill" and had to "dose himself continually", is supported by a news item in the *Krönungsjournal für Prag*, reporting the premiere of the opera: "The composition is by the famous Mozart and does him honour, though he did not have much time for writing it and was also the victim of an illness, during which he had to complete the last part."

Yet the better one comes to know the score and the more one experiences it in performance, the less limited it seems, the more one recognizes that it has a quality, a tone, a beauty of its own that is the result of the way Mozart consciously and deliberately conceived it – of what he put into it, not of what he left out. Certainly we will be disappointed if we look for that consistent and seemingly effortless embodiment of drama in music and musical structure that is a glory of *The Magic Flute* and the Da Ponte operas and of *Idomeneo* itself. Even in remodelled form, as turned into a "real opera", with Metastasio's aria-based, simple-recitative-dominated original partly replaced by a more – in Mozartian terms – dramatic libretto, it provided little scope for that. The remodelling was far from complete. In many scenes the Metastasian system of simple recitative for the exploration of moral and emotional complexities and arias for the expression of a single, unvaried idea – so different from what Mozart had been doing up till then – was left intact. Only rarely, above all in the finale of Act 1, was the composer-dramatist free to let music take complete charge. Here the situation – Sesto racked by remorse, Vitellia by fear and self-hatred, as the Capitol burns and the people mourn the supposed death of the Emperor in awestruck tones that look back to *Idomeneo* and forward to the Requiem – called forth a special response: rapid and violent changes of key, crunching dissonances, sombre orchestration, far-off cries from the terrified populace, and then, dramatically, a hushed, solemn climax and the quietest of endings. By emphasizing the rebellion – which in Metastasio was referred to only in (simple) recitative and took place entirely offstage – it created a magnificent conclusion to the first of the two acts.

There is one further highly dramatic number, the trio "Vengo . . . aspettate . . . Sesto! . . . Ahime!" ("I'm coming . . . wait . . . Sesto! . . . O God!"), in which the vengeful, ambitious Vitellia, who has just sent her lover Sesto to kill the Emperor, learns that the Emperor has chosen her as his wife, while Annio and Publio attribute her confusion to astonished joy at Tito's unexpected decision: an extraordinary number, largely carried on sotto voce, with Vitellia's fragmented vocal line set above a skeletal accompaniment of alternating forte and piano, almost continual tremolando, stabbing accents and sudden brief roars for the full orchestra. But that was about as far as Mozart could go. He could and did write grand and incisive music for the ceremonial scenes: the triumphal march which first introduces Tito in the Forum, surrounded by senators and the Roman people; the splendid G major chorus in praise of Tito, in the amphitheatre (Act 2), music of imposing rhythmic force and harmonic drive; the final sextet and chorus of rejoicing, propelled by trumpet fanfares and resounding drum tattoos and rolls, where the alternation of solo voice (Tito), the five other soloists and the chorus is managed to brilliant effect; and, to introduce it all, the powerful overture which, framed by festive, slightly hectic exposition and recapitulation, foreshadows the tensions and conflicts of the drama in a long and agitated development section. The chief business of the drama, however, remained focused on the interaction of three characters, Tito, Sesto and Vitellia, and on their dilemmas and developing psychologies: Vitellia consumed with hatred of Tito, whose father, Vespasian, robbed her father of the throne, and ruthlessly exploiting the hold her beauty gives her over Sesto (in music characterized by wide vocal leaps, tense syncopations and fierce accents); Sesto torn between his enslavement to Vitellia and his admiration and love for Tito, his close friend; and Tito, endlessly revolving within himself the duties and burdens of kingship, the virtues of clemency, and the right response to Sesto's act of betrayal – a debate whose outcome needs no guessing, given the title of the opera, though a certain tension is sustained by the fact that the other characters, if not the audience, are left for several scenes in ignorance of Tito's decision to pardon Sesto and his fellow-conspirators.

This triangular drama is played out in a series of mostly static, formal arias, duets and trios and in long stretches of simple recitative, varied briefly by the accompanied recitatives: one each for Sesto and Vitellia, two for Tito. There was only so much Mozart could do, once he had committed himself to this particular scenario within so narrow a timeframe. His previous serious opera, *Idomeneo*, was shaped over a period of six months, not the six or seven weeks in which *Tito* came to birth.

All the same I do not see its simplifications, except in one or two cases, as a concession either to haste or to the formality of the occasion. This was how he heard it in his mind's ear. Maybe with more time he would have involved the orchestra in the great scene in Act 2 between Tito and Sesto, the hub of the drama and one of the acknowledged summits of Metastasio's art, where the Emperor tries by every means possible to persuade his friend to explain his crime, while Sesto, intent on protecting Vitellia, evades his increasingly urgent questioning. It might have made a memorable accompanied recitative, if not a vivid duet. Yet, as it is, left as simple recitative, it still offers rich opportunities to two artists who know how to act and declaim and who are directed sympathetically. And the effect of the strings stealing in softly with the first strains of Sesto's rondo, after so much secco recitative, is a magical moment.

The tenderness and directness of the rondo are characteristic of Mozart's *Tito*. Though there are remarkable sounds in the opera – new sounds, like the strange passage of two-part harmony near the end of Vitellia's soliloquy in Act 2, where the voice is accompanied only by the solo basset-horn in its lowest register – the instrumentation is generally much plainer than in any other mature opera of Mozart's. So is the harmonic language (though not more so than that of *The Magic Flute*: that was the way his style was tending). Despite this plainness, partly because of it, *La clemenza di Tito* has the high finish and purity of the finest neo-classical art.

In no other Mozart opera are there so many short numbers: the little friendship duet for Sesto and Annio is only twenty-four bars long, Tito's first aria sixty-five bars and his second sixty-three, the ravishing A major love duet for Servilia and Annio sixty-two, Annio's plea to Sesto to throw himself on Tito's mercy fifty-four, Publio's aria fifty-three (it is still too long), Servilia's charming minuet "S'altro che lacrime" ("If with tears only") fifty-two. Their brevity gave Mozart space to expand in the arias in which the three main characters express their feelings: Vitellia's deceitful, manipulative "Deh se piacer mi vuoi" and her big showpiece with basset-horn obbligato, Sesto's "Parto, parto, ma tu ben mio" with solo clarinet and his A major rondo, and, not least, Tito's third aria, "Se all' impero", where the Emperor exults in his clemency and his decision to pardon Sesto, a decision that is hard won, achieved only after a long inner struggle for emotional self-mastery expressed in passionate accompanied recitative – for Tito, as Mozart depicts him, is no mere cipher or lifeless symbol but a ruler of heroic generosity.

Mozart had no great reason to think kindly of Leopold II. In the all-forgiving Tito he may well rather have seen an emblem of masonic goodness and benevolence. Several scholars have recognized Mozart's Tito as sharing attributes with Sarastro. The German musicologist Paul Nettl speculates that some members of the Bohemian Estates – Counts Thun, Canal and Pachta, for example, who were all masons

– "may have been motivated by the same thoughts" as Mozart in their choice of subject for the coronation opera. In this connection, a much later account, apparently based on contemporary records, reports that Mozart visited the Prague lodge Truth and Unity at the Three Crowned Pillars several times while he was in the city (as indeed we would expect him to have done). "The last time he attended, the Brothers were standing in two rows, and when he entered he was greeted with the cantata *Die Maurerfreude* which he had composed in 1785 in tribute to Born. Mozart was deeply touched by this attention and, when he thanked them, said that soon he would offer Freemasonry a better act of allegiance."

Whether or not, in one's heart of hearts, one warms to *Tito*, its seriousness of approach, care of workmanship and nobility of tone are incontrovertible. There are not many perfunctory bars in the score. Though it appears not to have pleased the imperial party, it is a coronation opera any enlightened sovereign would be proud to be honoured by. Whether or not the Empress Maria Luisa really made the remark later attributed to her – "Una porcheria tedesca" (German pigswill) – the shallow judgement echoed down the years. It sorts well with the entry in her diary: "In the evening to the theatre. The grand opera is not so grand, and the music very bad, so that almost all of us fell asleep. The coronation went splendidly." But *La clemenza di Tito*, received now into the repertory all over the world, has had the last laugh.

Mozart and Constanze, with Süssmayr, set out on the morning of 25 August. Only a month before, Constanze had given birth to a son, Franz Xaver Wolfgang. (It is not known who looked after him in her absence – perhaps her mother or one of her sisters – but he seems to have been well enough cared for: he lived into his fifties.) As Robbins Landon remarks, Mozart must have been particularly anxious to have her company, and she in turn may have been worried about his health. "Mozart was now dangerously overworked"; the Prague opera, and *The Magic Flute*, were still unfinished, he had probably not begun on the Requiem (commissioned shortly before, in circumstances which remain problematical), and there was the promised clarinet concerto for Stadler to complete.

Robbins Landon's *1791: Mozart's Last Year* contains an evocative account of the three-day journey:

The last stagecoach ride to the city that had always particularly loved his music and encouraged him took place during the final week in August, when the Austrian countryside always looks its most beautiful: the harvest is being taken by men and women on high-wheeled carts, the fields are slowly beginning to turn brown, and the first touches of red and gold are beginning to appear on the leaves of the vineyards north of Vienna. But as the carriage climbs towards Znaim on the post-road, the fields are too windswept for vines; and barley, oats and hay fill the huge fields, sloping in slow curves upwards towards Bohemia.

The travellers arrived on 28 August and lodged either in town or at the Duscheks'. Mozart had much to do and only ten days to do it. He had to finish the score: not only the numbers that are written on Prague paper (Tyson's Type V), including the overture, the march and Tito's first aria, but very probably some of the arias on Type III which he had not been able to complete in the brief weeks between Guardasoni's return from Italy, bringing information about the cast, and the departure for Prague. Time being so short, each number was handed to the copyists as it was completed. And in the midst of last-minute composition he had also to rehearse the singers and the orchestra.

How good or bad was the performance which sent the royal party to sleep and which the inevitable Zinzendorf described as a "boring spectacle"? We don't know. The orchestra, which had played *Figaro* and *Don Giovanni* many times in the same theatre, is not likely to have let the composer down. Mozart clearly had high expectations of his Tito, Antonio Baglioni: Tito's third aria is if anything even more taxing than Don Ottavio's "Il mio tesoro", written for Baglioni (in the same key, B flat) and presumably sung by him to Mozart's satisfaction. The Vitellia, Maria Marchetti Fantozzi, was widely admired both for her voice and for her acting (the Emperor, according to Zinzendorf, was "enthusiastic about her"). Domenico Bedini, Sesto, was nearing the end of his career but was still well regarded, not least by Mozart himself. Niemetschek seems to have been in a minority in complaining, a few years later, that the performance suffered from "a wretched castrato and a prima donna who sang more with her hands than her throat". But he may have been right when he added that "this heavenly work" (in which "Gluck's dignity is united to Mozart's original art") was too simple to interest an audience "preoccupied with coronation festivities, balls and illuminations". The celebrations were on a prodigious scale, with a bewilderingly varied programme of events, including plays, operas, masked balls, banquets, garden parties, firework displays, circuses, fairs and magic shows, offered to a city bursting with visitors. *La clemenza di Tito* had to compete with dozens of other attractions and, on the day of the premiere, with the coronation itself, the immense procession winding for hours through the streets to the sound of massed bands and gunfire. What state of freshness and receptivity would anyone have been in that evening? Such audiences are not the most receptive at the best of times (think of the ill-fated first night of Britten's *Gloriana* at Covent Garden in 1953). Zinzendorf says he went to the theatre at five o'clock but that the royal party did not arrive till "after 7.30" ("after eight o'clock", according to one report). Perhaps it was "one of those nights": cast and orchestra – under-rehearsed, it may be – nervous and Mozart, unwell, below his best. A thumbs down from an emperor and empress with "a preconceived aversion to Mozart's composition" – as stated by Count Rottenhan, who was in the royal box – would have been enough to turn the audience against it and seal the fate of the performance.

Yet, paradoxically, the month-long festivities were full of Mozart. Salieri, in charge of the official church music, brought scores and parts of three Mozart masses with him (K258, 317 and 337) as well as the Offertorium Misericordias Domini, K222, and a chorus from *König Thamos* arranged as a Latin motet. On 1 September, at a dinner in the Empress's residence, the music was from *Don Giovanni*, arranged for wind ensemble. The following evening *Don Giovanni* itself was given by Guardasoni's company at the National Theatre "by highest request" – i.e. curiously, by order of the Emperor or the Empress or, if not, a senior member of the court – and attended by the royal couple, the house being "crammed full". Mozart was there, according to the writer Franz Alexander von Kleist (uncle of the poet Heinrich Kleist), who describes "a little man in a green coat, whose eye proclaims what his modest appearance would conceal" and "whose joy it is to see for himself with what delight his beautiful harmonies fill the hearts of the public".

His dance music too undoubtedly figured at the numerous balls given during these weeks, not least at the gala on 12 September when five orchestras numbering 300 musicians played in the various rooms. And *Tito* itself was repeated. Like many of the evening shows it was poorly attended at first but seems to have picked up later in the month. By then Mozart and Constanze had left Prague; but Anton Stadler, who had remained (he was playing the clarinet and basset-horn solos), wrote to tell him that the final performance, on 30 September, was received with "tremendous applause". Mozart's letter relaying the news to Constanze (she was again in Baden) continues:

Bedini sang better than ever. The little duet in A major which the two girls sing was repeated, and had not the audience wished to spare Madame Marchetti, a repetition of the rondo would have been welcomed. Cries of "bravo" were shouted at Stodla [Stadler] from the parterre and even from the orchestra. "What a miracle for Bohemia!" he writes, "but indeed I did my very best."

By a strange coincidence, Mozart adds, it was "on the very evening when my new opera was performed for the first time with such success".

By the time Mozart returned to Vienna the premiere of *The Magic Flute* was at most two weeks off. Before leaving for Prague he would have given Schikaneder the bulk of the score, so that it could be rehearsed in his absence, under the company's young music director Henneberg. Now he revised Pamina's aria, the Boys' A major allegretto and the farewell trio, and composed the march (provided for in the libretto but not yet written) and the overture, entering the latter two in the catalogue on 28 September, two days before the first night. Meanwhile he had taken over the musical rehearsals.

Even if the tales which circulated after his death about his late-night drinking bouts with Schikaneder were invented, as they probably were (none of the stories is earlier than 1803), he was on easy, friendly terms with the members of the troupe. The days leading up to the first performance, and thereafter, would have been filled with intense, concentrated work but at the same time relaxed and happy. He knew the company well and was content with the cast: Gerl, the Sarastro, for whose deep bass he had written before, Schack (Tamino), who was a good friend, the precocious Anna Gottlieb (Pamina), who five years before, aged only twelve, had sung Barbarina in *Figaro*, his sister-in-law Josepha Hofer for whose powerful soprano and brilliant high notes the Queen of Night was conceived, and Schikaneder himself, not only a practised comedian who would make the most of Papageno but also a good singer – according to a contemporary critic his voice was "pure and melodious, and he sings with simplicity and taste".

There is no information about the premiere. But *The Magic Flute* quickly became a hit and was packed out night after night. Thanks to Constanze's being again in Baden for the waters – she went on 7 October, with the baby, Wolfgang, and was joined there by her sister Sophie – we have first-hand testimony of its progress, in the three letters from Mozart that survive.

He has just returned from the opera, he writes in one of them, on "Saturday night at half past ten o'clock". "Although Saturday – post-day – is always a bad night, the opera was performed to a full house and with the usual applause and repetition of numbers. It will be given again tomorrow." Mozart was no longer conducting it – Henneberg had taken his place – but he was constantly in the audience. In another letter, written on the 7th (the day Constanze went to Baden), he has

this moment returned from the opera, which was as full as ever. As usual the duet "Mann und Weib" and Papageno's glockenspiel in Act 1 had to be repeated and also the trio of the boys in Act 2. But what always gives me most pleasure is the *silent approval*. You can see how this opera is becoming more and more esteemed. Now for an account of my own doings. Immediately after your departure I played two games of billiards with Herr von Mozart, the fellow who wrote the opera which is running at Schikaneder's theatre, then I sold my nag for fourteen ducats, then I told Joseph to get Primus to fetch me some black coffee, with which I smoked a splendid pipe of tobacco; and then I orchestrated almost the whole of Stadler's rondo [the finale of the clarinet concerto, K622]. [. . .] At half past five I went out by the Stuben Gate and took my favourite walk over the Glacis to the theatre. But what do I see? What do I smell? Why, here is Don Primus with the cutlets! Che gusto! Now I am eating to your health. It's just striking eleven. Perhaps you're already asleep. Sh! sh! sh! I won't wake you.

Saturday the 8th. You should have seen me at supper yesterday. I couldn't find the old tablecloth so I fished out another one, white as a snowdrop, and put in front of me the double candlestick with wax candles. [. . .] As I write, no doubt you are having a good swim. The friseur came punctually at six o'clock. At half past five Primus had lit the fire and he then woke me at a quarter to six. Why must it rain just now? I did so much hope you would be having lovely weather. Do keep good and warm, so that you don't catch cold. I hope these baths will help you keep well during the winter. Only the desire to see you in good health made me urge you to go to Baden. I already feel lonely without you – I knew I should. If I'd had nothing to do I should have gone off at once to spend the week with you; but I have no facilities for working at Baden, and I'm anxious as far as possible to avoid all risk of money problems – the most pleasant thing of all is to have a mind at peace. But to achieve that one has to work hard. And I like hard work.

A few days later, on the 13th, he took his mother-in-law and the seven-year-old Carl to the opera, having first collected Salieri and his mistress Cavalieri and deposited them in his box.

You can hardly imagine how charming they were [Salieri and Cavalieri] and how much they liked not only my music but the libretto and everything. They both said it was an *operone* [grand opera], worthy to be performed for the grandest festival and before the greatest monarch, and that they would often come to see it, as they had never seen a more beautiful or delightful show. Salieri listened and watched most attentively and from the overture to the last chorus there was not a single number that did not call forth from him a bravo! or bello! It seemed as if they could not thank me enough for my kindness. They had been intending to go to the opera yesterday; but they would have had to be in their places by four o'clock. As it was, they saw and heard everything in comfort in my box. When it was over I drove them home and then had supper at Hofer's with Carl. Then I drove him home and we both slept soundly. Carl was absolutely delighted at being taken to the opera. He is looking splendid.

With the clarinet concerto virtually done, the work he referred to presumably meant the Requiem.

I have just swallowed a delicious slice of sturgeon which Don Primus, my faithful valet, brought me, and as I have a rather voracious appetite today I have sent him to fetch some more if he can. So during this break I shall go on writing to you. This morning I worked so hard at my composition that I went on till half past one. Then I dashed off in great haste to Hofer's, so as not to lunch alone, and found Mamma there too. After lunch I went straight home and composed again till it was time to go to the opera. Leutgeb begged me to take him again and I did.

Despite the work on the Requiem, *The Magic Flute* still loomed large:

The Adambergers had a box this evening. (?Adamberger) applauded everything most heartily. But he, the know-all, showed himself such a thorough Bavarian that I couldn't stay, or I should have had to call him an ass. Unfortunately I was there just when the second act began, that is at the solemn scene. He laughed at everything. At first I was patient enough to draw his attention to one or two passages. But he laughed at everything. I couldn't stand it any longer – I called him a Papageno and cleared out. But I don't think the fool realized what I meant. Then I went into another box where Flamm and his wife happened to be. There everything was very pleasant and I stayed till the end. But during Papageno's aria with the glockenspiel I went backstage as I felt a sort of impulse today to play it myself. Well, just for fun, at the point where Schikaneder has a pause, I played an arpeggio. He was startled and looked into the wings, and saw me. When he had his next pause, I didn't play an arpeggio. This time he stopped and wouldn't go on. I guessed what he was thinking and again played a chord. He then struck his glockenspiel and said "shut up!" – at which everyone laughed. I'm inclined to think our byplay taught many of the audience for the first time that Papageno doesn't play the instrument himself. By the way, you've no idea how charming the music sounds when you hear it from a box close to the orchestra – much better than from the gallery. As soon as you get back you must try it for yourself. [. . .] Kiss Sophie for me. I send Süssmayr a few good nosepulls and a proper hair-tug and Stoll a thousand greetings. Farewell. The hour has struck. We'll meet again.*

---

* The last eight words are a quotation from *The Magic Flute* – the farewell trio.

There are no letters from the second half of October to reflect the continued fortunes of the opera. Constanze was back. But Zinzendorf noted a "huge audience" when he saw it from Count and Countess Auersperg's box on 6 November, the twenty-fourth performance. His comment on the work was "music and stage designs pretty, the rest an unbelievable farce". Some newspapers could not forgive Mozart for his spectacular success. *Der Heimliche Botschafter* crossly announced that "Herr Schikaneder will before long have an opera performed which will far surpass *Die Zauberflöte* [...] entitled *Helen und Paris*" (this was by Peter Winter, a sworn enemy of Mozart's). And a Viennese news item in the Berlin *Musikalisches Wochenblatt* reported that "the new comedy with machines, *Die Zauberflöte*, with music by our kapellmeister Mozart, which is given at great cost and with much magnificence of scenery, is failing to have the hoped-for success, the contents and language of the piece being altogether too bad. We now daily await the arrival of the new imperial kapellmeister, Cimarosa, who is said to be bringing some excellent singers with him from St Petersburg. It looks as though no very advantageous epoch is in prospect here for German composers and musicians."

After all, this was Vienna. But the theatre was full every night and the opera was given three or four times a week; and it was not only the middle classes and the artisans who flocked to it. Mozart was enjoying the operatic triumph of his career.

Epilogue

In the event he would not enjoy it for long.

The circumstances surrounding Mozart's final illness, death and burial are still impossible to determine with certainty, even after the strenuous disentanglings and clarifications of Carl Bär, Braunbehrens, Stafford, Robbins Landon and others. Legend was already at work almost as the swollen body was placed on its bier in the little room on the first floor of the house in Rauhensteingasse where the young musician Ludwig Gall remembered seeing (if he actually did see) "the dead Master", "lying in a coffin, in a black suit with a cowl down over the forehead hiding the blond hair and the hands folded over his breast". An ordinary death, very possibly from recurrence of a disease that could have carried him off years before or from a common infection aided by energetic blood-letting by his doctor, was simply too mundane a cause for the extinction of so rare a spirit. It could not have been so haphazard, so cruelly accidental. There had to be other explanations, stranger, perhaps sinister.

Everyone, not excluding his grieving widow, would add their faithfully remembered testimony to the tale. We cannot be sure if Mozart really told Constanze, as they sat together in the Prater on a fine autumn day towards the end of that October, that he felt he had been poisoned and was writing the Requiem for himself. By the time she told Niemetschek (who recounted the story), she too had been drawn into the myth-making process.

Only a bare outline of those final weeks can be attempted. The score of the clarinet concerto must have been sent no later than about 9 or 10 October, to reach Stadler in time to be copied and rehearsed for his concert on the 16th. Mozart then worked on the Requiem, interrupting it only to compose the Little Masonic Cantata, K623, for two tenors, bass and orchestra, which had been commissioned by his lodge New Crowned Hope to celebrate their moving to a new hall. He conducted it at the inaugural ceremony on 18 November. By then, in all probability, the Introit of the Requiem was fully scored and some of the rest nearly complete or written in short score. Then about two days later Mozart took to his bed, apparently not to leave it again before he died, at five minutes to 1 a.m. on Monday 5 December.

How did the hours pass during those fifteen days? What was the detailed course of the disease? How much was he able to do – to talk – to communicate, of his intentions for the Requiem, of other things? We long to know; but the accounts of those who were there – Constanze, her sister Sophie, Eybler, Schack – most of them set down many years later or relayed at second or third hand, are too inconsistent and contradictory (sometimes contradicting themselves) to give us much idea.

In one, Mozart, during all his illness, is "completely conscious till two hours before his death", in another he has "periods of unconsciousness". In one, his mind remains clear throughout, in another he has hallucinations, imagining he is at a performance of *The Magic Flute*: "Almost the last words he whispered to his wife were: 'Sh! Hofer is taking the high F – now my sister-in-law is singing her second aria. [. . .] how powerfully she hits the B flat and holds it!'" Constanze remembered that only "a few moments before [his death] he had spoken so gaily". But she also remembered that his last words expressed his sorrow at leaving his family unprovided for, then "suddenly he began to vomit – it spat out of him in an arch, brown – and he was dead".

None of this inconsistency is surprising, least of all in the reminiscences of Constanze and of Sophie; the whole dreadful experience must have been inexpressibly traumatic. In Nissen's biography of Mozart Constanze is described as climbing into the bed and clinging to the corpse in the hope of catching the disease; in Sophie's account Constanze "could not tear herself [from the body], beg her as I did".

Sophie also says that Mozart's last movement before he died was "an attempt to express with his mouth the drum passages in the Requiem". Though that sounds fanciful, it is perhaps not the kind of circumstantial detail that anyone would invent or believe they witnessed when they didn't. It raises the larger question: could Mozart on his sickbed – as was fervently believed ever afterwards – have tried out parts of the score, especially in the early days of the illness? It is possible. Several eyewitnesses speak of it, though their accounts don't agree. One even recalls a full-dress rehearsal, with Mozart singing alto, Schack bizarrely taking the soprano line falsetto, and Franz Hofer and Gerl tenor and bass. Sophie recalled "Süssmayr at M's bedside, with the well-known Requiem lying on the coverlet and Mozart explaining how he should complete it after his death". According to Niemetschek (echoed by Nissen), he had the score of the Requiem brought to his bed. "'Didn't I say I was writing the Requiem for myself?' This he spoke, and looked over the whole attentively, with tears in his eyes. It was the last painful farewell to his beloved art."

The unfinished work must have been much in his thoughts as he lay there, day after day, and there would surely have been discussions about it; but we have to be, prosaically, on our guard against such seductive stories. That someone so sick, with badly swollen hands and in acute discomfort, could have been – as Sophie claimed – writing part of the Requiem "on the very day he died" is to say the least improbable. These stories, which resounded down the Mozart mythology, conferred a kind of redeeming aura on his death. But, as Stafford remarks, "in spite of romantic nineteenth-century paintings and novels, Mozart's death bed scene cannot have been noble, tranquil and sentimental. It will have been sordid, characterized by pain and fear."

More plausible are the homely details remembered by Sophie: that she and her mother, Frau Weber, made Mozart a special nightshirt which could be put on and taken off frontways, because in his swollen state he was unable to turn and could lie only on his back. She also recalled their making him a quilted dressing-gown to wear when he was better and was able to get up – for at that stage they didn't realize how serious the illness was, perhaps because at first it did not seem so bad, after all he had been ill before and had recovered; he too may have thought the same, till the last days.

Sophie clearly loved her brother-in-law, and it is her recollections, set down more than thirty years later, that, more than any others, have coloured subsequent published accounts of Mozart's end. Some of those recollections are obviously imagined, or garbled; but her impressions of his character are worth quoting:

I never in all my life saw M. in a temper, much less really angry. [...] Oh, how attentive M—t was when something was wrong with his dear wife. Thus it was once when she was seriously ill and I nursed her for eight long months. I was just sitting by her bed, Mozart too. He was composing at her side; I was observing her sweet slumber, which had been so long in coming. We kept as quiet as the grave so as not to disturb her. Suddenly an unmannerly servant came into the room. Moz. was terrified that his dear wife might be disturbed from her gentle sleep, tried to beckon the man to keep quiet, pushed the chair back behind him, but happened to have his pen-knife open in his hand. This impaled itself between the chair and his thigh in such a way that it dug in up to the handle in the thick flesh. Moz., who usually made such a fuss, did not stir but, biting back his pain, only signalled to me to follow him. We went to the room in which our mother was living secretly – we did not want the good Mozart [Constanze] to realize how ill she was, and that her mother was there in case there was a crisis. She bound him up and put oil of cubebs into his very deep wound; with this St John's oil she succeeded in healing him, and although he had to limp somewhat from the pain, he managed to conceal it and keep it from his dear wife.

What was Mozart's state of mind in those final days when he recognized that he would not recover – when, as one eyewitness reported him saying (like Hotspur in *Henry IV Part 1*), he could taste death "on his tongue"? Did he still think of death as "this best and truest friend of mankind", as "the key which unlocks the door of our happiness", as he had written consolingly in the last letter to his father that has survived, and as his Christian–masonic faith had taught him? Nissen said that Mozart "never became impatient" during his illness, but added, rather inconsequentially, that "as is usual with persons of delicate sensibility he was very afraid of death". Niemetschek, followed closely by Nissen, wrote of Mozart dying "peacefully but very reluctantly. [...] 'To leave my art [...] and my family, my poor children, just when I would be better able to care for them!'" A passage found in Nissen's notes but not used in the biography quotes Constanze as recalling that "he asked his wife what the doctor,

Closset, had said. She answered comfortingly but he contradicted her – 'That's not true' – and was very low-spirited: 'I must die just when I could look after you and the children. Oh, now I must leave you unprovided for.'"

That has the awful ring of truth. His future had been looking a lot more hopeful. If Constanze is right, a consortium of music-loving Hungarian nobles and a group of Amsterdam merchants were both proposing to subsidize him, and there was also the prospect that he might soon succeed Leopold Hofmann as kapellmeister of St Stephen's. It was not the time to die. His creative imagination was still running over. One of the myths that the early death fostered was of a Mozart who in the last months was exhausted in mind as well as in body, in terminal decline even before the final illness struck; he had said all that he had to say. But that is not the impression you get when you read the correspondence and listen to the late compositions. The writer of the letters quoted at the end of the previous chapter is in good heart and living life to the full; the creator of the finale of the clarinet concerto, music exuberantly, unstoppably inventive, or of the early movements of the Requiem – the sweetly gliding Recordare, the haunted opening of the work with its halting strings and plangent bassoon and soft, strange gleam of intertwined basset-horns interrupted by sudden forte and the harsh summons of trumpets and drums – is not exactly wanting in ideas or in the ability to shape and master them. As we have seen, he had several other substantial works in hand besides the Requiem.* Nearly all the remaining sixteen blank pages of the "Catalogue of all my works" were ready ruled on the right-hand side, waiting for the opening bars of the compositions that were to come to be inscribed on them. He had no thought of imminent death.

The symptoms mentioned in the various contemporary accounts – swelling, inflamed joints in hands and feet, spots on the skin, immobility, fever, vomiting – are most commonly thought to support a diagnosis of rheumatic fever, which Mozart had had twice as a child, and/or infective endocarditis, no doubt abetted by the emetics, bloodlettings and cold compresses which his doctor administered in obedience to the medical theories of the time.

* See p. 171.

Contrary to persistent legend, the corpse was not given a pauper's burial and flung into a pit, a communal grave. The third-class funeral chosen by Constanze, on van Swieten's advice, was one that most Viennese opted for, following Joseph II's reforms which had been aimed at curbing the costly and ostentatious burial customs popular in Vienna in the mid-1780s. Maybe, though, the myth is too deeply entrenched ever to be dug up and destroyed: it suits the notion of the divine visitant too well – the miraculous being who vanished as mysteriously as he had come. From time to time the news that Mozart's skull has been identified causes a brief sensation, only for it to be discovered that it is not his after all. In any case the mortal remains and their whereabouts are not of great importance. What is important, perennially, is not the skull but what was inside it, which lives on in the minds and hearts of unnumbered thousands for whom it is a reason for being alive.

Bibliography

Abert, Hermann, *Mozart's Don Giovanni*, trans. Peter   ABERT
Gellhorn, London, 1976

Bär, Carl, *Mozart: Krankheit, Tod, Begräbnis*, Salzburg,   BÄR
1966, 1972

Bauman, Thomas, *W. A. Mozart: Die Entführung aus*   BAUMAN
dem Serail (Cambridge Opera Handbooks), Cambridge, New York, Melbourne, 1987

Beecham, Sir Thomas, *A Mingled Chime: Leaves from*   BEECHAM
an Autobiography, London, New York, 1944

Brandenburger, Sieghard, ed., *Haydn, Mozart, Beet-*   BRANDENBURGER
hoven: Studies in the Music of the Classical Period
(essays in honour of Alan Tyson), Oxford, 1998

Branscombe, Peter, *W. A. Mozart: Die Zauberflöte*,   BRANSCOMBE
(Cambridge Opera Handbooks), Cambridge, New
York, Melbourne, 1991

Braunbehrens, Volkmar, *Mozart in Vienna, 1781–1791*,   BRAUNBEHRENS
trans. Timothy Bell, London, New York, 1990

Brown, Bruce Alan, *W. A. Mozart: Così fan tutte* (Cam-   BROWN
bridge Opera Handbooks), Cambridge, New York,
Melbourne, 1995

Carter, Tim, *W. A. Mozart: Le nozze di Figaro* (Cam-   CARTER
bridge Opera Handbooks), Cambridge, New York,
Melbourne, 1987

Da Ponte, Lorenzo, *Memoirs*, ed. Arthur Livingston,   DA PONTE 1
trans. Elisabeth Abbott, New York, 1929

    An Extract from the Life of Lorenzo Da Ponte,   DA PONTE 2
New York, 1819

Dent, Edward J., *Mozart's Operas: A Critical Study*,   DENT
London, New York, Toronto, 1947

Deutsch, Otto Erich, *Mozart: A Documentary Bio-* DEUTSCH
graphy, trans. Eric Blom, Peter Branscombe and
Jeremy Noble, London, Stanford, 1966

Einstein, Alfred, *Mozart: His Character, his Work*, trans. EINSTEIN
Arthur Mendel and Nathan Broder, London, New
York, 1946

Eisen, Cliff, *New Mozart Documents: A Supplement to* EISEN
O. E. Deutsch's Documentary Biography, Stanford,
1991

    Mozart Studies, ed. Cliff Eisen, Oxford, 1991   EISEN 1
    Mozart Studies 2, ed. Cliff Eisen, Oxford, 1997   EISEN 2

Glover, Jane, *Mozart's Women: his Family, his Friends,* GLOVER
his Music, London, 2005

Gutman, Robert W., *Mozart: A Cultural Biography,* GUTMAN
New York, London, 1999

Halliwell, Ruth, *The Mozart Family: Four Lives in a* HALLIWELL
Social Context, Oxford, 1998

Heartz, Daniel, *Mozart's Operas*, ed., with contributing HEARTZ
essays, by Thomas Bauman, Berkeley, Oxford, 1990

Hildesheimer, Wolfgang, *Mozart*, trans. Marion Faber, HILDESHEIMER
London, New York, 1983

Holden, Anthony, *The Man Who Wrote Mozart: The* HOLDEN
Many Lives of Lorenzo Da Ponte, London, 2006

Karhausen, Lucien, "Weeding Mozart's Medical His- KARHAUSEN
tory", in *Journal of the Royal Society of Medicine*, xci
(1998), 546–50

Kelly, Michael, *Reminiscences of Michael Kelly, of the* KELLY
King's Theatre and Theatre Royal, ed. Roger Fiske,
London, 1975

Kenyon, Nicholas, *The Faber Pocket Guide to Mozart,* KENYON
London, 2005

Kerman, Joseph, *Opera as Drama*, Berkeley, 1988, KERMAN
London, 1989

Koenigsberger, Dorothy, "A New Metaphor for KOENIGSBERGER
Mozart's *Magic Flute*", in *European Studies Review*,
vol. 5, no. 3, July 1975

Link, Dorothea, "Vienna's Private Theatrical and Musi- LINK 1
cal Life, 1783–92, as reported by Count Karl Zinzendorf", in *Journal of the Royal Musical Association*,
cxx, 122 (1997), 205–57

Link, Dorothea, and Nagley, Judith, eds., *Words about* LINK 2
Mozart: Essays in Honour of Stanley Sadie, Wood-
bridge, 2005

Mann, William, *The Operas of Mozart*, London, New MANN
York, 1990

Moberly, R. B., *Three Mozart Operas: Figaro, Don* MOBERLY
Giovanni, The Magic Flute, London, 1967

Moore, Julia, "Mozart in the Market-Place", in *Journal* MOORE
of the Royal Musical Association, cxiv (1989), 18–42

Mozart, W. A., *Briefe und Aufzeichnungen*, ed. Wilhelm BRIEFE
A. Bauer, Otto Erich Deutsch and Joseph Heinz Eibl,
7 vols., Kassel, 1962–75

    Letters of Mozart and his Family, trans. and ed. LETTERS 1
Emily Anderson, rev. Stanley Sadie and Fiona Smart,
London, 1988

    Mozart's Letters, Mozart's Life, ed. and newly LETTERS 2
trans. Robert Spaethling, New York, London, 2001

    Mozart's Thematic Catalogue: a facsimile, ed. Albi CATALOGUE
Rosenthal and Alan Tyson, London, 1990

Niemetschek, Franz, *Life of Mozart*, trans. Helen NIEMETSCHEK
Mautner, London, 1956

Nissen, Georg Nikolaus von, *Biographie W. A. Mozart's* NISSEN
nach Originalbriefen, Leipzig, 1828

Novello, Vincent and Mary, *A Mozart Pilgrimage, being* NOVELLO
the Travel Diaries of Vincent and Mary Novello in the
Year 1829, ed. Nerina Medici and Rosemary Hughes,
London, 1955

Porter, Andrew, *Wolfgang Amadeus Mozart: The Magic* PORTER
Flute, London, New York, 1980

Raeburn, Christopher, "Mozarts Opern in Prag", in RAEBURN
Musica, 13 (1959), 158–63

Rice, John A., *W. A. Mozart: La clemenza di Tito* (Cam- RICE
bridge Opera Guides), Cambridge, New York, Melbourne, 1991

Robbins Landon, H. C., *Mozart: The Golden Years*, LANDON 1
1781–1791, London, New York, 1989

    1791: Mozart's Last Year, London, New York, LANDON 2
1988

    The Mozart Companion, ed. H. C. Robbins Landon LANDON 3
and Donald Mitchell, London, 1965

The Mozart Compendium, ed. H. C. Robbins Landon, London, New York, 1990 — LANDON 4

Rochlitz, Friedrich, "Verbürgte Anekdoten aus Wolfgang Gottlieb Mozarts Leben", in *Allgemeine musikalische Zeitung*, 1–3 (1798–1801) — ROCHLITZ

Rosen, Charles, *The Classical Style: Haydn, Mozart, Beethoven*, London, New York, 1997 — ROSEN

Rushton, Julian, *W. A. Mozart: Idomeneo* (Cambridge Opera Guides), Cambridge, New York, Melbourne, 1993 — RUSHTON 1

W. A. Mozart: Don Giovanni (Cambridge Opera Guides), Cambridge, New York, Melbourne, 1981 — RUSHTON 2

Mozart: an Extraordinary Life, London (Associated Board), 2005 — RUSHTON 3

Mozart (Master Musicians), New York, forthcoming — RUSHTON 4

Sadie, Stanley, *Mozart: The Early Years, 1756–1781*, Oxford, New York, 2005 — SADIE 1

The New Grove Mozart, London, 1982 — SADIE 2

Wolfgang Amadé Mozart: Essays on his Life and his Music, ed. Stanley Sadie, Oxford, 1996 — SADIE 3

Shaw, George Bernard, *Shaw's Music: The Complete Musical Criticism*, ed. Dan H. Laurence, 3 vols., London, Sydney, Toronto, 1981 — SHAW

Smith, Erik, *Mostly Mozart: Articles, Memoirs, Rarities and Surprises*, Winchester, 2005 (privately published: to order copies call (UK) 01962 760287) — SMITH

Solomon, Maynard, *Mozart: A Life*, New York, London, 1995 — SOLOMON

Stafford, William, *Mozart's Death: A Corrective Survey of the Legends*, London, Stanford (*The Mozart Myths: A Critical Reassement*), 1991 — STAFFORD

Steptoe, Andrew, *The Mozart–Da Ponte Operas: The Cultural and Musical Background to Le nozze di Figaro, Don Giovanni and Così fan tutte*, Oxford, 1988 — STEPTOE

Stricker, Rémy, *Mozart et ses opéras: fiction et vérité*, Paris, 1980 — STRICKER

Till, Nicholas, *Mozart and the Enlightenment*, London, Boston, 1992 — TILL

Turner, W. J., *Mozart: The Man and his Works*, rev. and ed. Christopher Raeburn, London, 1965   TURNER

Tyson, Alan, *Mozart: Studies of the Autograph Scores*, London, Cambridge (Mass.), 1987   TYSON

Warrack, John, *German Opera: From the Beginnings to Wagner*, Cambridge, 2001   WARRACK

Zaslaw, Neal, *Mozart's Symphonies: Context, Performance Practice, Reception*, Oxford, 1989   ZASLAW

Notes

PREFACE

2   an over-deliberate tempo: andante, the tempo of the scene, generally stood for a quicker pace in the eighteenth century than in the nineteenth. We should, however, be on our guard against the more dogmatic claims of the early-music movement. Performance practice in the classical music world was much less uniform, more diverse than such claims commonly presuppose.

2   Shapiro . . .: *1599: A Year in the Life of William Shakespeare*, London, New York, 2005.

2   Greenblatt . . .: *Will in the World: How Shakespeare became Shakespeare*, London, New York, 2004.

3   *Responses*: London, New York, 1973, New York, 1983.

PROLOGUE

5   Misha Donat: in the Wigmore Hall's 1991 Mozart Bicentenary Festival programme book.

5   "If I could only impress . . .": D, 308, letter of December 1787.

5   Dittersdorf . . .: EISEN, 54 (document no. 86).

6   "too highly seasoned": D, 473.

6   "loquacious": D, 328.

7   "Who, going through . . .": Psalm 84.

7   As Charles Rosen says . . .: ROSEN, 325.

7   Schumann . . . "Grecian lightness": cf. ROSEN, 324: "Schumann's attitude to Mozart ends by destroying his vitality as it canonizes him."

8   Bernard Shaw: SHAW, II, 85 (11 June 1890).

8   to find Mozart superficial . . .: cf. Otto Jahn (quoted LANDON 1, 193): "Mozart seems cold at a certain period of our mental development."

9   the Chelsea Opera Group: see David Cairns, "1950–1965", in *In Concert: 50 years of the Chelsea Opera Group*, London, 2000.

9   Wagner . . .: in *Opera and Drama*.

11   in H. C. Robbins Landon's phrase: LANDON 3, 254.

11   the tangled web of myth: cf. STAFFORD, 264: "the traditional picture of Mozart is partly founded on gossip which quickly blossomed into legend and myth [. . .], a tradition which has fed upon itself".

12   "one of the most penetrating intellects . . .": Nicholas Till, in TILL, xi.

12   not . . . a womanizer: Maynard Solomon is inclined to believe the stories that began circulating after M's death (SOLOMON, 445–51). Later he speaks of M's "apparent inability to remain faithful to Constanze".

12   "Addio, ben mio . . .": L, 278 (26 September 1777, PS to a letter of M's). Albi Rosenthal, in a letter to *The Times* written in response to *Amadeus*, pointed out that such language, far from being peculiar to M, was normal and endemic in the speech of the Salzburg and adjoining southern Bavarian region.

12   "I am happier", etc.: L, 305, 587, 867, 968.

13   the *Idomeneo* quartet: L, 699, 27 December 1780.

13   Karoline Pichler's account: D, 556–7.

13   W. J. Turner: in TURNER, 109. Turner's book is nonetheless full of interesting opinions and unusual insights.

14   "an ordinary musician . . .": BRIEFE, II, 274.

14   the craftsmanship . . . industry: cf. ROSEN, 308, on Susanna's "Deh vieni": "there are many sketches for this exquisite and subtle aria, and its perfection was not easily arrived at".

14   in Alan Tyson's words: TYSON, 46.

14   the rising chromatic passage: in this case, more a matter of the notation than of the notes. See Wolf-Dieter Seiffert, "Mozart's 'Haydn' Quartets: an Evaluation of the Autographs and the First Edition", in EISEN 2, 175–200.

15   *The Impossible Adventure*: trans. Edward Fitzgerald, London, 1953, 309–10.

15   "speak to unborn generations . . .": Franz Alexander von Kleist, quoted D, 432–3.

CHAPTER 1: IMITATION, ASSIMILATION

17   15 [Frith] St: now no. 20, but the house has long since been replaced.

17   documentary proof of his age: obtained by B from the Salzburg cathedral register of births, with the help of the Bavarian ambassador (see D, 100). Was

this why M was unable to produce his birth certificate when the musicians' benefit society of Vienna demanded it as a condition of being admitted?

17   Charles Burney: quoted EISEN, 4 (document no. 4).

18–20   Barrington: published in the Royal Society's *Philosophical Transactions*, lx, 54–64, London, 1771.

20   Joseph Yorke: quoted EISEN, 9–10 (document no. 13).

20   "completely unrecognizable . . .": BRIEFE, I, 211, 12 December 1765.

21–2   Schachtner: quoted D, 451–4.

22   "soaked in music . . .": L, 587, 31 July 1778.

22   ambitions . . . take second place: cf. HALLIWELL, xxi and passim. For a hostile view of Leopold and his motives and actions see SOLOMON, passim.

22   "when Wolfgang makes new acquaintances . . .": L 463, 5 February [1778].

22   Nannerl said the same . . .: D, 462.

23   Erik Smith has argued: "Mozart in Chelsea", in SMITH, 119.

23   Nannerl was emphatic . . .: D, 462.

23   Cliff Eisen . . .: EISEN 2, vi.

23   "they treat me like a beginner . . .": L, 587.

23   *Musikalisches Wochenblatt*: quoted D, 431–2.

23   Michael Kelly: KELLY, 116.

23   "curious, attentive . . .": BRAUNBEHRENS, 367.

25   it "may be dismissed . . .": DENT, 19.

25   "we need not occupy . . .": EINSTEIN, 395.

26   Leopold's bitter complaints: e.g. D, 80–83.

26   Einstein remarks . . .: EINSTEIN, 395.

26   Bruno Walter's phrase: made while rehearsing the Linz symphony (recorded on an LP of the 1950s).

26   as Leopold Mozart warned: e.g. L, 681, 696.

28   "dramatic musician . . . when one has stated": EINSTEIN, 395, 416–17.

29   the Tanzmeisterhaus: the family moved there in 1773.

30   "Oh, if only we had clarinets . . .": L, 638, 3 December 1778.

31   Georg Benda's *Medea*: see L, 631, 12 November 1778.

CHAPTER 2: "SUCH GREAT THINGS IN SO SMALL A HEAD"

33   Carl Theodor's court: see Eugene K. Wolf, "The Mannheim Court", Chapter VIII in *Man and Music: The Classical Era, from the 1780s to the end of the 18th century*, ed. Neal Zaslaw, London, 1989, 213–39.

33 Charles Burney's words: quoted Wolf, op. cit.

34 Such innovations . . . *Günther van Schwarzburg*: see WARRACK, 127, 113–17.

34 . . . impressed Mozart: see L, 361, 8 November 1777.

34 . . . composing . . . for Mannheim musicians: e.g. the concert arias K295 for Raaff and K486 (295a) for Dorothea Wendling.

35 Constanze told [the] Novello[s]: NOVELLO, 94.

35 Constanze also recalled: NOVELLO, 115.

35 "Remember how much . . .": L, 462, 4 February 1778. His "dearest wish": L, 362, 8 November 1777.

35 . . . Heartz has argued: Daniel Heartz, "Mozart, his father and *Idomeneo*", *Musical Times*, 119 (1978), 228–31.

35 "the old ones" the best: L, 558, 3 July 1778.

36 Grimm . . . Idomenée: quoted HEARTZ, 5.

36 Its theme of human sacrifice: *Musical Times*, op. cit.

36 "who would believe . . .": L, 698, 27 December 1780.

36 "working for me tirelessly": L, 648, 31 December 1778.

37 Max Loppert: in the 2003 Glyndebourne Festival programme book.

37 "a kind of creative shock": Daniel Heartz, op. cit.

38 as Heartz observes: HEARTZ, 27.

40 On 8 November . . .: L, 660.

40 "sung through her two arias . . .": L, 664, 15 November 1780.

40 Five days later: L, 662, 13 November 1780.

41 "To Act 1 scene 8 . . .": L, 663, 13 November 1780.

41 a long . . . reply . . . from Leopold: L, 666, 18 November 1780.

41 "In the last scene of Act 2 . . .": L, 664, 15 November 1780.

41 "The aria [for Ilia] . . .": ibid.

42 ". . . can no longer show off in such an aria": ibid. Cf. M's letter of two years earlier (L, 552).

42 "The aria is not at all . . .": L, 674, 29 November 1780.

42 Leopold agreed: L, 681, 4 December 1780.

43 "I assume that you will choose . . .": L, 700, 29 December 1780. M adopted L's idea (assuming that he hadn't already had it himself).

43 Raaff was "as infatuated . . .": L, 677–8, 1 December 1780.

43 "we both want gentler . . .": L, 682, 5 December 1780.

44 "The scene between father and son . . .": L, 693, 19 December 1780.

44 "Raaff and dal Prato . . .": L, 698, 27 December 1780.

45 "Raaff is delighted": L, 701–2, 30 December 1780.

46 "a block of ice": Metastasio's word is "freddissimo" (quoted MANN, 254, STRICKER, 129).

46 "molto amato castrato . . .": L, 664, 15 November 1780.

46 "disgracefully badly": L, 669, 22 November 1780.

46 "we went through the quartet . . .": L, 701, 30 December 1780.

47 Count Seeau . . . ("the Mannheim people . . ."): L, 662, 13 November 1780.

47 "one and all" for him . . .: L, 670, 24 November 1780.

47 "I am glad to see you . . .": L, 665, 15 November 1780.

47 "cannot tell . . . how delighted . . .": L, 677, 1 December 1780.

47 "When you call at Dorothea Wendling's . . .": L, 683, 1 December 1780.

47 "Fiala has just . . .": L, 687–8, 15 December 1780.

48 "join me in Munich soon . . .": L, 690, 16 December 1780.

48 "placed in the room . . .": L, 707, 11 January 1781.

48 "I am delighted . . .": L, 669, 22 November 1780.

48 "as there is no extra ballet . . .": L, 662, 13 November 1780.

49 "to make the necessary arrangements . . .": ibid.

49 in Heartz's phrase: HEARTZ, 33.

50 a newspaper report: quoted D, 191–2.

50 "awkwardly placed": L, 708, 18 January 1781.

50 Its loss was "much regretted . . .": ibid.

50 "Varesco need know nothing . . .": ibid.

51 "would have arranged . . . in the French style": L, 765, 12 September 1781.

52 "desperate fight": L, 706, 10 and 11 January 1781.

52 Idomeneo ". . . a work dispossessed": HEARTZ, 34.

53 Alfred Einstein described . . .: see Chris Walton, "The performing version by Richard Strauss and Lothar Wallerstein", in RUSHTON 1, 89.

53 Desmond Shawe-Taylor . . . the New Statesman: 4 February 1956.

53 Edward Dent . . .: DENT, 45.

54 a museum piece . . . to be revived: DENT, 263.

54 Charles Rosen's assertion: ROSEN, 167. See also KERMAN, 85: "only sporadically dramatic".

64 a surviving performing score: see RUSHTON 1, 404.

67 in Dent's words: DENT, 63.

CHAPTER 3: VIENNA AND A NEW LIFE

69 to "wipe his arse": L, 690, 16 December 1780.

69 enjoy them too much: ibid.

70 good fortune . . . "waiting to welcome" him: L, 736, 6 May 1781.

70 "I like being here": L, 721, 4 April 1781.

70 "This is a splendid place . . .": ibid.

70 "the land of the clavier": L, 739, 2 June 1781.

70 the "beautiful Stein pianoforte": L, 718, 24 March 1781.

70 "what surprised . . . me . . .": L, 722, 8 April 1781.

70 played *Idomeneo*: see L, 736, 26 May 1781.

71 "Clear out – scoundrel . . . !" L, 728, 9 May 1781.

71 "I hate the Archbishop . . .": L, 729, ibid.

71 free to make his way in Vienna: STEPTOE, 79–80, suggests that Countesses Thun and Rumbeke may have influenced M's decision to leave the archbishop's service.

71 begging Leopold's "permission": L, 726, 28 April 1781.

71 "from my youth up . . .": L, 783, 15 December 1781.

72 "Having done my duty . . .": L, 815–16, 23 August 1782.

72n "As His Grace the Prince": L, 758, 10 August 1781.

73 "It saddens me . . .": L, 763.

73 "C'est un talent décidé": L, 789, 22 December 1781.

74 "If you really believe . . .": ibid.

74 "The voice of nature speaks . . .": L, 783, 15 December 1781.

74n coveting an expensive red coat: L, 823, 28 September 1782.

75 "more useful . . . in Vienna . . .": L, 733, 16 May 1781.

75 In September 1781 . . .: L, 767–8, late September.

75 the "many necessary alterations . . .": L, 796, 30 January 1782.

75 "I received today your letter . . .": L, 811, 31 July 1782.

76 shown him . . . *Zaïde*: see L, 725, 18 April 1781.

76 "well in with the Emperor": L, 745, 16 June 1781.

76 the Emperor . . . ended the court's monopoly: by the so-called *Spektakelfreiheit*.

77 "It is the heart that ennobles . . .": L, 747, 20 June 1781.

77 "How I wish you could see . . .": L, 751, 4 July 1781.

78 "rushed to his desk": L, 755, 1 August 1781.

78 seven-eighths German: Pushkin used to enjoy poking fun at the paucity of Russian blood in the modern Romanovs.

79–80 "As the role of Osmin . . .": L, 768–70, 26 September 1781.

81 "The verse, I agree . . .": L, 772–3, 13 October 1781.

81 "up to his eyes in work": L, 770, 26 September 1781.

82 Stephanie . . . "had something ready": L, 776, 3 November 1781.

82 Part at least of . . . K361: see Alan Tyson, *Neue Mozart-Ausgabe X: Supplement 33*.

82 "The six gentlemen who performed it . . .": L, 776, 3 November 1781.

82 They "asked for the street door . . .": ibid.

83 "in an opera the poetry . . .": L, 773, 13 October 1781.

84 "right after Easter": L, 796, 30 January 1782.

84 on the advice of Countess Thun: M had lent her the score of *Idomeneo* (see L, 748).

84 their first serious quarrel: see L, 802–3, 29 April 1782.

84 no reserved seats to be had: see L, 808, 20 July 1782.

85 "I thought it advisable . . .": L, 828, 19 October 1782.

85 "The whole town is delighted . . .": L, 884, late November 1784.

85 the popularity of *Die Entführung* [abroad]: see LANDON 4, 188.

85 "the Bohemians began . . .": NIEMETSCHEK, 33.

86 "Far too beautiful . . .": NIEMETSCHEK, 32, D, 499.

86 using one Mozart opera as a stick . . .: a bad habit of Hildesheimer's.

86 Mozart is sometimes accused . . .: e.g. by John Stone in LANDON 4, 155.

87 "sacrificed to the flexible throat . . ." L, 769, 26 September 1781.

87 "Mozart at his loveliest . . .": DENT, 79.

88 As . . . Bauman points out: BAUMAN, 77–82.

88 "As death, when we . . .": L, 907, April 1787.

89 "in the style of Turkish music": L, 755, 1 August 1781.

89 the main motif . . .: BAUMAN, 81.

91 as Beecham called him: BEECHAM, 155.

91 "we must take advantage of it . . .": L, 768, 26 September 1781.

91 deliver "with a fullness . . .": quoted BAUMAN, 68.

94 "together [they] create . . .": BAUMAN, 89.

94 Dent maintained . . .: DENT, 75.

94 "get through his devotions": DENT, 81.

95 "enormously long . . .": DENT, 81.

95 "songs [far] outside the scale . . .": DENT, 82.

95 Shaw . . . "rules of thumb": SHAW, III, 146 (28 February 1894): "The fact is, there are no rules, and there never were any rules, and there never will be any rules of musical composition except rules of thumb; and thumbs vary in length, like ears."

96 what Weber called: see *Carl Maria von Weber: Writings on Music*, ed. John Warrack, trans. Martin Cooper, Cambridge, New York, 1981, 265.

97 "Every nation has its own opera . . .": L, 839, 5 February 1782.

98 he seems to have composed two arias: see ibid.

98 Count Rosenberg . . .: see L, 832, 21 December 1782.

CHAPTER 4: LORENZO DA PONTE AND THE PERFECT MARRIAGE

99 "Another short letter! . . .": L, 847–8.

99 Baron Raimund Wetzlar: on M's Jewish friends see GUTMAN, 562–5.

100 Da Ponte's office: where Da P lived at the time of *Figaro* remains a mystery (later he seems to have had an apartment in the Wieden), but presumably, as poet to the court opera, he would have had an office at the Burgtheater.

101 Barisani . . . in Mozart's album: quoted D, 289.

101 the Duscheks: see L, 897.

102 "Please keep on reminding Varesco . . .": L, 849, 21 May 1783.

102 "not the slightest knowledge . . .": L, 853, 21 June 1783.

102 a letter written by Mozart: L, 861–2, 6 December 1783.

102 Some of the eight numbers: for the probable date of the composition of *L'oca* see TYSON, 77–9, 101–2.

102 "my only reason for not objecting . . .": L, 861, 6 December 1783.

103 You can feel his scorn: L: 864–5, 24 December 1783.

103 "the *same aria* . . .": Wodehouse fans will be reminded of "Jeeves and the Song of Songs".

103 a letter of July 1783: L, 855, 5 July.

104 in Robbins Landon's words: LANDON 1, 96.

105 the first hundred bars of . . . K488: see TYSON, 19, 32.

105 as Charles Rosen says: ROSEN, 228.

105 Mozart's pet starling: see D, 225. It lived till June 1787.

106 dissonances [in K467]: Leopold M (BRIEFE, III, 490, 14 January 1786) was puzzled by some of them: "several passages simply do not harmonize unless one hears all the instruments playing together"; he wondered whether the copy had been wrongly transcribed. Colin Davis has pointed out to me that the second violin and viola at one moment play the harmonies of the Annunciation of Death motif in *The Ring*.

106 tuttis of "brilliant violence": ROSEN, 235.

107 a work which began with *Don Giovanni* . . .: Ian Lake made this observation to me when we were rehearsing K466 for a performance we gave in 1995.

107 Another letter in March: 870–72, 20 March 1784.

107 "like a cross-section . . .": LANDON 1, 107.

108 (if Michael Kelly is to be believed): KELLY, 11.

108 The letters [Leopold] wrote to his daughter: see L, 885–9 and BRIEFE, III, 372ff.

112   The attendance record: D, 243, 244.

112   a letter of Leopold's . . . to Nannerl: L, 883, 14 September 1784.

112   two entries in Mozart's album: D, 289, 296.

113   "Kapellmeister Mozart": D, 230.

113   Haydn . . . (as reported to Nannerl): L, 886 [16 February 1785].

114   "I shall bring back several . . .": ibid.

114   "I shall buy everything . . .": L, 888, 12 March 1785.

114   "He is up to his eyes . . .": L, 893, 11 November 1785.

114   "The journalist . . .": L, 893, 3 November 1785.

115   learned to write quartets: Mozart was fully aware of the debt (cf. NIEMETSCHEK, 32: "Mozart often referred to [Haydn] as his teacher").

115   "My dear Constanze . . .": L, 801, 20 April 1782.

116   in Rosemary Hughes's words: *Haydn* (The Master Musicians), London, 1989, 152.

116   (in Rosen's phrase): ROSEN, 287.

116   the six "Haydn" quartets: cf. Hans Keller, in LANDON 3, 102: "Mozart made a special effort, in view of his expert dedicatee, to whom he would also be psychologically prepared to confide his deepest secrets."

116   Joseph II's interest in *Figaro*: for the idea that M "was being employed as a mouthpiece for the reform policies of the Josephinian court", see STAFFORD, 246.

116   a note to Count Pergen: D, 235.

117   Johann Rautenstrauch: ibid.

118   Joseph's correspondence with Count Rosenberg: see Otto Michtner, *Das alte Burgtheater als Opernbühne*, Vienna, 1970.

118   fetching [Paisiello] in his carriage: see L, 880, 9 June 1784.

119   *Figaro* is an opera of reconciliations: see Jessica Waldoff and James Webster, "Operatic Plotting in *Le nozze di Figaro*", in SADIE 3, 263.

119   "it [*Figaro*] will cost him . . .": L, 893, 11 November 1783.

120   as Rosen says: ROSEN, 323.

122   Figaro . . . important lesson: cf. ROSEN, 313: "one of the most revealing moments is when the valet, misled by Susanna, becomes as blind with jealousy as his master".

122   Nicholas Hytner: in an interval talk on BBC Radio 3 in February 1989.

125   Susanna "moves from the irony . . .": Jessie Waldoff and James Webster, op. cit., SADIE 3, 272.

126   what Erik Smith calls . . .: BRANSCOMBE, 114.

130   the form of the [Susanna/Marcellina duet]: by S. Lavarie, quoted CARTER, 24.

130   Mozart "relies upon an obviously . . .": Michael F. Robinson, "Mozart and the *opera buffa* tradition", in CARTER, 30–32.

130   "major statements by minor characters . . .": RUSHTON 2, 54.

131   Some have claimed: e.g. Nicholas Kenyon in "Mozart the ambiguous mirror", in *About the House* (Covent Garden), Christmas, 1988.

132   in Tim Carter's words: CARTER, 147.

132   Count Rosenberg, as reported by Leopold Mozart: L, 893, 11 November 1785.

133   Michael Kelly described him . . .: KELLY, 130.

133   *Pfeffer und Salz*: D, 270.

133   *Wiener Realzeitung*: D, 278.

134   Niemetschek's contention: NIEMETSCHEK, 34.

134   "Mozart was on stage": KELLY, 131.

135   post a notice at the Burgtheater: D, 275.

CHAPTER 5: PRAGUE AND "THE OPERA OF ALL OPERAS"

136   a merry party: described in L, 904, 15 January 1787.

136   "real entertainment": ibid.

136   *Prager Oberpostamtszeitung*: D, 284.

137   "I neither danced . . .", L, 903.

137   the theatre was "so crowded . . .": ibid.

137   Niemetschek . . . "The theatre": NIEMETSCHEK, 36.

138   (according to Nancy Storace . . .): L, 906, 1 March 1787.

139   Mozart "insisted . . .": DA PONTE 2.

141   "Having found these subjects . . .": DA PONTE 1.

141   Nancy Storace's farewell concert: Though there is no record of M's taking part, it is virtually certain that it was he who played the piano part in the concert aria "Ch'io mi scordi di te", K505, composed (the catalogue states) "for Mlle Storace and me". See also EISEN, 39–40 (document no. 64).

142   "I can guess the reason": L, 908 n. 4, 10–11 May 1787.

142   "finely and correctly written": D, 312.

143   the "brilliant idea": L, 902, 17 November 1786.

143   "I am still receiving reports . . .": L, 902, 12 January 1787.

143   "forgo this happiness . . .": L, 904, 15 January 1787.

143   Attwood . . . "a definite engagement": L, 906, 1 March 1787.

144   Rushton . . . "tapped a dark force": RUSHTON 2, 2.

145   as Andrew Steptoe remarks: STEPTOE, 204.

146   "How can anyone say . . . ?": quoted ABERT, 43.

146   what Ernest Newman called . . .: in a newspaper article (source not traced).

147–8   Goethe . . . recalled: quoted ABERT, 33–4.

148   a symphony by J. C. Bach: Haydn's Symphony No. 78 in C minor has been claimed as a source, but far more direct is the opening of the C minor slow movement of Bach's G minor symphony, op. 6 no. 6: 3/4 time, unison strings, and beginning with the identical sequence and pattern of notes in C minor: C, E flat, A flat, G, F sharp. Bach follows the F sharp with a G. M of course added the upward leap to E flat; but later in the movement (bars 302–5) we find Bach's exact motif.

150   "to have learned the language of ghosts . . .": quoted D, 341.

151   the swapping of hats and cloaks: found also in both Molière and Cicognini.

151   "a really serious treatment . . .": DENT, 159.

151   "perhaps the most beautiful [number] . . .: DENT, 165.

152   "a masterpiece of construction": DENT, 161.

152   only "Mozart could have achieved . . .": HEARTZ, 215.

153   As Rushton says: RUSHTON 2, 46.

154n   espoused by Einstein: see, for example, EINSTEIN, 439.

156   as Einstein says, sui generis: in the preface to the Eulenberg miniature score.

157   steeped in irony: cf. David Cairns, "Irony in Music before Mahler", in *Gustav Mahler et l'ironie dans la culture viennoise au tournant du siècle*, actes du colloque de Montpellier, 16–18 juillet 1996, 2001, 31, 32. See also Donald Mitchell, "Ironies of Love and Death", in the same proceedings, 281–96.

157   (in the Prague score): in the Vienna *Don Giovanni* "Or sai chi l'onore" is separated from "Fin ch'han dal vino" by Ottavio's "Dalla sua pace", written to replace his Prague aria "Il mio tesoro". Modern performances of the opera generally conflate the two versions by including both tenor arias, as well as Elvira's magnificent, and psychologically penetrating, Act 2 scena (Vienna), thus producing a hybrid. Beautiful and characteristic though these new numbers are, there is a case for preferring the tauter, dramatically more compelling Prague version – ending as it does, too, with the scena ultima, which may well have been shortened, or cut altogether, in Vienna.

157   other catalogue arias: see John Platoff, "Catalogue arias and the 'Catalogue Aria'", in SADIE 3, 296–311.

161   not melody but "the mysteries of harmony": RUSHTON 2, 119.

161 "As the Statue refuses . . .": ibid.

162 Nicholas Till: TILL, 197–228.

163 Luigi Bassi . . . told Stendhal: quoted EISEN, 52 (document no. 83). Stendhal adds: "On this subject, Bassi told me three or four little anecdotes which, however, I must refrain from including at this point."

164 a profound misunderstanding: for discussion of the scena ultima see Michael F. Robinson, "The alternative endings of Mozart's *Don Giovanni*", in Mary Hunter and James Webster, eds., *Opera Buffa in Mozart's Vienna*, Cambridge, New York, Melbourne, 1997.

165 "In the first place, the stage personnel . . .": L, 911, 15 October 1787. Cf. Zinzendorf, quoted D, 301: *Figaro* "not at all appropriate for fêting a newly married woman".

166 "as arranger of Mozart's two operas . . .": HEARTZ, 169.

166 "We never sang this number . . .": quoted HEARTZ, 172.

166 Bruno Walter said: in conversation with Hilda Oldberg, who told the author.

167 Heartz also argues: HEARTZ, 169–70.

167 confirmed by Constanze herself: NOVELLO, 95–6; see also NIEMET-SCHEK, 63–4, where N calls the story "common knowledge in Prague".

167 "a good many notes fell under the desks": ABERT, 13–14.

167 The *Prager Oberpostamtszeitung*: D, 303.

168 "Long live Da Ponte . . .": quoted D, 302.

168 she locked him in: ABERT, 16–17.

168 Another anecdote recalls: ABERT, 16 n. 1.

CHAPTER 6: CATECHISMS OF LOVE

169 "a man's reputation . . .": L, 739, 2 June 1781.

169 "this exhausting labour": L, 940, *c.* 12 June 1790.

169 Alan Tyson's study: TYSON, 135.

170 a letter of Leopold's: BRIEFE, III, 618, 8 December 1786.

170 Tyson . . . fragments of masses: TYSON, 26–7.

170 Mozart "is writing church music": D, 325.

171 "the string quartet . . .": TYSON, 47.

171 At his death, Tyson reckons . . .: TYSON, passim.

171 Till . . . the intriguing notion: TILL, 297.

172 Constanze's later testimony: NOVELLO, 81.

172 "Yesterday . . . to the Neumanns": L, 921–2, 13 April 1789.

173 "meagre reward": L, 925, 16 May 1789.

173   "distributing . . . free tickets": quoted LANDON 1, 206.

173   "his fortepiano playing . . . without payment": EISEN, 59 (document no. 93).

173   "This is music . . .": Rochlitz's anecdotes have been rightly examined with much scepticism and many of them disproved, most recently and authoritatively by Solomon in EISEN 1, but the story of M looking through the parts of Bach's motets has, to me, the ring of truth.

174   "in many noble . . . houses . . .": D, 347.

174   Mozart tells Puchberg: L, 916, c. June 1788.

174   "All lovers of music": D, 332.

175   "I am pleased to see . . .": quoted LANDON 1, 173.

176   According to Constanze: NOVELLO, 127.

176   Salieri . . . composing: see RICE, 10–13.

176   "expressly to prevent an artist . . .": D, 430.

176   "Salieri's plots . . .": L, 935, December 1789.

177   knew Mesmer: from visits to Vienna in 1768 and later.

178   *L'arbore di Diana*: for its influence on *Così* see Dorothea Link, "*L'arbore di Diana*: a model for *Così fan tutte*", in SADIE 3, 362–73.

178   The self-references: see the chapter "Citation, Reference and Recall" in HEARTZ, 229–53.

180   "the surprising combination . . .": ROSEN, 317.

181   "*Così fan tutte* is the best . . .": DENT, 190, 192, 206.

182   "This is not a pleasant . . ." BRAUNBEHRENS, 342.

182   "Da Ponte poked fun . . .": BROWN, 7–8.

182   "Mozart [said Stendhal] . . .": in the booklet of the 1986 Philips recording of *Figaro* (conducted by Neville Marriner).

182   "A current of violence . . .": Germaine Greer in a television broadcast of April 1990.

183   "The opera is a bitter-sweet tale . . .": TILL, 233, 242.

183   "Romantic critics . . .": HEARTZ, 222.

183   "what Fiordiligi's . . .": HEARTZ, 242.

184   the enigma of *Così*: a theory propounded in an article in the *Spectator* c. 1960, then amplified for the Glyndebourne programme book of 1978.

187   the despair of Cassandra: in the tonic minor, E flat.

187   echoed by Beecham: BEECHAM, 94.

190   "a deadly experiment . . .": Unfortunately I have failed to locate the source of this quotation.

191   in Joseph Kerman's words: KERMAN, 92–3, 98.

192   the biggest recorded . . . for that season: see Dexter Edge, "Mozart's reception in Vienna, 1787–1791", in SADIE 3, 66–117.

193 Louise Villeneuve: the arias K 578, 582, 583.

193 Zinzendorf: see Dexter Edge, op. cit.

CHAPTER 7: MOZART THE VISIONARY

194 "too strong meat": D, 549 (from DA PONTE 1).

194 on the death of Gluck: M's appointment was on a lower level than G's – G was "wirklicher k.k. Hofcompositeur" – and at less than half the salary. But G was at the height of his fame.

195 [Mozart] petitioned: L, 938–9, c. May 1790 (draft).

195 "strong aversion": D, 411.

195 "What a credit to the Viennese Court . . .": L, 947–8, early November 1790.

195 "made a great fuss of": ibid.

195 talks of coming back to Germany: ibid.

196 Abbé Stadler's recollection: NOVELLO, 170, 347 n. 123.

196 Johann Tost: he may have commissioned K593.

196 According to one report: D, 379, LANDON 2, 18–19.

196 a "merry meal": LANDON 2, 19.

196 John Bland . . . made contact: D, 368.

196 a letter from . . . O'Reilly: D, 377–8.

197 advertised his chamber organ: EISEN, 65 (document no. 105).

197 an opera on *The Tempest*: EISEN, 65–7 (document no. 106).

197 Count Rasumovsky: D, 406–7.

198 K595 also, possibly . . .: see Dexter Edge, op. cit., SADIE 3, 89–90.

198 Mozart petitions the Vienna City Council: L, 949, c. 25 April 1791, D, 395.

198 "As I was doing Mozart's hair . . .": LANDON 2, 28.

198 "a little man . . .": D, 375.

199 "The reason I am still here . . .": L, 947.

199 Wilhelm Backhaus: EISEN, 65 (document no. 104).

199 "Papa . . . you are not prepared . . .": Dies, quoted LANDON 2, 19.

199 "I've just this moment received . . .": L, 754, 6 June 1791.

200 an aria for . . . Josepha Hofer: K580. In the end the production did not take place.

200 Schikaneder "has bought a . . . popgun . . .": L, 680, 2 December 1780.

201 an aria . . . a production of Schikaneder's: this long-lost piece, "Die neugeborne Ros' entzückt", has recently been discovered, though in incomplete form, and has been published, ed. Christoph Wolf and Faye Ferguson,

with facsimile, by the Internationale Stiftung Mozarteum, Salzburg, 1996. It will appear in a supplementary volume of the Neue Mozart-Ausgabe.

201 *Der Stein der Weisen*: see David Buch, "Mozart and the Theater auf der Wieden: New attributions and perspectives", in *Cambridge Opera Journal*, vol. 9, no. 3 (November 1997), 195–232 (especially 198–202).

202 *Der Fagottist* . . . "nothing to it": L, 954, 12 June 1791.

202 he enjoyed . . . *Anton bei Hofe*: L, 952, 6 June 1791.

202 Schikaneder['s] . . . orchestra: see LANDON 2, 123.

203 "planned . . . carefully . . .": BRANSCOMBE, 89.

203 As Peter Branscombe has shown: BRANSCOMBE, passim.

204 Carlo Gozzi: for his influence see ROSEN, 318–21.

204 *Dschinnistan*: in his preface to the collection, Wieland says that he mixed the lofty and the popular (folk material and its fantastic elements) expressly to serve a higher purpose (see LANDON 4, 150).

205 Ignaz von Born's essay: see BRANSCOMBE, 20–25.

205 "the surviving evidence . . .": BRANSCOMBE, 3.

205 "massively indiscreet": " 'Singspiel' and Symbolism", in ENO Opera Guide 3 (1980), 11–16.

205 "testifies to an intimate knowledge . . .": HEARTZ, 259.

205 "Masons in north Germany . . .": HEARTZ, 277.

205n Gieseke: he may have contributed a line or two during rehearsals. According to BRANSCOMBE, 88–9, his Viennese plays and librettos show little originality or distinction.

206 Maria Theresa: the identification, even if not intended by the authors, was soon being made widely.

206 What decided Mozart and Schikaneder: They may have been encouraged by the success of *Das Sonnenfest der Brahminen*, a singspiel by Müller and the freemason Karl Friedrich Hensler (1790). Whereas Kotzebue's *Die Sonnenjungfrau* had to be purged of all masonic elements in order to be put on at the Burgtheater, *Das Sonnenfest*, with its high-minded humanitarian sentiments and unambiguous denunciation of religious intolerance, was given at the Leopoldstadttheater uncensored. See HEARTZ, 258–9.

206 "Mozart and Schikaneder risked . . .": LANDON 2, 60.

206 "the opportunity to communicate . . .": TILL, 271–2, 321.

208 "If all liars . . .": cf. TILL, 306.

210 Mozart's "infinite care to create . . .": HEARTZ, 270.

213 [Mozart] "abandons none of the pretensions": ROSEN, 332.

214 as Bauman demonstrates: HEARTZ, 283–6.

218 the excited state of his imagination: the orchestral epilogue, in its sudden thoughtful piano after a bar of confident forte, casts a new light on

T's character. See BRANSCOMBE, 114, for Erik Smith's eloquent bar-by-bar musico-dramatic account of the form of the aria.

219 as his name suggests: curiously, it appears as "Manostatos" in M's autograph.

221 He tolerates the anomaly: rather as God, in Goethe's *Faust*, tolerates Mephisto and uses him for his purposes: see BRANSCOMBE, 213.

222 "the only music yet written . . .": SHAW, III, 744 (18 March 1927).

223 the allegro, in which the trials: Bauman in HEARTZ, 286–97. The allegro is "deeply implicated in the central conflicts of the opera it introduces".

227 his old friend Baron Wetzlar: see J. Arthur, " 'NN' revisited: new light on Mozart's late correspondence", in BRANDENBURGER, 127–45.

228 three others . . . apparently revised: see TYSON, 35.

CHAPTER 8: PROPAGANDA AND PARABLE

229 The contract: EISEN, 67–8 (document no. 107).

229 If Salieri is to be believed: see EISEN, 68–9 (document no. 108) and LANDON 2, 84–8.

231 Tyson's analysis of the paper-types: TYSON, 48–60.

231 the eighteen days: NIEMETSCHEK, 41, 64 ("in the travelling coach on the way from Vienna" – mistranslated as "to Vienna").

232 Opera seria . . . alive and thriving: see especially "Mozart and his Italian contemporaries", in HEARTZ.

233 a text with reassuring messages . . .: "to represent the ideal, the Enlightenment, which should be in stark contrast to the alarming events in France" (LANDON 2, 100).

233 to rule "in association with the aristocracy . . .": Nicholas Till, "*La clemenza di Tito* and Enlightened Despotism", in the programme booklet for English National Opera's production of the work, 2005.

234 "in Prague Mozart fell ill": NIEMETSCHEK, 43.

234 *Krönungsjournal für Prag*: D, 405.

234 Certainly we will be disappointed: cf. ROSEN, 164: "a work of exquisite grace and rarely redeemed dullness".

237 Paul Nettl speculates: quoted LANDON 2, 100.

238 "The last time he attended . . .": quoted LANDON 2, 119.

238 "In the evening to the theatre": EISEN, 70 (document no. 109).

238 Franz Xaver Wolfgang: much used to be made of the fact that the first two names were those of Süssmayr, Constanze's putative lover. They were

also those of Gerl, Sarastro in the first *Magic Flute*. We may make of that what we will. It is worth noting that Franz Xaver was a common combination of baptismal names.

238 "Mozart . . . dangerously overworked": LANDON 2, 97.

239 "The last stagecoach ride . . .": LANDON 2, 98.

239 Zinzendorf described . . .: see LINK I, op. cit.

239–40 "a wretched castrato . . .": see RAEBURN, and LANDON 2, 117–18.

240 "after eight o'clock": D, 405.

240 "this heavenly work": before it fell into critical disrepute, *Tito* was one of M's most popular operas in the early nineteenth century.

240 "a preconceived aversion . . .": D, 411.

240 *Don Giovanni* . . . "by highest request": D, 402, 411.

240 "crammed full": D, 403.

240 Franz Alexander von Kleist: D, 433.

241 "Bedini sang better than ever": L, 967 [7–8 October 1791].

241 none . . . earlier than 1803: see STAFFORD, 19, 97–8.

242 his voice was "pure and melodious . . .": quoted PORTER, iii.

242 "Saturday night at half past ten . . .": L, 968 [?8–9 October 1791].

244 "I have just swallowed . . .": ibid.

244 "The Adambergers had a box . . .": ibid. See J. Arthur, op. cit.: he deciphered the name under Nissen's erasure, but was uncertain whether the "thorough Bavarian" refers to Adamberger or not. Adamberger, the first Belmonte, was from Bavaria.

245 Zinzendorf noted a "huge audience": D, 412.

245 *Der Heimliche Botschafter*: ibid.

245 a Viennese news item: D, 409.

EPILOGUE

246 Ludwig Gall: quoted LANDON 2, 168.

246 Niemetschek (who recounted the story): NIEMETSCHEK, 43.

247 Mozart "completely conscious . . .", etc.: for this and the many other, different accounts of M's last days, see D, NOVELLO, NIEMETSCHEK, NISSEN, STAFFORD.

249 "I never in all my life . . .": D, 526.

249 "this best and truest friend . . .": L, 907 [4 April 1787].

250 Hungarian nobles . . . Amsterdam merchants: NIEMETSCHEK, 45.

250 abetted by the emetics . . .: see KARHAUSEN.

Index